I needed a practical guide for pastors, counselors, and laypeople them understand the dynamics of gospel-rich conversations with struggling Christians. Now I've found it! Both rich in theology and Scripture, and at the same time very practical, Bob Kellemen's *Gospel Conversations* is a powerful tool for everyone who wants to think more carefully about how to help others. It skillfully equips God's people to have heartfelt, empathic, engaging, Christlike, servant-hearted, thoughtful, and gospel-centered conversation.

> DR. DEEPAK REJU, President, Biblical Counseling Coalition; Pastor, Biblical Counseling and Families, Capitol Hill Baptist Church, Washington, DC

Gospel Conversations is just what pastors, local church leaders, and compassionate laywomen and men need as we serve and minister to those God has placed around us. We come in contact with people who are suffering and struggling each and every day. *Gospel Conversations* will equip us all to better speak *both* truth *and* love in a way that is winsome *and* wise.

> STEVE VIARS, Senior Pastor, Faith Church, Lafayette, IN; author, *Putting Your Past in Its Place*

As a pastor who strives to equip others in the church to do what is covered in *Gospel Conversations*, I was affirmed, enlightened, challenged, and encouraged by Bob's winsome and relentless gospel focus revealed in this incredible work. I highly recommend *Gospel Conversations* for your library and as a field guide for your ministry. It displays the very best of Bob Kellemen — the instruction of a coach, the love of a pastor, and the wisdom of a teacher.

> DR. ROBERT K. CHEONG, Pastor of Care, Sojourn Community Church, Louisville, KY; author, *God Redeeming His Bride: A Handbook for Church Discipline*

I really appreciate Bob's love of people and his desire to teach others how to be relationally wise with a goal of growth in Christlikeness. *Gospel Conversations* takes "one anothering" seriously and teaches us how to put into practice honest, in-depth, and grace-saturated relationships with others. In other words, truly biblical relationships. Thanks, Bob, for guiding us to be more relationally competent to counsel. Don't just read *Gospel Conversations* — practice it, and your church can move from Sunday morning surface relationships to truly dealing with the realities of life on a fallen planet.

> DR. ERNIE BAKER, Professor of Biblical Counseling, the Master's College; fellow, the Association of Certified Biblical Counselors; author, *Help! I'm in a Conflict*

Gospel Conversations is comprehensive, compassionate, clear, and correct in its insight into God's Word and wisdom in the arena of biblical counseling. The book not only explains the "how" of counseling, it does an excellent job in explaining the "what" and the "why." It will significantly impact lay people, pastors, and students for years to come in the arena of biblical counseling.

Dr. Nicolas Ellen, Professor of Biblical Counseling,
College of Biblical Studies, Houston, TX; author, *With All Your Heart*

Bob Kellemen is a master trainer of counselors and *Gospel Conversations* is a training masterpiece. Distilling thirty years of counseling training, this book is much more than a training manual. It is a treasury of wise biblical soul care. Bob's approach to counseling is clear, comprehensive, compassionate, and compelling. I found his Four Dimensions of Comprehensive Biblical Counseling Equipping and the wealth of helpful self-counseling and other-counseling questions especially helpful. I plan to reread *Gospel Conversations* soon as I seek to improve my own counseling training at my church. I enthusiastically recommend it to everyone who aspires to counsel fruitfully and help others do the same.

Pat Quinn, Pastor of Counseling Ministries,
University Reformed Church, East Lansing, MI

I am thankful for Bob Kellemen's *Gospel Conversations* equipping manual, which has been carefully designed to apply practical principles of gospel-centered biblical counseling in a small-group setting. What is taught in this book is founded upon careful exposition of Scripture and is rooted in sound theology that has stood the test of time throughout church history. I also appreciate the way *Gospel Conversations* boils down the key points into "tweet-sized" statements, memorable word pictures ("climb into the coffin"), and lists that summarize the principles he is emphasizing.

Dr. Jim Newheiser, Pastor, Grace Bible Church, Escondido, CA;
Executive Director, Institute for Biblical Counseling and Discipleship

Gospel Conversations is a gift to the counseling community at large. It is theologically rich, gospel-soaked, hope-filled, and practically presented. As a Christ-centered approach to counseling, it offers anyone interested in reaching the hearts of hurting people a solid opportunity to be equipped to do so. I highly recommend it to pastors, churches, educators, and missionaries as well as anyone wanting to be equipped or to equip others. I am grateful for the privilege to apply this in my church.

DR. DWAYNE R. BOND, Lead Pastor of Wellspring Church;
CEO and Founder of Proximus Group

Everyone has favorite authors, people whose books you'll read because you know the content will be solid, innovative, and biblical. Bob Kellemen is one of those authors for me. *Gospel Conservations* is the book I need every counselor, every Christian in my church to read. Drawing on over three decades of pastoral and counseling ministry, Bob has dedicated his life to equipping biblical counselors for the work of ministry in the church. The work you hold in your hands is the fruit of Bob's labor and ministry which seeks to honor Christ and see others transformed into His image. From personal and private preparation for conversation to the actual engagement, Bob skillfully, compassionately, and biblically navigates us through everyday conversations aimed at Christlike change. In a culture dominated by technologically mediated conversations, Bob's call to gospel conversations is both refreshing and convicting. Read this book, work through it with a small group of people committed to interpersonal ministry, and watch as the Spirit works through our conversations to transform us into the image of Christ. Could there be any more important work for you and me as we labor until Christ comes?

JONATHAN HOLMES, Counseling Pastor, Parkside Church;
author, *The Company We Keep: In Search of Biblical Friendship*

Bob Kellemen has crafted a relational masterpiece with *Gospel Conversations*. It is an excellent resource for caring for the souls of hurting people. Bob emphasizes the need to equip by following Christ's model of disciple making: training the whole person to be a thoroughly equipped biblical counselor. I have personally benefited from the soul-to-soul, relational counseling style put forth in this book. Truth balanced by love and compassion is the foundation on which *Gospel Conversations* is based. Rich with applied theology, this book will be required reading for our biblical counseling trainees.

JULIE GANSCHOW, Founder, Reigning Grace Counseling Center;
author, *Living Beyond the Heart of Betrayal: Biblically Addressing the Pain of Sexual Sin*

Bob Kellemen's book is a robust, relational, comprehensive training manual. While you can work through it on your own, this manual has much to offer in a group setting to grow all participants to be equipped to compassionately, biblically counsel for Christ. Even if you have been counseling for years, *Gospel Conversations* offers significant insights from the Scriptures about how to counsel that will help a veteran counsel in a more soul-to-soul manner in accordance with the Scriptures. I've been counseling for decades and am being greatly helped by *Gospel Conversations*.

KEN LONG, Executive Pastor, Grace Fellowship Church, Florence, KY;
contributing author, *Christ-Centered Biblical Counseling*

"I'm not a counselor" is an all too common and erroneous statement. We are all counselors. Some of us counsel from behind our steering wheel or from our couch while watching our favorite sport. We offer counsel of some kind every day. The issue is whether we are good counselors. More importantly, are we biblical counselors? Our counsel is only as good as it is biblical. Much of what fosters the thought that we are not counselors is our judgment that we don't know how to talk to people about their particular trial or sinful habits. Bob Kellemen, in *Gospel Conversations*, provides the church with an invaluable resource to help people appreciate their fundamental role as a counselor. Not only that, it also offers the reader training in practical relational skills for becoming an equipped biblical counselor.

ANDREW ROGERS, Pastor of Soul Care, College Park Church

Gospel Conversations

Also by Robert W. Kellemen

Gospel Conversations

EQUIPPING BIBLICAL COUNSELORS

HOW TO CARE LIKE CHRIST

Robert W. Kellemen

Foreword by Brian Croft

ZONDERVAN

Gospel Conversations
Copyright © 2015 by Robert W. Kellemen

This title is also available as a Zondervan ebook. Visit www.zondervan.com/ebooks.

Requests for information should be addressed to:

Zondervan, 3900 *Sparks Dr. SE, Grand Rapids, Michigan 49546*

Library of Congress Cataloging-in-Publication Data

Kellemen, Robert W.
    Gospel conversations : how to care like Christ / Robert W. Kellemen.
       pages cm. — (Equipping biblical counselors)
    Includes bibliographical references and index.
    ISBN 978-0-310-51615-6 (softcover)
    1. Counseling – Religious aspects – Christianity. 2. Bible – Psychology. I. Title.
    BR115.C69K445 2013
    253.5 – dc23   2015003153

All Scripture quotations, unless otherwise indicated, are taken from The Holy Bible, *New Interna-tional Version*®, *NIV*®. Copyright © 1973, 1978, 1984, 2011 by Biblica, Inc.® Used by permission. All rights reserved worldwide.

The identities and situation of the individuals described in this book have been disguised in order to protect their privacy.

Any Internet addresses (websites, blogs, etc.) and telephone numbers in this book are offered as a resource. They are not intended in any way to be or imply an endorsement by Zondervan, nor does Zondervan vouch for the content of these sites and numbers for the life of this book.

Published in association with the literary agency of Wolgemuth & Associates, Inc.

Cover design: Christopher Tobias / tobiasdesign.com
Cover photo: Anthony Bradshaw / GettyImages.com
Interior design & composition: Greg Johnson/Textbook Perfect & Kait Lamphere

Printed in the United States of America

HB 02.07.2023

Contents

Foreword

No one was more surprised than I was to be asked to run the newest center on church revitalization at the Southern Baptist Theological Seminary. Besides the fact that there are many gifted and qualified people affiliated with this institution, I personally have no formal theological training or degrees. So why me?

They explained how crucial it was that the vision for this new center be driven by the practical, daily trench work of church revitalization that I knew well, not just a theoretical approach. They understood that to reach pastors in the trenches and to train students for this important work, they needed practitioners. They needed real pastors who had done this hard work in declining, struggling churches and have survived to tell about it to be the teachers, trainers, and motivators. In light of this, I gladly accepted.

There is an essential lesson that must be learned from this to be truly effective in all local church ministry: the theoretical must move to the practical. Faithful preaching must lead to piercing application. The truths of the gospel must permeate the deeper places of the heart in a raw and honest way. Otherwise, those truths become a mental exercise that stay on the surface of the soul and only bring an illusion of change without true healing.

This is especially true with the ministry of soul care. To treat the deep brokenness of the soul with heady theories and spirited debates is like a heart surgeon thinking a successful heart transplant has been accomplished by merely trimming a scab off one's chest. The soul must be reached to do effective soul care. Since the gospel of Jesus Christ is the only thing that gives us hope, healing, and life to our souls, the gospel must infiltrate the soul for true lasting healing to come in the midst of the layers of pain, scars, and hurt that each of us lug around in the crevasses of our souls. This cannot be done without a knowledgeable guide who is also a skillful practitioner — someone who has a strong grasp on the saving power of the gospel yet knows the interworking of the soul to know how to reach its depths with that gospel and help others do the same in a real, authentic way.

The book you hold in your hand uniquely does both. Bob Kellemen is overqualified to teach and lecture on all facets of biblical counseling, evidenced not just in the myriads of letters at the end of his name, but in the respect and reputation he has earned among his academic colleagues and fellow biblical counselors. But more importantly, Bob has a unique gift to take the truths of the gospel he knows so well and skillfully move them to the heart and help others do the same.

Gospel Conversations: How to Care like Christ is one of the finest demonstrations of that skillful movement I have ever read. It is a practical, well-balanced, and an incredibly useful tool that will press others to be real, raw, and honest in the safety of Christian community, which is essential to get to those deeper places in our souls.

One word of counsel: Bob understands the best way to learn how to care for souls is by doing it and allowing others to do the same for you. Do not settle into this book as a distant reader with your heart on the shelf. Bob will not allow it. He wants and even expects you to participate and have your own soul nourished, challenged, and met by the sweet, real, and forgiving presence of Jesus.

This book is all you will need to guide and train others to minister the gospel to the soul. But if you will take the risk of engaging in this book with your own soul as intended, I am confident you will not only more fully learn how to help others care for souls, but you will also experience the healing balm of the gospel for your own soul in a new and fresh way.

BRIAN CROFT, Senior Pastor, Auburndale Baptist Church; Founder, Practical Shepherding; Senior Fellow, Mathena Center for Church Revitalization, SBTS

Acknowledgments

Gospel conversations involve much more than something someone shares in an "official counseling session." Gospel conversations can and ought to be normal parts of everyday life. No one in my life exemplifies this more than my wife, Shirley. Shirley — you apply the gospel of Christ's grace to my life every day, not only in words, but even more so in attitude and action. If anyone has ever been "Jesus with skin on" to me — it is you, Shirley. Thank you.

Over the years, I've worked with several publishers/editors, and have enjoyed each working relationship. Ryan Pazdur of Zondervan has not only been an editor, but a sounding-board, and a friend. Thank you, Ryan, for the work you and your team have done to make *Gospel Conversations* a much better book than it would have been without your help.

My agent, Andrew Wolgemuth, of Wolgemuth & Associates, Inc., has truly become a great friend. We pray for each other. We care about each other's lives and families. Andrew has the rare blend of a sharp mind, business acumen, and a loving heart. Thanks, Andrew!

INTRODUCTION

Christlike Care

For two decades I've offered local church seminars on how to care like Christ. I originally called the seminar "What to Do After the Hug." People who attend seminars on counseling, just like people who read books on counseling, have a heart to care, but they often share that they feel ill equipped to know how to care in a Christlike way.

You might think this is true of "laypeople," but not of pastors. However, numerous studies indicate that pastors, even after graduation from seminary, feel inadequately prepared for the task of pastoral counseling.[1]

Our need to learn how to care like Christ is common to all Christians. The author of Hebrews recognizes this when he exhorts believers to consider how to spur one another on toward love and good deeds (Heb. 10:24). Like all believers, the Hebrew Christians were struggling with suffering (Heb. 10:32 – 34) and battling against temptations to sin (Heb. 3:12 – 14). Throughout Hebrews, the author directs believers back to Christ and his gospel of grace — applied daily — as their sure hope and practical help (Heb. 1:1 – 9; 2:1 – 4, 14 – 18; 3:1 – 11; 4:14 – 16; 10:19 – 23).

The two books in the Equipping Biblical Counselors Series — *Gospel-Centered Counseling* and *Gospel Conversations* — are written in obedience to this command to give careful thought and consistent attention to how to use the gospel to encourage one another to resist temptation and to respond to suffering with love for God and one another. *Gospel Conversations* provides an intensive, relational, hands-on equipping manual. Through it you will develop twenty-one biblical counseling relational skills so you can *care like Christ*. (See figure 1.1 at the end of this introduction.)

The two books in the Equipping Biblical Counselors Series—*Gospel-Centered Counseling* and *Gospel Conversations*—are written in obedience to this command to give careful thought and consistent attention to how to use the gospel to encourage one another to resist temptation and to respond to suffering with love for God and one another.

What Is a "Gospel Conversation"?

What do gospel conversations look like and sound like? It will take this entire book to answer that question fully, but here's my one-sentence summary:

> Gospel conversations promote personal change centered on the person of Christ through the personal ministry of the Word.

Jay Adams rightly summarized that "All counselors have one goal in common: change . . ." and "use verbal means to bring about the change."[2] Biblical counseling is change through talking—but not just any type of talking. It is talking or conversation that relates Christ's gospel story to our life story.

I've been equipping biblical counselors in the local church and seminary settings for three decades. I summarized those thirty years in *Soul Physicians*:

> I have doggedly pursued the fundamental question: *What would a model of biblical counseling and discipleship look like that was built solely upon Christ's gospel of grace? What does the gospel offer? What difference does the gospel make in how we live, how we relate, and how we offer help?*[3]

The essence of gospel conversations is helping one another to understand and apply the gospel to the details of our lives as saints who struggle with suffering and sin. Through your active participation in this training manual, you'll learn how to use four biblical compass points to speak gospel truth in love—gospel conversations:

- *Sustaining: "It's Normal to Hurt"*—Learning how to weep with those who weep by offering biblical sustaining care for hurting people.
- *Healing: "It's Possible to Hope"*—Learning how to give hope to the hurting by offering biblical healing comfort and encouragement for suffering people.
- *Reconciling: "It's Horrible to Sin but Wonderful to Be Forgiven"*—Learning how to be a dispenser of Christ's grace by offering biblical reconciling for people struggling against besetting sins.

+ *Guiding: "It's Supernatural to Mature"* — Learning how to disciple, coach, and mentor by offering *guiding* wisdom for people growing in Christ.

How Do We Get from Here to There?

Gospel Conversations is a local church curriculum map. It is a best-practice manual for equipping God's people to care like Christ — to change lives with Christ's changeless truth. But how do we learn to care like Christ? Is it just a "brain dump" where you read *about* gospel conversations?

Whenever I equip biblical counselors, I begin our learning time with the "big idea." I'll often state it like this to the group, "If you forget everything else today, remember this ..." Here's the big idea of *Gospel Conversations*. If you forget everything else in this book (I pray that you don't), remember this:

> We learn to become competent biblical counselors by giving and receiving biblical counseling in the context of real and raw Christian community.

We don't learn to be effective counselors simply by reading a book — no matter how profound the book. We don't learn to be skilled people-helpers simply by engaging in role-play scenarios or even by watching experienced counselors — though both of these are very helpful methods. We learn to be effective biblical counselors through face-to-face gospel ministry where we speak the truth in love to one another.

Here's the most important piece of advice I can offer you as you work your way through *Gospel Conversations*: Do not try to use *Gospel Conversations* simply as text to read or a lecture to give. That is not how I designed it. I've designed *Gospel Conversations* as an experiential training manual that promotes real and raw, vulnerable and open relationships among your equipping group members.

A Relational Training Manual

Gospel Conversations is "not your father's textbook." Though you can use it individually, I've structured it ideally for use in a small group lab setting where you can engage one another — by giving and receiving biblical counseling in the context of community. The book's extensive content is to be *experienced*, not simply read or taught. Trust me — I am every bit as concerned about content as you are. There's no "dumbing down" here.

Here's an idea of what that might look like. Your group facilitator directs the group's attention to a question, perhaps about a counseling scenario mentioned in one of the chapter lessons. The group starts interacting, and at first it is somewhat "surface." But as they share a bit more, the group facilitator detects that one group member is responding much more personally. So the leader asks, "Becky, it seems like this question has stirred up some deep thoughts and feelings for you. Would it be okay if we shifted from a more academic discussion to a more personal one? Would you like us to help you think through what's going on for you and in you right now?"

That's different, isn't it, from how we sometimes work through a discussion guide. Just as the group facilitator in the vignette above *invited* Becky to "go deeper," so I would invite your group to consider going deeper, going personal. Of course, that requires that your group develops trust — that your group is not just a "class studying biblical counseling," but fellow members of the body of Christ ministering to one another as you speak and live gospel truth in love.

A Kid in His Dad's Oversized Suit

I will never forget the first evening I spent with the first group of men and women I was training in biblical counseling. Among the twelve trainees was my wife, but everyone else was between five and twenty-five years older than I was. This was back in the day when pastors wore a suit and tie — even on a Wednesday night. I was doing just fine during the first hour of our training — the lecture/interaction hour (where we explored and applied content similar to what you will find in the book that accompanies this one, *Gospel-Centered Counseling*). After a short break, we switched our chairs from rows to a circle and were about to begin our first counseling small group lab.

Suddenly, an overwhelming image struck me. I pictured myself as a ten-year-old boy dressed in Dad's oversized suit, the sleeves dangling over my hands, and my legs too short for my feet to touch the floor. The image shouted to me, "You are so ill-equipped to train this group, and the experiential lab part of this class is going to expose you as a novice, as the unprepared rookie that you are!"

My first inclination was to ignore the image and to pretend that all was fine. Instead, I made one of the most significant decisions of my young ministry. I shared that mental image with the class. Rather than act like I had it all together, I decided to "walk the talk." I had told each of them during the recruiting process that we were going to get real and talk honestly about life. And that first night we did, and we were never the same because of it. We connected. We bonded. We spoke the truth in love to one another.

Can you guess what I discovered? I wasn't the only person in our biblical counseling training group who felt intimidated. Person after person shared their story of trepidation. We laughed and cried. We shared Scripture about our identity in Christ. We prayed. We went way over time … and nobody noticed (except the nursery worker who was watching our newborn daughter, Marie). That day set the tone for our entire time together because that day we gave and received biblical counseling in the context of real and raw community.

How to Use Your *Gospel Conversations* Training Manual

I understand that some of you are ready to jump right into chapter 1. I appreciate your excitement. Since this is not your father's training manual, could I encourage you to take ten minutes to read the next few pages? I'm confident it will be well worth your time.

The Transformational Small Group Climate and How to Cultivate It

Throughout this book, I use the words "lab," "small group," and "small group lab" interchangeably. The word "lab" used alone can have a clinical feel to it. Instead of real life, lived together *experiential* learning, you might picture an artificial and forced connection — more like *experimental* learning. When I say "small group – oriented training," some of you might think that we are training people to be only or primarily small group leaders. But putting together "small group lab" is meant to convey that *community is the container for equipping in biblical counseling competency.* The authentic, intimate small group environment provides the fertile soil in which we nurture competent biblical counselors.

In teaching, if we become overly dependent upon a lecture mode and content communication, we suck the life out of our biblical counseling training. In small group labs, if we become overly dependent on skill development, we suck the air out of the one-another community environment. If it is only a place for discussing case studies, or observing experts counsel, or just for practicing skills through role-playing, the lab becomes a sterile environment. While all of these are essential components of lab work, they must exist within a genuine, secure small group community.

In lab training, my first goal is to cultivate a climate where we experience biblical counseling together. We grow more like Christ as we receive soul care for our suffering and our struggle against sin. We become more competent biblical counselors as we sustain, heal, reconcile, and guide *one another* in our small group lab.

How do we do this? It begins with a mind-set, with a vision communicated consistently. We are not a pack of lab rats. We are image bearers. We are here not simply to learn skills but to minister to one another. Then we must model that vision. I did that when I shared with my first training group my image of myself as a ten-year-old boy in my father's oversized suit. In my very first seminary small group lab, two of my students had so caught the vision that on the very first day, they invited me to open up. One was a pastor's wife, one was a pastor, and as the lab began, they asked me what the transition was like from pastor to professor and who was building relationship into my life now.

Rather than dismiss their care and concern so I could focus on the lesson plan, I shared openly. The group focused on me. I was on what became affectionately known as "the hot seat." The hot seat refers to any time the group shifts its focus from discussing the material in *Gospel Conversations* to offering biblical counseling within the group.

By responding to their invitation, I modeled the priority of "presence" — staying in the moment, dealing with what was happening in the room, focusing on the people in the group and the relationships among the group members. Whether in the seminary setting or the local church setting, I have found that you rarely need to role-play, because when you prioritize presence, you experience and engage in live biblical counseling with one another.

Authentic community is caught and learned by experience more than it is taught or read. When I consult, churches often bring me on-site to lead a small group lab. In a lab we will be talking about a question from *Gospel Conversations* or dabbling in a role-play assignment. I'll say something like this: "Bill, that question seems like it really hits home for you. Would you like to talk about it a bit more at a personal level?"

After an hour of the group counseling Bill on "the hot seat," he'll likely say, "Wow! In an instant, we moved from talking *about* counseling to my *being* counseled." And someone else will chime in, "Bill, thank you for your courage to be so vulnerable and open. Not only did it help you personally, but I learned more in the one hour of our counseling you than I would ever learn in hours of reading about counseling."

This also illustrates the need to invite intimacy, not to force intimacy. While some labs stay clinical forever, I have observed others that are so bent on experiencing deep relationships that people feel guilty if they are not ready to go deep, or they feel coerced into going deeper faster than they were ready. Knowing the difference is not always easy, but it begins with creating a safe environment — safe to go deep *or* safe not to go deep until a group member is ready.

Transformational Small Group Lab Methods and How to Implement Them

Don't think that "the hot seat" is all you do. The goal is not to turn a spontaneous, divinely appointed connection into a method. A grace-oriented community where group members feel safe to speak the truth in love is the context for using a variety of lab-based methods. Since we want to avoid the mechanical implementation of lab methods, it can be helpful to consider a variety of ways that you can use *Gospel Conversations* so that you learn biblical counseling in the context of giving and receiving biblical counsel.

- Come to your lab small group having read assigned content sections of *Gospel Conversations*. Your lab leader will facilitate discussions and respond to questions about principles and methods of biblical counseling. Be prepared for these interactions to quickly "morph" into real-life counseling situations.

- Come to your lab having completed the built-in application/interaction sections — called "Maturing as a Biblical Counselor" — spread throughout each chapter lesson. You'll find three different categories in these sections: self-counsel, counseling others, and counseling one another.

  - *Self-Counsel Questions:* Come to your lab having completed the character development questions — called "Self-Counsel" — in *Gospel Conversations*. Your lab can then use this section of *Gospel Conversations* in several ways. Sometimes you will pair up with a lab encouragement partner to share. Other times you can start with a particular question, yet always stay open to the discussion soon morphing into "the hot seat." Other times the leader can simply invite people to share: "Is there a particular question that raised something in your heart and life that you want us to help you with?"

  - *Counseling Others Questions:* Come to your lab having completed questions related to counseling competency development — called "Counseling Others." Some of these require you to share how you might respond to a person with a particular issue. Others ask you to evaluate or discuss a case study. Still others suggest role-plays that you can practice with your encouragement partner or that you can practice in the group. As always, be open to these role-play scenarios developing into real-life counseling issues.

- *Counseling One Another Questions:* Come to your lab prepared for the third type of interaction questions — called "Counseling One Another." As you think through how to personally apply material, four options will be suggested. Your group could spread out over the room, break out with a lab partner, and privately counsel one another. Or one person could volunteer to be counseled by the entire group. Or one person could volunteer to be counseled by the lab facilitator as the group observes. Or you could have one person volunteer to be counseled by a group member while the lab facilitator provides occasional guidance and the group observes. After the counseling concludes, be sure to "debrief" by talking about what you learned in your personal life and as a biblical counselor. If you are working through this material individually, then respond to these *counseling one another* questions in writing, being sure to write down an action plan for growth.

- The important principle to remember with your *Gospel Conversations* training manual is that it is your servant, not your master. It is a guide to prompt discussion, not a list of questions you must cover in an allotted amount of time. Allow the material to prime the pump and get the discussion going, and then use your biblical counseling skills to invite one another to go deeper.

- Hold one another accountable for having read and engaged the material thoroughly before class, and then you don't have to be concerned with covering everything in class.

We can categorize additional lab-training methods by thinking through increasing levels of on-the-job training and intensity.

- *Discuss Case Studies:* The leader facilitates a discussion of a case study with background information and presenting problem and has the group explore relevant biblical principles (theory) and how they would intervene and interact (methods).

- *Practice "Meta-Skills":* The facilitator gives group members specific, brief assignments to practice specific skills such as listening or spiritual conversations. Often it is helpful to do this in triads: one person is the counselor, one person is the counselee, and a third person provides feedback. Then you rotate so that each person has occupied each role.

+ *Use Triad Role-Play Counseling:* This combines and goes beyond case studies and meta-skills. The facilitator shares a prepared case study, then one student plays the counselee, another student plays the counselor, and a third student provides feedback.

+ *Use Group Observation Role-Play Counseling:* Here, instead of just one person observing, the entire class observes one student role-play counseling another, and then they all provide feedback.

+ *Use Observation of Live Counseling by the Trainer:* Either a class member, a church member, or a member of the community is counseled live by the trainer while the class observes. After the session ends, the trainer/counselor, the counselee, and the class interact about what they observed and learned, and they ask questions for clarification and instruction.

+ *Use Live Counseling by the Trainee with the Trainer Sitting In:* The class observes while a trainee counsels either another class member, a church member, or a member of the community. The trainer/supervisor is in the room and periodically offers feedback, shares probing questions, and occasionally and briefly counsels and hands things back to the trainee. Everyone interacts about the counseling afterward.

+ *Use Live Counseling by the Trainee without the Trainer Sitting In:* The trainer and the class observe the student counseling someone live, and all interact at the end of the session.

Some of the live counseling will be preplanned and may occur in a room with a microphone and a one-way mirror if your facilities allow for that. At other times, the live counseling occurs spontaneously through "the hot seat" method described previously.

Frequently, when you are discussing the live counseling, the trainee/counselor will end up on "the hot seat." A group member might note, "Barb, you seemed a tad disengaged in the counseling session. Did you sense that at all?" Perhaps Barb acknowledges her disengagement and the group invites Barb to ponder with them what may be happening in her heart that she wants to work on. Or, going even deeper, Barb may not acknowledge that she was relationally distant. Other group members might express a similar experience of Barb keeping them at arm's length. As the discussion unfolds, Barb will begin to disengage from the group. As the leader, you may discern that the timing is not right and you may need to address this later. Or you may invite Barb to either discuss it now with you in front of the group or later in supervision.

"Barb, it seems that you may be disengaging a bit with us even while we give you feedback about disengaging. Would you like to talk with me about that now, or would you like to interact with me about that later during supervision? Or would you like to think about it, ponder it, pray about it, and maybe share with us next week?"

At this point, your small group lab has come full circle. You have created a safe place to speak the truth in love. Barb spoke the truth in love to her counselee, but it raised issues in Barb's life. Now you have invited Barb to allow you and the group to enter her life. This is the essence of transformational small group lab-oriented training in biblical counseling — learning to become biblical counselors by giving and receiving biblical counseling in the context of real and raw Christian community.

Transformational Meetings with a Paul, a Barnabas, and a Timothy

The Christian community developed in the lab can and should be extended outside the lab time. I recommend that you use the time-honored and biblical threefold equipping model of:

+ Meeting with a Paul or Priscilla: A lab supervisor/mentor.
+ Meeting with a Barnabas or Ruth: A lab encouragement partner/ spiritual friend.
+ Meeting with a Timothy or Naomi: A protégé/counselee.

Transformational Supervision/Mentoring Meetings

The supervisory role is multifaceted. If you are the lab facilitator/leader, during meetings with trainees, always seek to help them to mature in the four areas of biblical content, Christlike character, counseling competence, and Christian community (see chapter 3). Spend time discussing questions about the content you have covered and its application to life. During these meetings, provide sustaining, healing, reconciling, and guiding biblical counseling. These meetings assist in the development of Christlike character. They also develop counseling competencies, since one of the best ways to learn to be a biblical counselor is to be counseled by an experienced biblical counselor.

During the course of your training, you can have encouragement partners record themselves counseling each other. Part of supervision can involve listening to portions of recordings and then helping trainees to assess and develop their counseling. As with the labs, many times the way trainees counsel can end up opening windows to their own heart issues. So, listening to a tape can quickly shift to talking about the trainee's own life.

Transformational Encouragement Partners/ Spiritual Friendship Meetings

Your group facilitator/trainer can pair up group members as encouragement partners/spiritual friends and have them meet at least every other week for an hour. During these meetings, they provide mutual sustaining, healing, reconciling, and guiding — biblical counseling through gospel conversations. They are also focused on developing counseling competencies. At times they will work through role-play assignments from *Gospel Conversations*. Most of the time they take turns counseling one another with real-life issues.

Transformational Protégé Counselee Meetings

As group members begin to develop their counseling competency, they can, under the facilitator's/trainer's supervision, be assigned protégés to counsel. The facilitator can screen and assign counselees based on their issues and the expertise of the trainee. All such meetings should be recorded. After the biblical counseling session, you can listen to your recording and evaluate yourself (see appendix 8.3). The group facilitator/trainer can listen to portions of the tape with you and together you assess and evaluate your biblical counseling.

Where We've Been and Where We're Headed

Counseling is complex because people and relationships are complex. However, learning how to relate in truth and love is not "rocket science"; it is biblical wisdom lovingly applied. So, to reduce complexity, I'll conclude each chapter with a "Twitter-size" tweet — a one-sentence summary of the main point of each chapter lesson. Here's my summary of our introduction to *Gospel Conversations*:

> • We learn to become competent biblical counselors by giving and receiving biblical counseling in the context of real and raw Christian community.

That's where we've been — learning the "how-tos" of how to care like Christ. We're headed next to the foundations of biblical counseling — four chapters that prepare us for robust, relevant, relational biblical counseling.

Figure 1.1

Biblical Counseling Relational Competencies Overview

Sustaining Relational Competencies: *GRACE*

G	Grace Connecting	Counseling Incarnationally
R	Rich Soul Empathizing	Climbing in the Casket
A	Attuned Gospel Listening	Hearing Life Redemptively
C	Comforting Spiritual Conversations	Sustaining Theological Trialogues
E	Empathetic Scriptural Explorations	Sustaining Biblical Trialogues

Healing Relational Competencies: *RESTS*

R	Redemptive, Relational Mind and Soul Renewal	Cropping Christ Back into the Picture
E	Encouraging Communication	Celebrating the Empty Tomb
S	Scriptural Treatment Planning	Pursuing Christlikeness
T	Theo-Dramatic Spiritual Conversations	Healing Theological Trialogues
S	Stretching Scriptural Explorations	Healing Biblical Trialogues

Reconciling Relational Competencies: *PEACEE*

P	Probing Theologically	Examining the Heart Biblically
E	Exposing Heart Sins	Confronting Lovingly and Wisely
A	Applying Truth Relationally	Connecting Intimately
C	Calming the Conscience with Grace	Dispensing Grace
E	Enlightening Spiritual Conversations	Reconciling Theological Trialogues
E	Empowering Scriptural Explorations	Reconciling Biblical Trialogues

Guiding Relational Competencies: *FAITH*

F	Fanning Into Flame the Gift of God	Envisioning Our New Identity in Christ
A	Authoring Empowering Narratives	Putting on New Covenant Living
I	Insight-Based Action Plans	Co-Creating Homework That Works
T	Target-Focused Spiritual Conversations	Guiding Theological Trialogues
H	Heroic Scriptural Explorations	Guiding Biblical Trialogues

Maturing as a Biblical Counselor

Self-Counsel and Group or Partner Interaction

1. *Gospel Conversations* requires you to be "real and raw," "open and vulnerable." To benefit from this workbook, you will need to be willing to look at your own life and be open to the counsel of others in your small group training lab. How prepared are you for that level of transparency? Does a group like this excite you? Intimidate you?

2. What impact are you hoping that *Gospel Conversations* will have on you personally— in your growth as a Christian?

3. What impact are you hoping *Gospel Conversations* will have on your growth as a biblical counselor? How do you hope to use this equipping in the lives of other people?

4. Share some of your fears and apprehensions as it hits you, "I'm going to counsel people?"

5. Share some of your joy and anticipation as it hits you, "I'm going to counsel people!"

FOUNDATIONS OF BIBLICAL COUNSELING

FOUNDATIONS OF BIBLICAL COUNSELING

When someone is being trained for the pulpit ministry of the Word—preaching—they rarely begin with the "how-to" class called "homiletics." In a homiletics class, the preacher-in-training learns how to develop and present a sermon. However, long before someone takes their first homiletics course, they've typically taken scores of foundational courses — Bible, theology, Greek, Hebrew, and many more. The art of preaching is built upon a deep and rich foundation.

Training in the personal ministry of the Word — counseling — is similar. Before we are prepared to learn the "how to" of counseling, we must learn the "why" and "what" of counseling. The art of counseling is built upon a deep and rich foundation. In *Gospel Conversations*, that won't involve scores of courses, but it will involve four foundational chapters. Before you work through the last eight chapters of *Gospel Conversations* where you will learn twenty-one biblical-counseling relational competencies, you will benefit from the following four chapters on the foundations of biblical counseling:

- Chapter 1: 5 Biblical Portraits of the Biblical Counselor: Sharing Scripture and Soul
- Chapter 2: 8 Ultimate Life Questions for Biblical Counseling: Listening to Scripture and the Soul
- Chapter 3: 4 Résumé Qualifications of the Biblical Counselor
- Chapter 4: 2 Guideposts and 4 Compass Points of Biblical Counseling

Gospel Conversations is an equipping manual, and I'm a coach at heart. Equippers, coaches, and teachers appreciate concrete, measurable objectives. I call them SOLOs: Student-Oriented Learning Objectives. Here are the SOLOs that will be our target as we learn the foundations of biblical counseling.

- *Active participants in the reading and application of chapters 1 – 4 will be able to:*
  - Speak the truth in love by sharing Scripture and soul (truth and relationships) like the apostle Paul did as a brother, mother, father, child, and mentor (chapter 1).
  - Apply the whole Bible story to the whole person's whole story by relating Christ's gospel story to people's earthly story (chapter 2).

- Identify and begin developing the four biblical characteristics that qualify them to be a competent biblical counselor (chapter 3).
- Follow a biblical and historical GPS that serves as a guide for the biblical counseling journey of helping saints who are enduring suffering and battling sin to pursue sanctification in Christ (chapter 4).

If you are working through *Gospel Conversations* with a group of people, then to meet these learning objectives, you will want to do the following prior to meeting with your small group training lab:

- Chapter 1: 5 Biblical Portraits of the Biblical Counselor: Sharing Scripture and Soul
  - Read pages 31 to 46.
  - Respond to all questions on pages 34 – 35, 42 – 44, and 46.
  - Read, meditate on, and study 1 Thessalonians 2.
  - Optional: Read the introduction of *Gospel-Centered Counseling*.
- Chapter 2: 8 Ultimate Life Questions for Biblical Counseling: Listening to Scripture and the Soul
  - Read pages 47 to 76.
  - Respond to all questions on pages 49 – 50, 60 – 63, and 69.
  - Read, meditate on, and study Genesis 1 – 3 and Revelation 19 – 22.
  - Optional: Read chapters 1 – 2 and 6 – 7 of *Gospel-Centered Counseling*.
- Chapter 3: 4 Résumé Qualifications of the Biblical Counselor
  - Read pages 77 to 94.
  - Respond to all questions on pages 78, and 92 – 94.
  - Read, meditate on, and study Romans 15:14 in context (12:1 – 16:27).
  - Optional: Read chapters 3 – 4 of *Gospel-Centered Counseling*.
- Chapter 4: 2 Guideposts and 4 Compass Points of Biblical Counseling
  - Read pages 95 to 118.
  - Respond to all questions on pages 97, 109, and 116 – 118.
  - Read, meditate on, and study 2 Corinthians 1:3 – 11.
  - Optional: Read chapters 8 – 9 of *Gospel-Centered Counseling*.

CHAPTER 1

5 Biblical Portraits of the Biblical Counselor: Sharing Scripture and Soul

Picture Trudy and Tony. Referred to you from another church, you've never met them before today. They've come to you after already having seen a divorce attorney. Trudy tells you that she is "100 percent motivated to be in counseling" and "desperately wanting to see our marriage saved." Tony is meeting with you because he feels it's his obligation to "make one more attempt to save this marriage."

What do Trudy and Tony need from you *first?* Do they need *truth* — scriptural insight about sacrificial love applied to their marital relationship? Or do they need *love* — to connect with you, to build a relationship with you so that they are ready to hear truth from you?

Which is most important in biblical counseling? Is the ministry of the Word primary and loving relationships secondary? Or is the relationship central, and you need to wait to share truth until you've established a trusting relationship?

Are these even the right questions? Do the Scriptures divide truth from relationship in ministry? Does the Bible speak in terms of ranking truth and love? Wouldn't that be somewhat like asking, "Which counselor is least effective: The one who ignores the greatest commandment to love God and others, or the one who ignores commands to counsel from the Word?"

The Bible never pits truth against love. It never lays them out on a gradation or ranking system. The Bible presents equal couplets: truth/love, Scripture/soul, Bible/relationship, truth/grace.

Maturing as a Biblical Counselor

Self-Counsel and Group or Partner Interaction

1. Why does it seem so hard to "blend" truth and love? Which do you tend more toward: The truth side or the love side? Why? What implications might that have for your growth as a biblical counselor?

2. In your life, who has modeled well truth *and* love as they have ministered to you? What impact has their blending of truth *and* love had on your life? On how you do ministry?

3. How would you answer these questions about what has priority in biblical counseling?

   a. Which is most important in biblical counseling? Is the ministry of the Word primary and loving relationships secondary? Or is the relationship central, and we wait to share truth until we've established the trusting relationship?

   b. Are those even the right questions? Do the Scriptures divide truth from relationship in ministry? Does the Bible speak in terms of ranking truth and love?

4. In addition to 1 Thessalonians 2, where would you go in Scripture to answer this question: Does the Bible teach that only the message matters, or does it teach that the messenger's character and the messenger's relationship to the hearer also matter greatly?

Counseling Others

5. If you were meeting with Trudy and Tony, what do you think they would need from you during your first meeting? What would your counseling with them during the first meeting "look like" and focus on?

Speaking the Truth in Love

And yet ... we're forced to ponder these questions about truth and love in every counseling session. I was forced to ponder the issue again recently when I listened to an excellent closing session at a biblical counseling conference. The message was biblical, relevant, and powerful. The wise, godly speaker wrapped the entire message around the theme that the power in our ministry comes solely from the power inherent in God's Word.

His concluding illustration put an exclamation point on his theme as he shared about the Christmas present he purchased for his daughter. The gift arrived two days before Christmas, delivered by "the UPS guy." The speaker's daughter, hearing the UPS truck pull into the driveway, bolted to the door to meet the delivery man. She snatched the package from his hands and raced to place it under the tree, not the least bit focused on the UPS guy. The speaker concluded with the phrase, "We're just the UPS delivery guy. The real gift, the great present, is the Word that we deliver. We're just the UPS delivery guy!"

I joined the crowd in "Amen!" I loved the illustration. I "got" the theme — the power is in the Word of God!

But then ... later that evening, I started asking myself, "Is that the complete biblical picture? Don't we always say that God calls us to speak the truth in love (Eph. 4:15), to make our love abound in knowledge and depth of insight (Phil. 1:9 – 11), and to share not only the gospel but our very own souls (1 Thess. 2:8)? Does the Bible really teach that only the message matters, or does it teach that the messenger's character and the messenger's relationship to the hearer also matter greatly?"

Once these questions started whirring through my mind, I couldn't sleep. Thinking about 1 Thessalonians 2:8 regarding sharing Scripture and soul, I turned in my Bible to 1 Thessalonians 2. As I read those twenty verses, five portraits of the biblical counselor emerged from the pages of my Bible. I saw then what I share with you now:

> Biblical counseling involves gospel conversations where we engage in soul-to-soul relationships as brothers, mothers, fathers, children, and mentors who relate Christ's gospel story to our friends' daily stories.

God calls us to love well and wisely. That's why, in biblical counseling, we must weave together in our ministries what is always united in God's Word — *truth and love* — comprehensive biblical wisdom *and* compassionate Christlike care. Biblical counseling is not either/or: *either* be a brilliant but uncaring soul physician *or* be a loving but unwise spiritual friend. God calls us to be wise *and* loving biblical counselors.

Not Just the UPS Delivery Guy

We are more than just the UPS delivery guy. According to 1 Thessalonians 2, God calls us to share his Word with the love of a brother, mother, father, child, and mentor. This is vital to our ministries today, just as it was vital to Paul's ministry in Thessalonica. Based on 1 Thessalonians 2:2 – 3, 5 – 6, commentator Leon Morris notes that

> it is clear from the epistle that Paul had been accused of insincerity. His enemies said that he was more concerned to make money out of his converts than to present true teaching. The accusation would be made easier in virtue of the well-known fact that itinerant preachers concerned only to feather their own nests were common in those days. Paul was being represented as nothing more than another of this class of preaching vagrants.[4]

Morris goes on to explain that in Paul's day,

> holy men of all creeds and countries, popular philosophers, magicians, astrologers, crack-pots, and cranks; the sincere and the spurious, the righteous and the rogue, swindlers and saints, jostled and clamored for the attention of the credulous and the skeptical.[5]

That's why the unity of Scripture and soul, truth and relationship was so vital to Paul. In writing to the Thessalonians, Paul is saying, "You doubt my credentials? Then be a good Berean who examines the message and the messenger — what I say, who I am, and how I relate to you." It's the identical message that Paul sends to every young minister anywhere. If you want to validate your ministry, then "Watch your *life and doctrine* closely. Persevere in them, because if you do, you will save both yourself and your hearers" (1 Tim. 4:16, emphasis added).

Paul writes 1 Thessalonians 2 to affirm his ministry as from God and to affirm the nature of all ministry from God by modeling the sharing of Scripture and soul, by embodying truth in love. It is God's plan to use his Word powerfully when we share it *truthfully and lovingly* — like a brother, mother, father, child, and mentor.

Portrait #1: The Love of a Defending Brother

Paul uses the Greek word for "brother" twenty-one times in 1 and 2 Thessalonians. He starts his first letter to the believers in Thessalonica by letting them know that he always thanks God for them: "For we know, brothers loved by God, that he has chosen you" (1 Thess. 1:4). Paul is saying they are siblings in God's family by grace. Imagine hearing from the great apostle Paul that you are family; you are equals — equally loved by God by grace.

Could our counselees say this of us? "I experience you as a beloved brother embracing me as a fellow, equal member of God's forever family by grace."

Paul's use of the word "brothers" is not limited to a family context, but also extends to an army/military context in the sense of a band of brothers who have one another's backs. Paul says it like this in 1 Thessalonians 2:1–2: "You know, brothers, that our visit to you was not a failure. We had previously suffered and been insulted in Philippi, as you know, but with the help of our God we dared to tell you his gospel in spite of strong opposition." The word "opposition" means agonizing and struggling together. It was used of teammates training together and of soldiers fighting together in warfare.

Though persecuted, Paul courageously shares because he cares. Paul describes his counseling ministry in similar language in Colossians:

We proclaim him, admonishing and teaching everyone with all wisdom, so that we may present everyone perfect in Christ. To this end I labor, struggling with all his energy, which so powerfully works in me. I want you to know how much I am struggling for you. (Colossians 1:28 – 2:1a)

Because I sell a lot of books out of my home, I know my UPS delivery guy quite well. While he sometimes struggles to lift those boxes up my stairs, it is *not* because he sees me as a brother or a teammate.

Notice that in 1 Thessalonians, Paul dares to share *the gospel* with his Christian brothers and sisters, and in Colossians, Paul labors out of love to proclaim

Christ to his believing brothers and sisters. Paul's brotherly relationship is *not* devoid of truth content; it is richly focused on Christ's gospel of grace.

> Could our counselees say this of us? "I experience our relationship as a band of brothers, and I experience you as a teammate who fights for me and agonizes on my behalf as you relate Christ's grace to my life."

Portrait #2: The Love of a Cherishing Mother

In the first portrait, Paul says to his counselee, "I've got your back, bro!" In this second portrait, Paul speaks as a mother who says, "I long for you with a nourishing and cherishing affection." We read of Paul's motherly love in 1 Thessalonians 2:7: "But we were gentle among you, like a mother caring for her little children."

Paul describes his gentle relational ministry as like a nursing mother, literally describing the tender nourishing of a breast-feeding mother. The word "caring" highlights cherishing, keeping warm, tenderly comforting. The Reformer John Calvin portrays the scene beautifully: "A mother nursing her children manifests a certain rare and wonderful affection, inasmuch as she spares no labor and trouble, shuns no anxiety, is worn out by no labor, and even with cheerfulness of spirit gives herself to her child."[6]

In 1 Thessalonians 2:9 we learn the nature of the nourishment Paul shares: "... while we preached the gospel of God to you." Paul's motherly love is not simply touchy-feely love devoid of content. It is passionate love filled with the meat of God's Word applied to people's lives. Paul speaks in similar motherly language in Galatians 4:19: "My dear children, for whom I am again in the pains of childbirth until Christ is formed in you." And he shares similar affectionate language in 2 Corinthians 6:11 – 13: "We have spoken freely to you, Corinthians, and opened wide our hearts to you. We are not withholding our affection from you, but you are withholding yours from us. As a fair exchange — I speak as to my children — open wide your hearts also."

> Could our counselees say this of us? "I experience you as a nursing mother nourishing me with gospel truth through tender, cherishing love."

Paul continues his theme of motherly affection in 1 Thessalonians 2:8: "We loved you so much that we were delighted to share with you not only the gospel of God but our lives as well, because you had become so dear to us." I call this a "ministry sandwich," because Paul sandwiches loving them so much and being "dear to us" around sharing Scripture and soul. The phrase "we loved you so much" means to long for, to affectionately desire, to yearn after tenderly. "Delighted" means to joyfully serve out of pleasure and not out of a sense of duty or obligation. "Share" emphasizes imparting generously and personally. Morris summarizes Paul's words well: "But the real sharing of the gospel implies the total committal of the preacher [I would add "counselor"] to the task. If they give a message, they also give themselves."[7]

Speaking about 1 Thessalonians 2:8, Milton Vincent, author of *A Gospel Primer for Christians*, describes well who we are, how we relate, and what we share: "We are significant players in each other's gospel narrative, and it is in relationship with one another that we experience the fullness of God in Christ.... The greatest gift I can give to my fellow-Christian is the gospel itself."[8]

Could our counselees say this of us? "I experience you as an affectionate, generous mother giving me Scripture and your very own soul because I am dearly loved by you."

Portrait #3: The Love of a Shepherding Father

Paul's third portrait of the biblical counselor communicates, "I love you individually and uniquely with a guiding love." We see this beginning in 1 Thessalonians 2:11: "For you know that we dealt with each of you as a father deals with his own children." The original Greek highlights the individual, focused attention that Paul gives each person he ministers to — each of you, his own children. Morris notes that this is not just general group concern, but individual pastoral care.[9] To Paul, no one was simply a number or an item on a "to-do" list.

Could our counselees say this of us? "I experience you as a father focused on me with individual pastoral attention."

Paul further describes his fatherly focused attention with these words: "... as a father deals with his own children, encouraging, comforting, and urging you to live lives worthy of God, who calls you into his kingdom and glory" (1 Thess. 2:11 – 12). Paul's ministry is *not* a one-size-fits-all ministry. To those in need of hope, Paul offers encouraging care — coming alongside to help and to en-courage: to implant courage into. To those struggling with loss, Paul offers comforting care — consoling the grieving and fainthearted, sharing in their sorrows. To those in need of insight and direction, Paul provides guidance by urging them — discussing application of truth to the specifics of their lives. Paul offers person-specific, situation-specific, and need-specific counsel (see also Eph. 4:29; 1 Thess. 5:14; and Rom. 12:15).

Could our counselees say this of us? "I experience you as a wise and caring father, shepherding me with exactly what biblical wisdom I uniquely need at the specific moment."

Portrait #4: The Love of a Longing Child/Orphan

Paul now turns his portraits upside down. Previously he has described his relationships as a brother to a sibling, a mother to her infant children, and a father to his individual children. What a contrast as he now communicates the love of an orphaned child bereaved of his parents. "But, brothers, when we were torn away from you for a short time (in person, not in thought), out of our intense longing we made every effort to see you" (1 Thess. 2:17).

"Torn away" is a phrase used of a child left bereft by separation from a parent — an orphan. The church father Chrysostom depicts the word powerfully: "He sought for a word that might fitly indicate his mental anguish. Though standing in relation of a father to them all, he yet utters the language of orphan children that have permanently lost their parent."[10] It reminds us of our Paul's description of his leave-taking with the Ephesian elders.

> When he said this, he knelt down with all of them and prayed. They all wept as they embraced him and kissed him. What grieved them most was his statement that they would never see his face again. Then they accompanied him to the ship. After we had torn ourselves away from them, we put out to sea and sailed straight to Cos. (Acts 20:36 – 21:1)

And what was the *content* of Paul's relational ministry to the Ephesian believers? It was gospel truth for daily sanctification.

> You know that I have not hesitated to preach anything that would be helpful to you but have taught you publicly and house to house.... However, I consider my life worth nothing to me, if only I may finish the race and complete the task the Lord Jesus has given me — the task of testifying to the gospel of God's grace. Now I know that none of you among whom I have gone about preaching the kingdom will ever see me again.... For I have not hesitated to proclaim to you the whole will of God.... Remember that for three years I never stopped warning each of you night and day with tears. Now I commit you to God and to the word of his grace, which can build you up and give you an inheritance among all those who are sanctified. (Acts 20:20, 24 – 25, 27, 31 – 32)

Could our counselees say this of us? "I experience you as longing for me so much that when we are apart, you grieve like an orphan."

When torn away, here's how Paul responded: "Out of our intense longing we made every effort to see you" (1 Thess. 2:17b). We could translate the tense and the language of the original like this: "We experienced such nonstop, eager desire to reconnect with you that we endeavored exceedingly to see you!"

Let's be honest. There are some counselees whose struggles are so difficult, and whose way of relating so troublesome and self-centered, that at times we think, "Couldn't someone else counsel this person?" In those moments, we need to pray for the Spirit to empower us with the type of love and longing that Paul writes about in 1 Thessalonians 2:17.

Could our counselees say this of us? "I experience you as desperately longing for deep connection with me as a child longs for connection with a parent."

Portrait #5: The Loving Respect of a Proud Mentor

Paul's final portrait of the personal ministry of the Word comes in a military context. He writes in 1 Thessalonians 2:18, "For we wanted to come to you — certainly I, Paul, did, again and again — but Satan stopped us." "Stopped us" literally means a cut in the road — an obstacle placed in the road by a military opponent to impede or slow the advance of oncoming troops.

Paul continues in this military context in 2:19: "For what is our hope, our joy, or the crown in which we will glory in the presence of our Lord Jesus when he comes?" Paul now paints the image of the conquering king or general. Typically that general would gladly, and not-so-humbly, claim all the accolades for himself. Instead Paul turns to the "lowly private" and says, "You earned the victor's crown. The glory wreath! You are a spiritual warrior. Well done!" Sometimes we so focus on confronting the sins of our counselees that we forget that they are, by God's grace, saints — victorious in Christ. And we forget to celebrate with them their victories.

Could our counselees say this of us? "I experience you as a mentor so proud of who I am in Christ that you give me a spiritual medal of honor."

As if to put an exclamation point on his respect for them, Paul concludes, in verse 20, "Indeed, you are our glory and joy." Paul loves them and is proud of them. He publicly honors them for their esteemed service. They are spiritual champions in Christ.

Could our counselees say this of us? "I experience you as a mentor so proud of who I am in Christ that I am your pride and joy."

Maturing as a Biblical Counselor

Self-Counsel and Group or Partner Interaction

1. Regarding Portrait #1: The Love of a Defending Brother:

   a. Could your counselee say this of you? "I experience you as a beloved brother embracing me as a fellow, equal member of God's forever family by grace."

   b. Could your counselee say this of you? "I experience our relationship as a band of brothers, and I experience you as a teammate who fights for me and agonizes on my behalf as you relate Christ's grace to my life."

   c. What needs to happen in your heart and ministry to grow as a biblical counselor who exhibits the love of a defending brother?
   Drop my ego, my agenda, initially, but be one who is truly concerned, listening carefully

2. Regarding Portrait #2: The Love of a Cherishing Mother:

   a. Could your counselee say this of you? "I experience you as a nursing mother nourishing me with gospel truth through tender, cherishing love."

   b. Could your counselee say this of you? "I experience you as an affectionate, generous mother giving me Scripture and your very own soul because I am dearly loved by you."

   c. What needs to happen in your heart and ministry to grow as a biblical counselor who shares the love of a cherishing mother?
   I must thoroughly believe and know that the tender, sacrificial motherly love

3. Regarding Portrait #3: The Love of a Shepherding Father:

   a. Could your counselee say this of you? "I experience you as a father focused on me with individual pastoral attention."

   b. Could your counselee say this of you? "I experience you as a wise and caring father, shepherding me with exactly what biblical wisdom I uniquely need at the specific moment."

   c. What needs to happen in your heart and ministry to grow as a biblical counselor who offers the love of a shepherding father?

      Wise, measured

4. Regarding Portrait #4: The Love of a Longing Child/Orphan:

   a. Could your counselee say this of you? "I experience you as longing for me so much that when we are apart you grieve like an orphan."

   b. Could your counselee say this of you? "I experience you as desperately longing for deep connection with me as a child longs for connection with a parent."

   c. What needs to happen in your heart and ministry to grow as a biblical counselor who embodies the love of a longing child/orphan?

      Earnestness, hopeful

5. Regarding Portrait #5: The Loving Respect of a Proud Mentor:

   a. Could your counselee say this of you? "I experience you as a mentor so proud of who I am in Christ that you give me a spiritual medal of honor."

b. Could your counselee say this of you? "I experience you as a mentor so proud of who I am in Christ that I am your pride and joy."

c. What needs to happen in your heart and ministry to grow as a biblical counselor who demonstrates the loving respect of a proud mentor?

Encouragement, Comraderie

"Truth Telling" and "Building Relationships" Are Not Counseling Skills

Recall our initial discussion in this chapter regarding which has priority: truth telling (truth) or building relationships (love). One of the reasons we separate these concepts rather than unite them is because we think of them as counseling skills, techniques, competencies, or a stage in counseling. That's a mistake.

In 1 Thessalonians 2:1 – 20, Paul is not talking about a process of relationship building in the way that we might talk about "establishing rapport." We would use "establishing rapport" as a counseling stage or skill. Instead, Paul is talking about a caring heart that loves out of a family relationship: as a brother, mother, father, child, and mentor. For Paul, and for us, a family relationship with a counselee is not a stage; it is a heart attitude.

Nor is Paul in 1 Thessalonians 2:1 – 20 talking about a process of truth telling the way we might talk about "instruction in counseling." We would use "instruction in counseling" as a counseling stage or skill. Instead, Paul is talking about truth telling as a comprehensive gospel-centered worldview that provides the wisdom for gospel conversations — speaking truth in love — truthing and loving.

Truth and love are not counseling techniques, competencies, skills, or stages. Truth and love are the united framework and heart commitment out of which we counsel. They are broader terms that emphasize scriptural wisdom and Christlike love as the foundation for our approach to biblical counseling and our approach to our counselees.

Counseling relational competencies are not bad. In fact, in *Gospel Conversations* we will develop twenty-one biblical relational competencies. My point is that these relational competencies must be truth/love competencies — they must flow from a heart of Christlike love and a mind growing in Christlike wisdom.

So we can ask, "With Trudy and Tony, do we wait to share truth until we build relationship?" That question assumes that when we say "build relationship," we are thinking of a counseling skill or stage. But if we are thinking of "build relationship" as a heart issue, then we would say it like this: "We wait to counsel anyone until our heart is progressively moving toward a heart of love like a brother, mother, father, child, and mentor." The Christlike character of the counselor is the issue. If my character does not increasingly reflect the Christlike relational love of a brother, mother, father, child, and mentor, then I need to "switch chairs." I need to become the counselee, the disciple.

Or, we can ask, "With Trudy and Tony, if I have a Christlike heart of love, is 'truth telling' the first thing I do in my counseling relationship with them?" Again, that question assumes that when we say "truth telling," we are thinking of a counseling skill or stage. But if we are thinking of "truth telling" as a comprehensive, gospel-centered worldview, then we would say it like this: "We wait to counsel anyone until our mind is growing in knowledge of God's truth so that we can share Scripture with the wisdom of a brother, mother, father, child, and mentor." The Christlike biblical content/conviction of the counselor is the issue. If my biblical wisdom is not increasingly reflecting Christlike wisdom, then I need to "switch chairs." I need to become the counselee, the disciple.

"Truth telling" is not the first thing I do in counseling any more than "relationship building" is the first thing I do. Typically, the first thing I do is *pray that I will listen well and wisely out of a heart of love and a mind filled with gospel truth*.

Where We've Been and Where We're Headed

Here's our tweet-size summary for chapter 1:

+ It is God's plan to use his Word powerfully when we share it truthfully and lovingly — sharing Scripture and soul like a brother, mother, father, child, and mentor.

Is that all there is to being competent to counsel? Chapter 2 suggests that we not only need to share Scripture and soul, we also need to listen to the Scripture and the soul. In chapter 2, we'll learn that in biblical counseling, the whole Bible story must impact the whole person's whole story.

Maturing as a Biblical Counselor

Counseling One Another

- If you are working through this material individually, then respond to these questions in writing, being sure to write down an action plan for growth.

- If you are working through this material in a lab small group, then with the entire group, or with a lab partner, or with the lab facilitator counseling one group member, or with a lab member counseling another lab member, use these questions as a starting place for giving and receiving biblical counsel.

1. We should wait to counsel anyone until our heart is progressively moving toward a heart of love like a brother, mother, father, child, and mentor. If my character does not increasingly reflect the Christlike relational love of a brother, mother, father, child, and mentor, then I need to "switch chairs" and become the counselee.

   a. How well are you loving others?

   I believe that I could love others well. Especially. now that I am aware of opportunity that God might bring to me

   b. Are there areas where you need to "switch chairs" and become the counselee so that your character can increasingly reflect Christlike relational love? If so, what issues do you want to address to become more Christlike in how you love others?

2. We should wait to counsel anyone until our mind is growing in knowledge of God's truth so that we can share Scripture with the wisdom of a brother, mother, father, child, and mentor. If my biblical wisdom is not increasingly reflecting Christlike wisdom, then I need to "switch chairs" and become the counselee.

   a. How well are you applying Christlike wisdom to your life and ministry?

   Good, I believe

   b. Are there areas where you need to "switch chairs" and become the counselee so that your counsel can increasingly reflect Christlike wisdom? If so, what issues do you want to address to become more Christlike in how you think about life issues?

CHAPTER 2

8 Ultimate Life Questions for Biblical Counseling: Listening to Scripture and the Soul

Think with me about how someone might *interpret* the main message of our first lesson. "What a helpful reminder that I need to share Scripture *and* soul. God calls me to love others as brothers, mothers, fathers, children, and mentors as I relate the gospel story to people's life stories. So ... as long as I have a loving heart toward my counselee and pick the right Bible verses to share with my counselee, then I will be a competent biblical counselor!"

Ponder how someone might *apply* the main message of our first lesson. With one counselee, they listen compassionately to their counselee's story of anxiety and then turn confidently to Philippians 4:6 to teach their counselee not to be anxious for anything, but in everything to make their request known to God. With another counselee, they listen compassionately to their counselee's story of emotional abuse from their spouse and then turn confidently to Romans 8:28 to instruct their counselee in the truth that God works everything — including emotional abuse — together for their good. With Trudy and Tony, they listen compassionately as Trudy and Tony share about their marriage difficulties and then turn confidently to Ephesians 5:21 – 33 to interact about biblical roles in a Christlike marriage. Then they wrap up their afternoon of counseling by sincerely and humbly thanking God for empowering them to speak the truth in love.

Maturing as a Biblical Counselor

Self-Counsel and Group or Partner Interaction

Several years ago, "Tim" shared his story with me. His uncle had repeatedly sexually abused him while he was in elementary school. Tim never told anyone about the damage in his soul until he finally found the courage to tell a pastoral counselor. Hear Tim's words:

> Bob, it was incredibly hard. I felt so ashamed, but I got the words out—sobbing as I shared. The second I finished, my counselor whipped out his Bible, turned to Genesis 3, and *preached a thirty-minute message on sin.* Bob, it wasn't even a good sermon! But worse than that, I knew that I was a sinner. I'm clueless as to how my pastoral counselor intended to relate that passage to my situation. At that second, did I need a sermon on my personal sin?

1. Has anyone ever interacted with you like Tim's counselor? What did it feel like? What were the results?

   Yes. It felt like my hurt was not heard or appreciated. I stopped listening and grew resentful.

2. What view of the Bible and of "people helping" might have motivated Tim's counselor?

   Truth without love

3. What view of the Bible guides *your* biblical counseling?

   Loving with truth
   Listen to understand and empathize
   Speak truth from a heart of empathy and understanding

4. What biblical content/information/wisdom does a person need to know in order to be a biblical counselor?

The more the better

While Philippians 4:6, Romans 8:28, and Ephesians 5:21 – 33 are powerful scriptural verses, has this counselor truly "done biblical counseling"? Has this counselor fulfilled the essence of God's biblical counseling mission statement to speak the truth in love and to share Scripture and soul?

One of the caricatures of biblical counseling states that it promotes the mentality of "one verse, one problem, one solution." Others have characterized biblical counseling as "take two verses and don't call me in the morning." Still others have judged biblical counselors to be sincerely loving (both of the Bible and people) but seriously simplistic.

We could respond to these caricatures defensively by telling ourselves, "Those people making those judgments simply don't trust the *sufficiency* of Scripture like *we* do!" Or we could ask, as we are doing in this chapter, "What does the Bible teach about the robust, rich, and relevant use of Scripture? What does it look like and involve to share Scripture and soul in a Christ-centered, comprehensive, and compassionate way?"

In chapter 1, I summarized my answer like this:

+ Biblical counseling involves gospel conversations where we engage in soul-to-soul relationships as brothers, mothers, fathers, children, and mentors who relate Christ's gospel story to our friends' daily stories.

+ It is God's plan to use his Word powerfully when we share it truthfully and lovingly — sharing Scripture and soul like a brother, mother, father, child, and mentor.

I can summarize my answer in chapter 2 with these two tweet-size statements:

- In biblical counseling, the gospel is the controlling lens through which we understand and interpret our counselee's life story.
- In biblical counseling, the whole Bible story impacts the whole person's whole story.

Taken together, these four summaries teach us that in order to *share* Scripture and soul well and wisely, we must *listen* well and wisely to Scripture *and* to the soul. We must listen competently and compassionately to the Bible's grand redemptive story *and* to our counselee's life story.

As biblical counselors, we stand between two worlds: the eternal/heavenly story narrated in God's Word *and* the temporal/earthly story narrated by our counselee. Picture the skilled biblical counselor "pivoting" constantly back and forth between these two stories and journeying with counselees as together they navigate these two stories.

Throughout *Gospel Conversations*, we will learn twenty-one biblical counseling relational competencies. In this chapter we learn the "metacompetency" that shapes every other counseling competency — *listening well and wisely to Scripture and the soul*. If we fail to listen to the main narrative of God's Word, then counseling competencies can become nothing more than secular skills and techniques. If we fail to listen competently and compassionately to the main themes of our counselee's earthly story, then counseling competencies can become nothing more than rote, routine soulless tools from a counseling toolbox. Since none of us has any interest in secular skills and soulless tools, let's ponder and learn how to listen to Scripture and the soul.

Listening Well to Scripture's Grand Redemptive Narrative

In *Gospel-Centered Counseling*, I label the one verse, one problem, one solution approach "the concordance approach" — where we use the Bible as a topical index of various verses for various problems.

> Some follow the *concordance* approach. The stereotype goes something like this: "I'm a committed Christian. I want to help you with your struggle. You have a problem. I'll use my Bible concordance to find God's answer." Some have called this the "one-problem, one-verse, one-solution" approach. There's confidence in the Bible, but its application lacks an understanding of the complexity of life and the rich nature of God's Word.[11]

The concordance approach to Scripture views the Bible as an answer manual, the biblical counselor as the answer man/woman, and biblical counseling as giving the right biblical answer to a person's questions about life. Those descriptions raise a host of questions that we must address. Does the Bible describe itself as an "answer manual," or, as I will suggest, as a grand redemptive narrative? And what difference does that description make? Is the biblical counselor the answer man/woman (just the UPS delivery guy) or a brother, mother, father, child, and mentor who shares Scripture and soul? And what difference does that description make? Is what makes biblical counseling biblical how many Bible verses we quote per session, or is it something richer?

Grasping the Bible's Grand Redemptive Narrative

Here's my premise: If we are to view the Bible accurately and use the Bible competently, then we must understand the Bible's story the way God tells it. And God tells his story and ours as the *drama of redemption*. To listen well to Scripture and to avoid the "concordance approach" to biblical counseling, we need to understand the main theme of Scripture: *a gospel narrative of relationship*.

The Bible presents a grand narrative in which God is both the Author and the Hero, with the story climaxing in Christ. God begins by telling the story of relationship initiated in Genesis 1 – 2 and relationship rejected in Genesis 3. After those first three chapters, the rest of the Bible tells the story of God wooing us back to his holy and loving arms, all the while fighting the Evil One who wants to seduce us away from our first love.

Ever since Genesis 3, *life is a battle for our love* — the ageless question of who captures our heart — Christ or Satan. In *Soul Physicians*, I encapsulated all of life as *a war and a wedding*.[12] Others have described it picturesquely as *slay the dragon; marry the damsel*. The Bible calls it "the gospel." Our counseling is sterile and dead if we see the Bible as an academic textbook or a concordance of problems. But if we view and use the Bible as the story — the gospel-centered drama — of the battle to win our hearts, then our biblical counseling comes alive.

Biblical counseling is biblical when the central message, the sweeping redemptive narrative of the Bible, becomes the controlling lens through which we look at all of life. We understand people, diagnose problems, and prescribe solutions through the Bible's gospel/grace grid. We share Scripture and soul by listening to what the Scripture's grand redemptive narrative communicates about the soul. That's what I mean by *the whole Bible story impacting the whole person's whole story*. It's also why I describe biblical counseling as gospel conversations where we engage in soul-to-soul relationships as brothers, mothers, fathers, children, and mentors who relate Christ's gospel story to our friends' daily stories.

Biblical counseling is biblical when the central message, the sweeping redemptive narrative of the Bible, becomes the controlling lens through which we look at all of life.

God's Story Interprets Our Story

How do we move from Scripture to our life script? Michael Horton, in *The Gospel-Driven Life*, helpfully frames our thinking. "Do I define the Jesus story or does it define me?"[13] Horton points out that we attempt to define our own stories not only by the answers we give but by the questions we ask.

> This is where we typically introduce the Bible as the "answer to life's questions." This is where the Bible becomes relevant to people "where they are" in their experience. Accordingly, it is often said that we must *apply* the Scriptures *to daily living*. But this is to invoke the Bible too late, as if we already knew what "life" or "daily living" meant. The problem is not merely that we lack the right answers, but that we don't even have the right questions until God introduces us to his interpretation of reality.[14]

We have it backward. We want our story to interpret God's story, when in truth God's redemptive story interprets and defines our story. In *Gospel-Centered Counseling* and *Gospel Conversations*, we turn to God's Word not simply to find answers for daily living, but first to discover God's ultimate questions about life — questions every counselor must address.

Listening to the Creator of the Soul

We understand the person sitting in front of us by first understanding what the Creator of the soul says about souls — about life, people, problems, and solutions. In my study of Scripture, I've found that the Bible's grand gospel narrative defines for us *eight ultimate life questions*. In *Gospel-Centered Counseling*, I outlined these questions as:

+ The Word: Where do we find wisdom for life in a broken world?
+ The Trinity/Community: What comes into our mind when we think about God? Whose view of God will we believe — Christ's or Satan's?
+ Creation: Whose are we? In what story do we find ourselves?
+ Fall: What's the root source of our problem? What went wrong?
+ Redemption: How does Christ bring us peace with God? How does Christ change people?

- Church: Where can we find a place to belong and become?
- Consummation: How does our future destiny with Christ make a difference in our lives today as saints who struggle against suffering and sin?
- Sanctification: Why are we here? How do we become like Jesus? How can our inner life increasingly reflect the inner life of Christ?[15]

Together, these *eight ultimate life questions* seek to answer the biblical counselor's foundational question: "What would a model of biblical counseling and discipleship look like that was built solely upon Christ's gospel of grace?" Additionally, these questions and their biblical answers arm us with biblical wisdom categories for thinking deeply about life and for applying Scripture robustly to life.

Two hallmarks of the modern biblical counseling movement have always been the *sufficiency of Scripture* and *progressive sanctification*. In the outline of life's eight ultimate questions, those two issues serve as bookends. By starting with the Word of God, we humbly submit to God's wisdom about life in our broken world. By ending with sanctification, we acknowledge that we build our answer to the question, "How do we become like Jesus?" upon God's answers to all the preceding questions — upon God's grand redemptive narrative.

Many theologians and biblical counselors have summarized the Bible as a CFR Narrative: Creation, Fall, Redemption. This summary offers a wonderful picture of the grand movement of the Bible's gospel story.

My six questions between my two bookends offer an expanded, robust portrait of the biblical narrative for biblical counseling. Instead of CFR, it is the "CCFRCC Narrative of the Drama of Redemption."

- Bookend One: The Word — The Sufficiency of Scripture for Biblical Counseling
  - Prologue: **C**ommunity — Before the Beginning/Eternity Past
  - Act I: **C**reation — In the Beginning
  - Act II: **F**all — The End of the Beginning
  - Act III: **R**edemption — Eternity Invades Time
  - Act IV: **C**hurch — In the Fullness of Time
  - Epilogue: **C**onsummation — After the End/Eternity Future
- Bookend Two: Progressive Sanctification — The Goal of Biblical Counseling[16]

In *Gospel-Centered Counseling*, I explored, chapter by chapter, each of life's ultimate questions *as they relate to our lives and ministries as biblical counselors.* My task in this chapter is not to repeat the sixteen chapters of *Gospel-Centered Counseling*. However, I do encourage you to read *Gospel-Centered Counseling* as I will be using the theology of life and biblical counseling from that book as a foundation for the methodology of counseling in this book.

Listening to Scripture *about* the Soul

In this chapter, I want to use those questions and summary answers to illustrate, through my counseling with Tony and Trudy, how to listen to the Scriptures about the soul. People often talk about "meeting people's felt needs" in preaching and in counseling. While it was helpful and compassionate for me to hear Tony's and Trudy's "felt needs," the Bible communicates their ultimate needs, their ultimate life questions, and life's ultimate answers.

Listening to Stories about the Source of Wisdom: The Word

As I counseled Trudy and Tony, it became clear early on that their sources of wisdom were worlds apart. Though both claimed Christ as Savior, if I had directly asked Tony, "Where do you find wisdom for life in a broken world?" he would not have answered, "God's Word." Yes, God's Word was authoritative for "spiritual matters" for Tony, but he did not see how the Bible related to his marriage, his feelings, or his search for happiness.

The source of truth wasn't a "felt need" for Tony. It wasn't even on his radar. But Tony was living by *a* source of truth — what made him feel complete, manly, happy. That wasn't only his radar; it was a magnet that attracted him irresistibly. Before we could go very far in counseling, I laid out for Tony my conviction that *we discover wisdom for how to live life in a broken world from the wisest person who ever lived — Christ.* Tony, ever blunt, told me, "If you can show me how that works in the *real* world, more power to you."

In response, I leaned over, acted like I was lifting something extremely heavy from the floor, leaned back up, looked Tony in the eyes, and replied, "I'm picking up the gauntlet, accepting your challenge. But it won't be my power that will demonstrate the relevance of God's Word — it will be God's power ..."

Listening to Stories about Our View of God: The Trinity

If I had focused only on Tony's felt needs (such as happiness and a wife who encouraged him and made him feel manly), I never would have pondered, "What comes into Tony's mind when he thinks about God?" Or, "Whose view of God and of life is Tony believing — Christ's or Satan's?" But everything Tony said about his life, his attraction to a coworker, his disdain for his wife — it all communicated a sub-biblical view of God, a sub-Christ view of God. Tony's God was not a God who so loved the world that he sacrificed his own Son. Tony's God was not a Savior who said, "Not my will, but thine be done." Tony's god was a genie-in-a-bottle god who wanted Tony happy at all costs.

Detecting those themes and threads in Tony's story did not mean that I blurted out, "You're worshiping the wrong god!" It did mean that I was listening with one ear to Tony's unstated but implied view of God and with the other ear to Christ as the perfect narrative and image of God. And it did mean that we probed together passages like Luke 15 and the prodigal and pharisaical sons to see what their "felt needs" were, what their views of God looked like, and how the true God offered them true life.

Running through my mind as I related God's story to Tony's story were these truths: (1) To know the God of peace and the peace of God, Tony must know his triune God in the fullness of his holy love demonstrated in the cross of Christ. (2) Because Satan attempts to plant seeds of doubt about God's good heart, God was calling me to crop the Christ of the cross back into Tony's picture.

Listening to Stories about People: Creation

Tony clearly had a felt need to answer the question, "Who am I?" The world might have diagnosed Tony as being in the throes of a classic "mid-life crisis." He had wrapped up his identity in his job, his kids, and his wife, and as everything was crumbling around him, Tony felt lost, empty, lonely, worthless. But, oh, how this coworker made him feel important, wanted, needed, intelligent ...

I didn't ignore those feelings in Tony. Not in the least — I wanted to hear his story, understand it from his eyes, from his soul. But I certainly did not ignore God's story — the story that asks a different question than "Who am I?" God's story asks, "*Whose* am I?"

If I had asked Tony, "Whose am I?" he would have honestly answered me, "Right now, I am *hers!*" He was captivated by his coworker. Likely the only thing stopping Tony from moving from an emotional affair to a physical affair was his coworker's reticence because she also was married.

So, over the course of time, Tony and I talked about "cisterns and springs" — as in Jeremiah 2:13 where God charges his people with the two sins of forsaking him, the spring of living water, and digging broken cisterns that could hold no water. This woman was Tony's broken cistern, and it was Tony's faulty view of God (see Jer. 2:5, 19) that made her seem more attractive to him than God was.

Listening to Stories about Our Core Problems: The Fall

Tony was shrewd. He said, "So, are you saying, like I always hear from the pulpit at my church, that I'm supposed to kill all desire?" As we interacted, I made it plain that God created us with deep desire — for him and for one another. And that the desire Tony needed to "kill" was the misdirected, sinful desire for this other woman, and the desire he needed to nourish was the pure desire for God and for his wife.

Tony was fierce in his conviction about the source of his problem. It was the church that killed desire. And it was his wife who was not satisfying his desire. In the course of counseling, I talked to Trudy about how she was relating to Tony. However, Trudy was *not* the root source of Tony problem. Tony was.

In answering together the question, "What went wrong in Trudy and Tony's marriage and in each of their hearts?" we looked to James 4:1 – 4, where God asks the great diagnostic question, "What causes fights and quarrels among you?" (James 4:1a). And we looked at God's great diagnostic answer:

> *Don't they come from your desires that battle within you? You want something but don't get it. You kill and covet, but you cannot have what you want. You quarrel and fight. You do not have, because you do not ask God. When you ask, you do not receive, because you ask with wrong motives, that you may spend what you get on your pleasures. You adulterous people, don't you know that friendship with the world is hatred toward God?"* (James 4:1b – 4a)

It was while we discussed this passage together that Tony began to break. It was now that he began to see not only his demandingness toward Trudy but his demandingness toward God. For the first time, Tony wept at the thought of how he was treating Trudy. And he wept as we pondered the biblical reality that the essence of sin is spiritual adultery — choosing to love anyone or anything more than God. Tony, like the prodigal son, began to "come to his senses" as he realized that spiritual adultery was behind his temptation toward marital adultery.

Listening to Stories about Solutions (Soul-u-tions): Redemption

By this point, Tony's story and God's story were merging — meeting at repentance, confession, and receiving grace. One of the most powerful "grace moments" was when Tony and I talked together with Trudy about the pain and suffering she had felt. Imagine the horrendous pain of being in a relationship with a man who repeatedly says, "I want *her*. I wish *you* could be like *her*."

But through it all, through Christ's strength, Trudy was committed to showering Tony with grace-love. Her grace brought tears not only to Tony's eyes but to mine as well as we celebrated together the "tastes of grace" that Trudy was offering her husband. Tony's ultimate need was peace with God, and he found it and more — peace also with his wife.

Of course, while repentance was the primary first step in Tony's life, he still needed ongoing power to change. Thus we explored the ultimate life question, "How does Christ change Tony?" We marveled at the truth that through regeneration Tony's new heart had a new "want-to," and through redemption his new heart had a new "can-do" — to put off his sinful desires and to put on his new Christlike desires for his wife and to sacrificially love his wife. The world talks about "solutions" — how *we* change. The Bible talks about "soul-u-tion" — how God changes us at the soul/heart level.

Listening to Stories about a Place to Belong and Become: Church

Tony, as I've noted, had some issues about church — his church and the universal church. As I listened to Tony's story, I detected that he had been subtly asking, "Where can I find a place to be affirmed — regardless of my behavior?" While the longing for belonging is a God-given one, it does not stop there. The church is a place to belong *and* become — to become more like Christ. Thus it is a place both of affirmation and of accountability, of comfort and care-fronting. For the story of Tony's changed heart and changed relationship to his wife to grow chapter after chapter, he needed his band of brothers in the church. I enjoyed listening to Tony talk about his renewed commitment to meeting with godly men at lunch and to rejoining his church's men's group. Tony was applying the biblical truth that sanctification is a community journey.

? where

Listening to Stories about Our Future Destiny: Consummation

Tony certainly didn't come into my pastoral counseling office and say, "Pastor Bob, my marriage is difficult, I've been tempted toward an affair, and I would like your help to know how eschatology (end-time events, heaven, eternity) might relate to my struggles today." However, I kept in the forefront of my mind the question, "How does Tony's future destiny with Christ make a difference in how he loves his wife like Christ *today?*" So I engaged with Tony in discussions that helped him to weigh, from a biblical perspective, living for immediate desires (the pleasure of sin for a season) versus "looking ahead to his reward" (Heb. 11:26) as Moses did.

Listening to Stories about Why We Are Here: Sanctification

As I listened to Tony during our first few meetings (marriage counseling and individual counseling), it was quite clear that his ultimate goal for counseling was quite different than mine. Like most counselees (like most of us), Tony fixed his mind on changing his circumstances and fixing his feelings. That's why he was with me in counseling and it was what motivated his life.

Little by little, as we interacted, I invited Tony to reflect on his goals — for counseling and for life. Gradually he shifted his focus from changing his circumstances to asking the Spirit to increasingly *change him into the image of Christ* — whether or not his circumstances changed.

Connecting Scripture and Soul

Theology matters. The Bible is relevant. The redemptive theme of the Bible is vital for our daily lives and our daily counseling.

As Tony's counselor, I did not see myself as his theology instructor. Instead, theology instructed and guided my thinking as I interacted with Tony. I listened to Tony's story theologically — that's what makes our biblical counseling truly biblical. Our understanding of the Bible's grand story enlightens us to understand people and to interpret their life stories through a biblical grid.

Data Collecting or Soul Connecting?

In the biblical counseling world, listening well in order to gather information has always been emphasized. However, I suggest that we use the phrase "soul connecting" rather than "data collecting." Out of context, "data collecting" or "gathering data" can sound like and communicate "the UPS delivery guy" instead of the soulful brother, mother, father, child, and mentor of 1 Thessalonians 2. Image bearers cannot be analyzed, dissected, examined, or studied. They can only be known, experienced, and loved.

Whatever we call it, it is vital that we listen well to our counselee's life story. And, as we've seen, listening well means *listening theologically*. Specifically, we need to listen well to people's *situational data* (what is happening around them and to them), and we need to listen well to people's *soul data* (what is happening in them as they respond to what is happening to them).

To listen well to situational data and soul data, we need to understand how God designed people. Knowing who God designed us to be provides us with our target or goal in counseling. The end goal of biblical counseling is *our inner life increasingly reflecting the inner life of Christ*. Christ is not only the exact image of God (Heb. 1:3); he is the perfect image of the healthy and holy image bearer. Our goal is not simply symptom relief, but Christlikeness. We are not solution focused; we are *soul-u-tion focused*.

A Biblical X-Ray of the Heart in the World

For us to move others toward this goal, we must grasp God's comprehensive original design for the human personality. Biblical counselors rightly talk frequently about the heart. But what is a comprehensive biblical understanding of the heart? In order to reflect God, relate to God, rule under God, and rest in God (Gen. 1:26 – 28), God designed image bearers as one comprehensive being with the following interrelated capacities of personhood:

- Relational Beings: Loving with Passion — Affections
  - Spiritual Beings: Communion/Worship
  - Social Beings: Community/Fellowship
  - Self-Aware Beings: Conscience/Shalom
- Rational Beings: Thinking with Wisdom — Mind-Sets
  - Rational Beings: Thinking in Images
  - Rational Beings: Thinking in Ideas/Beliefs
- Volitional Beings: Choosing with Courage — Purposes/Pathways
  - Volitional Beings: Heart Motivations
  - Volitional Beings: Actions/Behaviors

+ Emotional Beings: Experiencing with Depth — Mood States
+ Embodied Physical Beings: Living with Power — Embodied Personality
+ Embedded Life-Situational Beings: Engaging Our World — Embedded Socially
+ Everlasting Beings: Created by, like, and for God — *Coram Deo* Existence[17]

Figure 2.1 helps to capture the essence of our comprehensive nature. As you read the bullet points and ponder figure 2.1, *don't panic*. We'll explain, walk through, and illustrate every bullet point. In the rest of this chapter, this summary portrait of image bearers will serve as our guide for journeying with our counselees as we listen to their situational story and their soul story.

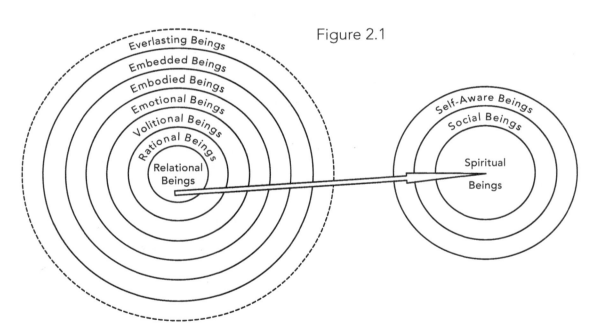

Figure 2.1

Maturing as a Biblical Counselor

Self-Counsel and Group or Partner Interaction

1. What would your tweet-size (140 characters) summary answers be to life's eight ultimate questions?

    a. The Word: Where do you find wisdom for life in a broken world?

    The Operators Manual

    b. The Trinity: What comes into your mind when you think about God?

    Sovereign, Wise, Good

    c. Creation: Whose are you?

    I am God's creation

    d. Fall: What's the root source of your problem?

    Neglecting #A, Rejecting #B Denying #C

    e. Redemption: How does Christ bring you peace with God? How does Christ change you?

    By changing your willing heart after turning it from stone to flesh

    f. Church: Where can you find a place to belong and become?

    g. Consummation: How does your future destiny with Christ make a difference in your life today as a saint who struggles against suffering and sin?

    Very joyful!!

    h. Sanctification: How do you become increasingly like Jesus?

    Abiding in Jesus and fighting against sin

Counseling Others

2. Think of a recent situation where you were counseling another believer. How could the following concepts shape your thinking about helping this person?

   a. The Word: To view the Bible accurately and use the Bible competently, we must understand the Bible's story the way God tells it—as a gospel victory narrative. We discover wisdom for how to live life in a broken world from the wisest person who ever lived—Christ.

   b. The Trinity: We must know the Trinitarian Soul Physician personally to be a powerful soul physician. To know the God of peace and the peace of God, we must know our triune God in the fullness of his holy love demonstrated in the cross of Christ.

   c. Creation: God designed our soul so that the whole, healthy, holy person's inner life increasingly reflects the inner life of Christ—relationally, rationally, volitionally, and emotionally. Our goal is to love like Christ (relational), think like Christ (rational), choose like Christ (volitional), and respond to our feelings like Christ (emotional).

   d. Fall: The essence of sin is spiritual adultery—choosing to love anyone or anything more than God.

   e. Redemption: Through regeneration our new heart has a new want-to; through redemption our new heart has a new can-do. Counsel Christians as saints—new creations in Christ.

   f. The Church: Sanctification is a community journey.

g. Consummation: As saints who struggle with suffering and sin, we must crop back into the picture our future purity and our future victory. The end of our story (eternity) impacts how we live out each chapter of our story today.

h. Sanctification: Sanctification is the art of applying our complete salvation empowered by God's grace, God's Spirit, God's Word, God's people, and God's future hope so we increasingly reflect Christ today.

Gathering Situational Data: Connecting Soul-to-Soul with the Outer Story

Think back to Tony. The first words out of his mouth during our first meeting were not, "Bob, I know that in the core of my being, I'm a spiritual being, designed to exalt and enjoy God. Help me to do that more and more like Christ." Like almost 100 percent of our counselees, Tony began not with his inner story (who he is in relationship to Christ), but with his outer story (what was happening to him).

We do people a disservice if we skip or race through their outer story. In fact, we are wise to start there and settle there for some time. Refer back to figure 2.1. As you look at the outer circle, you note that Tony is an everlasting being — God is his ultimate environment. We're aware of that and our counseling always consciously moves between God's eternal story and Tony's earthly story. But initially, Tony is most aware of the next circle — he is a "socially embedded being."

Tony would never use that language — and neither should we in a counseling session. However, as biblical counselors, we need to be aware of the concept of a socially embedded being. Biblical counselors seek to understand the influences that shape the responses of the human heart. Who we are is not a question we can ask without also seeking to understand the context in which we live.

As biblical counselors, we seek to recognize the complexity of the connection between people and their social environment. Thus, we seek to remain sensitive to the impact of suffering and of the great variety of significant

[handwritten margin note: To what extent? Greatly. Good relationship ⇒ happy heart. Bad relationship ⇒ unhappy.]

social-cultural factors (1 Peter 3:8 – 22) people have experienced. In our desire to help comprehensively, we seek to apply God's Word to people's lives amid both positive and negative social experiences — both now and in their past.[18]

As biblical counselors addressing the past and present relational experiences of our counselees, we are asking the *nurture* question: "To what extent do relationships affect how our heart (the inner person) responds to life?" While the Bible steers us away from social determinism (that our relational situation is the primary cause of our behavior), *[handwritten: the Bible]* it does clearly recognize the influence of other people on our lifestyle choices (Deut. 7:1 – 4; Prov. 13:20; Luke 6:40; Acts 4:13; 1 Cor. 15:33), and it compassionately identifies with the impact of suffering on the soul (Rom. 12:15; 2 Cor. 1:3 – 11). As biblical counselors, we seek to discern how Tony — as one complex, comprehensive person (body and soul/heart) — operates in a network of personal relationships situated within a society because we understand that he is a socially embedded being.[19]

Trialogues

To move from a *theology* of social beings to a *relational methodology* of engaging people's outer stories, I need to introduce a concept that will be central to almost every relational competency in this book — *trialogues*. A monologue is when I talk to you, teach you, or preach to you — I speak to you. A dialogue is when you and I engage in a back-and-forth, give-and-take conversation — we speak to each other. A trialogue is when there are three people in our conversation: the counselor, the counselee, and the Divine Counselor through God's Spirit and God's Word — together we listen to God.

Trialoguing is one of the major ways that we avoid the "concordance approach" to counseling. It is also a major way that counseling, or the personal ministry of the Word, is different from preaching/teaching, or the pulpit ministry of the Word. While the pulpit ministry of the Word is powerful and absolutely essential in our Christian lives, we should not think of biblical counseling as "preaching to an audience of one." The great beauty and benefit of the personal ministry of the Word is the give-and-take relationship that occurs.

In trialoguing, I take my theological understanding (God's story), listen to Tony's understanding of his situation (his life story), and then interact with Tony in ways that invite him to ponder how God's story interprets his story — this is the essence of a *gospel conversation*. That's why throughout *Gospel Conversations* we'll read hundreds of sample trialogues, often in one of two forms: scriptural conversations or spiritual explorations.

In a scriptural conversation, I consider *with* Tony how a specific passage might relate to his life story. For instance, when Tony was struggling to "kill" his desire toward "the other woman," we explored James 4:1 – 4 (as illustrated earlier in this chapter) and Hebrews 11:23 – 28. I did not "teach" Hebrews 11:23 – 38 to Tony. Instead, we read it together and then probed together questions like, "How do you think Moses was able to resist the temporary but very real pleasure of sin? How could Moses' response apply to your situation?"

He saw the greater reward with God — much greater than with Pharaoh

In caring spiritual conversations, I used biblical wisdom principles to engage Tony in discussions that helped him to think through his external and internal situation. Rather than necessarily looking at a specific section of Scripture, I explored with Tony biblical/theological/spiritual concepts that helped him to see God's perspective on his situation and his soul. For example, as Tony and I explored his image of God, we engaged in spiritual conversations like, "Where do you think you were recruited into this idea that God is a genie in a bottle and his number one concern is your happiness? Who modeled this idea for you? Does it seem to square with your understanding of the Bible? Of Christ?"

? Where did this come from?

In summary, scriptural explorations use specific applicable biblical passages to help people to relate God's truth to their circumstances. Spiritual conversations use broad theological concepts to prompt people to ponder more deeply their walk with God. Both use the Bible's grand redemptive narrative as the overarching context to understand and interpret our counselees' specific life stories — helping them to relate God's story to their stories.

Probing Trialogues for Exploring the Outer Story

Picture Tony and Trudy sitting down in front of you. You have very little information at this point about why they are even meeting with you other than a serious marital issue. Some basic introductory questions and trialogues could be of great help.

+ What situations, issues, or concerns bring you to counseling today?
+ Trudy and Tony, what would you each like to change about this situation?
+ What do you dream would be different about this situation?
+ What is your goal in talking today, Tony and Trudy? What results are you hoping for in counseling with me?
+ How will you know that our counseling has been successful, helpful?
+ Tony and Trudy, please give me a snapshot of your relationship.
+ What theme or title would you give to your situation?

Your goal at this point is threefold: (1) To help Tony and Trudy to clearly label their problem — what is their situational story? (2) To understand how they understand their problem — how do they see their story? (3) To empathize with them in their troubling story. We can't bring to bear God's story until we accurately and compassionately understand Tony's and Trudy's story.

Tracking Trialogues for Mapping the Influence of the Outer Story

We often approach life from "passengerhood." We don't feel like we are "more than conquerors." Tracking the influence of the situation helps Tony and Trudy to clarify their outer, external story. It also helps them to see that "the giant in the land" is something tangible, relational, and through Christ, conquerable. So, having used probing trialogues to identify the situational issues, now we can use tracking trialogues to *map the influence* of the problem on Tony and Trudy.

We start by helping them to *trace* their problem by using trialogues such as:

+ Tell me about the history of this struggle in your marriage? How long has this struggle existed? What have you done about this issue?
+ Tell me when the temptation with this other woman began, Tony.
+ What might happen if this problem were defeated? How would things be different for you if the issue were remedied?

We can also *track the influence* of the problem.

+ How do these struggles in your marriage affect each of you?
+ How is this problem depleting and defeating you?

It also can be very helpful to *explore the life support system* of the problem.

+ How might you be feeding this problem?
+ Are there any ways either or both of you are prolonging it?
+ Are there any ways you are contributing to the ongoing existence of this problem?

People need hope. *Tracking the influence of our counselee over* the problem can infuse hope.

+ When is the problem in your marriage a little bit less? What are you doing differently when this problem is not as severe? How will you and God keep these times of victory going and growing?

+ Imagine into the future. How do you see this problem being defeated?

+ Tell me about the time in your marriage before this stuff ever started.

+ Have you had other situations similar to this? What have you learned from these situations that might be helpful to you now?

Bridging Trialogues for Beginning to Relate God's Story to the Outer Story

Slowly we can begin to invite Tony and Trudy to ponder their story from God's perspective.

+ Could we explore any other ways of looking at this?

+ What would you like to see happen instead?

+ Tony and Trudy, I know you are both committed believers and active in your church. What do you think God's Word says about the source of your problems? What do you think God's perspective is on your situation?

+ Imagine that whatever you prayed about this issue, God would grant your request. What would you pray for? How would you know that God answered your prayers? What would be different? What would you be doing differently?

Biblical Counseling Forms for Gathering Situational Data

Good "paperwork" has an important place in biblical counseling. It should not replace face-to-face and soul-to-soul connecting, but it can supplement it. In appendixes 2.1 to 2.7, you'll find the following sample forms:

+ Appendix 2.1:   Biblical Counseling Initial Intake Form

+ Appendix 2.2:   Biblical Counseling Goals Form

+ Appendix 2.3:   Biblical Counseling Personal Information Form

+ Appendix 2.4:   Authorization for Release of Information: To

+ Appendix 2.5:   Authorization for Release of Information: From

+ Appendix 2.6:   Biblical Counseling Consent Form

+ Appendix 2.7:   Biblical Counseling Permission to Record and Review Form

Gathering Soul Data: Connecting Soul-to-Soul with the Inner Story

If we are going to help Tony and Trudy, we have to understand what's happening *to* them — their outer story, or situational data. But we never want to stop there as biblical counselors. We also need to understand *who they are* as they *respond internally* to what is happening to them externally.

There are numerous approaches to gathering personal, or soul, data. In the *medical model*, the therapist asks, "What disease does my client have?" In the *personality* model, the counselor asks, "What personality type is my counselee?" In the *psychodynamic* model, the psychologist asks, "What is my counselee's controlling unconscious like?" In the *brief therapy/solution-focused* model, the counselor asks, "How can I help my counselee to gain a more healthy perspective on the situation?"

In *Gospel Conversations*, we are following the *imago Dei* (image of God) model, and we are asking, "*How maturely or immaturely is my counselee living like an image bearer who is a relational, rational, volitional, emotional, and physical being?*" With Tony, we'd be asking, "As Tony responds to his outer story, is he increasingly reflecting the inner life of Christ by loving sacrificially like Christ (relational), by thinking wisely like Christ (rational), by choosing courageously like Christ (volitional), and by taking his emotions candidly to the Father like Christ (emotional)?"[20]

Throughout *Gospel Conversations*, we unite the inner life areas of relational, rational, volitional, and emotional (along with our physical being/responses) with the four counseling compass points of sustaining, healing, reconciling, and guiding (areas you first read about in the introduction and that you will learn more about in chapter 4). In the rest of this chapter, I'll introduce you to a way of thinking about people as they face suffering and battle temptations toward sin. The goal is to understand people like Tony and Trudy both biblically and "soulfully." That is, we move toward a biblical and *universal* way of understanding how any image bearer faces life while also moving toward a personal and *unique* understanding of how this person we are counseling is facing life.

Loving – Relational
Thinking – Rational
The Will – Volitional
Emotions – Emotional
Physical Health – Physical

Maturing as a Biblical Counselor

Self-Counsel and Group or Partner Interaction

Estrangement from Faith

1. Ponder a problem, struggle, or issue that you are facing in your life.

   a. Choose several of the "Probing Trialogues for Exploring the Outer Story" on pages 65–66 and relate them to your situation—your outer story.

   What do you dream would be different about this: She could talk to me. The History of this problem: began at age 9 when Faith decided that she could be the parent. Anne made comments about Faith was telling Anne what to do and when. Sometimes she would just take charge. She did not talk to parents making requests, she only made demands.

   b. Choose several of the "Tracking Trialogues for Mapping the Influence of the Outer Story" on pages 66–67 and relate them to your situation.

   We have spoken to worked with 2 or 3 counsellors. Only one explained trauma effects. This at least made sense, but not a cure.

   c. Choose several of the "Bridging Trialogues for Beginning to Relate God's Story to the Outer Story" on page 67 and relate them to your situation.

   What would it look like if God granted your prayers about your relationship w Faith? We would be able to play table games together and have dinner together

Counseling One Another

2. If you are working through this material in a lab small group, then be prepared to work through questions 1a, b, and c with the entire group, or with a lab partner, or with the lab facilitator counseling one group member, or with a lab member counseling another lab member.

Counseling Others

3. How could the concept of trialogues, scriptural explorations, and spiritual conversations change, impact, and strengthen your biblical counseling ministry?

Sustaining Probes and Disappointment

In sustaining, we're exploring *disappointing* life situations and how people respond to suffering in a fallen world. Think about Trudy and what it might be like to live day in and day out with a husband who repeatedly tells her, "You don't measure up to the 'other woman' I'm having an emotional affair with!" What is going on inside Trudy as she wrestles with a husband who candidly and readily admits to having an emotional affair and desires to have a physical affair? What biblical and relational way of thinking about life will help us to understand Trudy relationally, rationally, volitionally, emotionally, and physically as she responds to Tony? What questions do we want to be asking ourselves and interacting with Trudy about?

Gold Stuff

+ *Relational Probes:* Where is Trudy experiencing the greatest relational disappointment? What legitimate affections, longings, and desires are going unmet?

  + *Relational Spiritual with God:* What is Trudy longing for from God as she faces these disappointments? What would it look like for Trudy to turn to God and trust God's good heart even when life is bad?

  + *Relational Social with Others:* How is Trudy responding in her soul to the loss of her husband's committed affection?

  + *Relational Self-Aware:* How is Trudy's identity in Christ impacting her sense of self as she experiences these disappointments? How is hope deferred making her heart sick?

+ *Rational Probes:* Where is Trudy enduring the greatest mental doubt and anguish? What lying story is Satan hissing at her? What mind-sets control her evaluation of her loss? What disappointing images pervade her perspective?

+ *Volitional Probes:* How is Trudy responding and reacting in her actions to her situation? Is she withdrawing, lashing out, pretending, retaliating, trusting God, sacrificially and courageously loving her husband? Where is her "courage meter" — on all-time low, half-empty, almost full, ready to despair, desperately trusting?

+ *Emotional Probes:* How is Trudy responding and reacting emotionally to her suffering? What is she feeling? How aware is Trudy of her moods? How in control of her moods is she? What is the hurt like for her?

+ *Physical Probes:* How are Trudy's external situation and her inner-life responses impacting her physically? Is she depleted? Exhausted? Is she resting in and finding strength from God?

Healing Probes and Despair/Doubt

In sustaining, we probe Trudy's *hurts.* In healing, we probe her *hope.* Where is she placing her hope in the midst of situations that seem filled with despair? In sustaining, we face with Trudy the fact that life is bad. In healing, we probe whether Trudy is believing that God is also bad or whether she believes that God is good even when life is bad.

+ *Relational Probes:* Where is Trudy facing the greatest relational despair? How is she handling her unquenched thirsts? Where do I see glimpses of hope and evidence of grace in her responses?

  + *Relational Spiritual with God:* As Trudy faces the temptation to despair, is she saying, like Job's wife, "Curse God and die!" or is she saying, like Job, "The Lord gives and the Lord takes away; blessed be the name of the Lord"? Is she trusting or doubting God?

  + *Relational Social with Others:* As Trudy responds to the temptation to despair, is she demanding from others or is she ministering out of Christ's strength?

  + *Relational Self-Aware:* Are these temptations toward despair driving Trudy deeper into her identity and victory in Christ or into self-hatred and shame?

+ *Rational Probes:* Where is Trudy enduring the greatest mental battles? What is the battle like in her mind between Satan's lying, works narrative, and Christ's truth and grace narrative? How is Trudy sorting out questions about the goodness of God during the badness of life?

+ *Volitional Probes:* What would it look like for Trudy to respond courageously even as she feels deeply hurt? Where do I see evidence of her reengaging the battle by worshiping and ministering? Where do I sense that she is tempted to give up and give in to despair?

+ *Emotional Probes:* What would joy in the midst of sorrow be like for Trudy? Is she crying out to God? Is she soothing her soul in her Savior? Is she suffering *coram Deo* — with God — or suffering without God?

+ *Physical Probes:* What spiritual disciplines would assist Trudy to connect to Christ's resurrection power and thus empower her to yield the members of her body (Rom. 6) to Christ's service even while experiencing deep thirsts?

Reconciling Probes and Distancing

From reading earlier about Tony, it's obvious that he has some serious sin issues that need to be biblically and lovingly confronted. However, that does not mean that Trudy is automatically only the sufferer in this situation and not also facing temptation to sin. What theological thoughts about her sin and God's grace could guide us as we seek to understand her inner-life story?

+ *Relational Probes:* Where is Trudy distancing herself from God and others? Where is Trudy turning in on herself instead of turning upward to God and outward toward others?

  + *Relational Spiritual with God:* What false lover of the soul might Trudy be tempted to turn to as she responds to her husband's sin? Is she clinging to God or running from him? What would relational repentance and return look like in her life?

  + *Relational Social with Others:* As Trudy responds to others, is she reflecting the new person she is in Christ or the old person she was before Christ? What will Christlikeness look like for Trudy in this situation?

  + *Relational Self-Aware:* As Trudy gives in to sin, how can Christ's grace impact her soul? Will she believe Satan's lie that she must beautify herself, or will she believe Christ's truth that forgiveness and cleansing are in him alone?

+ *Rational Probes:* What idols of the heart might Trudy be tempted to pursue? What evidence do I detect of her buying Satan's lie? What old mind-sets does she need to put off? What would mind renewal look like in her situation? What new images of Christ and who she is in Christ does she need to put on?

+ *Volitional Probes:* Where is Trudy tempted to "kill and covet" (retaliate and manipulate — James 4:1 – 4)? What sinful patterns of response to Tony might she need to put off? What evidence do I see of godly patterns of response? How could God's grace empower her to respond courageously?

+ *Emotional Probes:* How is Trudy managing her moods? Is she failing to be self-aware? Is she lacking emotional control? How could she soothe her soul in her Savior?

+ *Physical Probes:* What spiritual disciplines would assist her to put off old ways and put on new ways? How are Trudy's distancing responses impacting her physically?

Guiding Probes and Defeating Sin

In reconciling, we probe sin and grace — possible areas of sinful responses in Trudy and infinite oceans of God's grace to Trudy. In guiding, we probe "sanctifying grace." The grace that saves is also the grace that empowers Trudy to defeat sin and temptation and live a Christlike life. We want to understand how Trudy is responding and could respond to her situation with Christ's resurrection power.

+ *Relational Probes:* Where is Trudy drawing near to God and others? How is Trudy's newness in Christ impacting how she relates to God and others?

    + *Relational Spiritual with God:* Where is Trudy most passionately loving God? Most faithfully clinging to and depending upon Christ and his resurrection power?

    + *Relational Social with Others:* Where is Trudy most sacrificially loving Tony? Where is she freely offering herself to Tony? What would mature relating to Tony look like and involve?

    + *Relational Self-Aware:* What new dreams is God stirring up in her soul? How can she fan into flame the reality that she does not have a spirit of fear, but of power, love, and wisdom?

+ *Rational Probes:* Where is Trudy already winning the battle for her mind? What evidence do I detect of her defeating Satan's lies? What spiritual mind-sets prevail in her heart? What new beliefs and images can Trudy be putting on? What will ongoing sanctification look like for her mentally?

+ *Volitional Probes:* What godly patterns of responding can I encourage Trudy to put on? What evidence do I see of Trudy following biblical purposes and Christlike pathways of speaking truth in love to Tony? How can she offer tastes of grace to Tony?

+ *Emotional Probes:* How can Trudy mature emotionally as a person who experiences life fully, deeply, and honestly? What does emotional maturity look like for her in this situation? How can she spread her joy to others?

+ *Physical Probes:* How are Trudy's godly affections, mind-sets, pathways, and mood states empowering her physically? How can I use her "physical energy meter" as a diagnostic tool to assess how well she is putting off old patterns and putting on new ones?

Where We've Been and Where We're Headed

As we've examined the foundations of biblical counseling, thus far we've seen that biblical counselors share Scripture and soul (chapter 1) and that biblical counselors listen to the Scripture and the soul (chapter 2). We've already seen our two tweet-size summaries of chapter 2:

+ In biblical counseling, the gospel is the controlling lens through which we understand and interpret our counselee's life story.

+ In biblical counseling, the whole Bible story impacts the whole person's whole story.

If chapters 1 and 2 provide the foundation of what biblical counselors do, then chapter 3 provides the foundation of what qualifies a person for biblical counseling. Specifically, we'll examine Romans 15:14 to explore four résumé qualifications of the biblical counselor.

Maturing as a Biblical Counselor

Self-Counsel and Group or Partner Interaction

1. Ponder a problem, struggle, or issue that you are facing in your life.

   a. Choose several of the Sustaining Probes from pages 70–71 and relate them to your inner story—your soul.

   b. Choose several of the Healing Probes from pages 71–72 and relate them to your inner story—your soul.

   c. Choose several of the Reconciling Probes from pages 72–73 and relate them to your inner story—your soul.

   d. Choose several of the Guiding Probes from pages 73–74 and relate them to your inner story—your soul.

Counseling One Another

2. If you are working through this material in a lab small group, then be prepared to work through questions 1a, b, c, and d with the entire group, or with a lab partner, or with the lab facilitator counseling one group member, or with a lab member counseling another lab member.

Counseling Others

3. How could the concept of relational, rational, volitional, emotional, and physical probes in the areas of sustaining, healing, reconciling, and guiding impact your biblical counseling ministry?

CHAPTER 3

4 Résumé Qualifications of the Biblical Counselor

Picture Trudy and Tony again. Ten minutes into your first meeting, Tony leans forward, looks you straight in the eyes, and says, "As you know, I've seen a divorce attorney already. The pastor at our church recommended that we see you before we make any final decisions. If I'm putting my future on the line, I want to know what makes *you* qualified to help us."

Pausing, gulping, you could do the "counselor thing." "Tony, I wonder what *you* think would qualify me to be of help to you and Trudy?"

Or you could do the "biblical counselor thing." "Tony, I'd be glad to address that, but first I'd like us to probe what heart issues might be behind your question."

Or you could briefly but directly respond to Tony's very direct question. If so, what would you say qualifies you to counsel Tony and Trudy?

Regardless of how we respond in the counseling session, Tony is raising a legitimate question. What qualifies us to claim the mantle of "biblical counselor"? Ask that question to a group of biblical counselors, and you'll receive a myriad of answers. High on the list would be "biblical wisdom" — robustly, richly, and relevantly knowing and understanding what the Bible says about life — and understanding people, diagnosing problems, and prescribing solutions biblically.

Suppose you shared that with Tony. "A major part of the reason I'm 'qualified' to help you is my commitment to the Bible as my sufficient source of wisdom for counseling you and Trudy in your relationship to Christ and your relationship to one another."

Maturing as a Biblical Counselor

Self-Counsel and Group or Partner Interaction

1. How confident are you that God's people can be equipped to be competent biblical counselors? On what do you base your confidence? What could increase your confidence?

2. How confident are you that *you* can become a competent biblical counselor? What can you do to further develop your confidence in your competency in Christ?

3. Before you read this chapter (or the introduction earlier), how would you have answered the question, "If you were sending your résumé to the Divine Counselor, what résumé qualifications would you include to demonstrate your eligibility to enter the ranks of 'biblical counselor'?"

4. What biblical passages and scriptural principles would you turn to in order to answer the question, "What qualifies a person to be a competent biblical counselor?"

5. If you were looking for someone to talk to about issues in your life, what qualifications would you look for?

Skeptical, Tony leans back, strokes his chin, and responds, "That's great. Now, could you tell me how that's working for you in *your* marriage?" While we may or may not respond directly to Tony's question, he raises a valid issue, doesn't he? The application of biblical wisdom to our lives, relationships, and ministries ought to be high on the list of qualifications for effective biblical counseling. God calls us not only to know his Word richly, but to apply his Word relevantly to our lives so that we grow in Christlike character.

Perhaps you choose to engage Tony briefly about his second question. "That's a fair question, Tony, and here's my summary response. By God's grace, my wife and I seek to apply God's truth to our marriage. While our marriage is imperfect, it is a growing marriage that honors Christ as we both seek to lovingly minister to each other so that we each become more like Jesus."

Tony nods approvingly. Squints. "Okay, thank you for your candor and for your patience with my questions. One more question, if it's all right. So, you know God's Word, you apply it to your life. How successful have you been in helping *others* with their marriages?"

Tony is raising another valid point. Rich knowledge of God's Word applied to our lives provides a powerful foundation for biblical counseling. But counseling, by very definition, involves engaging others and helping them in applying truth to their lives. So our competence as a counselor in sharing Scripture and soul — lovingly relating truth to life — is also vital. So we might say to Tony, "By God's grace, couples report that their marriages have been significantly helped as I've been able to compassionately care about couples and engage with couples biblically about their heart issues and their relationship ..."

Biblical content (rich knowledge of God's Word), Christlike character (application of gospel wisdom to our lives), and counseling relational competence (sharing Scripture and soul with others) unite with a fourth characteristic to qualify us to minister to others — Christian community. None of us believes that a formal hour per week meeting with another person is in itself sufficient for growth in grace. Growth is a community project, a congregational journey. Biblical counselors need to know how to embed themselves and those they help in a 24/7 relationship with Christ and the body of Christ.

How do we grow as biblical counselors who engage in soul-to-soul gospel conversations as brothers, mothers, fathers, children, and mentors? What résumé qualifications demonstrate our eligibility to enter the ranks of "biblical counselors"? What are the comprehensive training goals that we must pursue as we seek to share Scripture and soul and listen to the Scriptures and the soul?

Fortunately, the apostle Paul has already completed the biblical counselor's résumé. "I myself am convinced, my brothers, that you yourselves are full of goodness, complete in knowledge and competent to instruct one another" (Rom. 15:14). In this verse, the surrounding context, and other biblical passages, we discover the four résumé qualifications of a nurtured biblical counselor. They supply our biblical counseling equipping *goals and objectives*:

The Four Dimensions of Comprehensive Biblical Counseling Equipping		
• Christlike *Character:*	"Full of Goodness"	Heart/Being
• Biblical *Content*/Conviction:	"Complete in Knowledge"	Head/Knowing
• Counseling *Competence:*	"Competent to Instruct"	Hands/Doing
• Christian *Community:*	"Brothers/One Another"	Home/Loving

Equipping in Biblical Counseling

In my consulting in churches and educational settings about biblical counselor equipping, the primary weakness we identify is training that lacks one or more of the four dimensions addressed above. In fact, many training programs tend to highlight one dimension to the detriment of the other components of comprehensive biblical counseling training.

Some biblical counseling equipping tilts almost exclusively to biblical content. Trainees know the Word, which is essential, but they are mostly head and little heart (truth minus love). Lacking compassion, they share Scripture, but not soul. Lacking the competency to relate truth to life, they end up preaching *at* counselees rather than engaging counselees in scriptural explorations that empower counselees to apply truth to their lives.

Some biblical counseling training inclines the pendulum in the other direction and focuses almost exclusively on counseling competency. Training consists of the meticulous role-play practice of skills and techniques apart from an equal emphasis on biblical wisdom, Christlikeness, and loving engagement. Trainees have big hands, if you will, but underdeveloped heads and hearts.

Still other ministries focus on the character of the counselors and their spiritual formation, which is vital. But the mind-set assumes that somehow by osmosis the godly person will help others to become godlier. Churches and schools end up with trainees who are all heart, but are lacking in biblical insight and counseling abilities.

Additionally, some training in biblical counseling tends to be a tad tone-deaf to the community or relational aspect. Perhaps because of biblical counseling's appropriate emphasis on content and the Word, an inappropriate de-emphasis results. Training becomes classroom-like, didactic, and academic. Even the "lab," or skills component, is more oriented to technique development or case study discussions rather than relational depth and personal connection among group members. What is lacking is a nurturing environment that encourages group members to grow together in Christ through connecting with one another and communing with Christ. Since we counsel like we are trained, trainees end up more robotic than relational.

There are various explanations for one-dimensional equipping: the personality of the trainer, the training the trainer experienced, the educational philosophy of the trainer, and time limitations. Everything seeks to pull us away from comprehensive equipping.

This is why it is absolutely vital that we saturate our biblical counseling equipping with four-dimensional goals and objectives. We must commit to remain on the cutting edge of biblical counseling equipping by following Christ's disciple-making model of intentionally and comprehensively training the whole person: the heart (being/character), the head (knowing/content), and the hands (doing/competence) in the context of God's home (loving/community).

Our first task in becoming equipped biblical counselors is to laser focus on the four-dimensional biblical portrait. Consider the rest of this chapter your snapshot of the comprehensive résumé qualifications you are seeking to develop through your engagement with *Gospel Conversations*.

Confidence in Our Competence in Christ

Before we develop these four characteristics, we need to consider a common reaction. The moment we start talking about training "nonprofessionals" as counselors, we can expect pushback. People will raise numerous objections, sometimes vehemently, against our conviction that God's people (pastors and laypeople) can be competent counselors. We can respond to their pushback with God's Word, which settles the issue, and with research that validates the effectiveness of paraprofessional people helpers.

Confidence Based on God's Word: The Sufficiency of Christianity

Recall Paul's résumé for the competent biblical counselor: "I myself am convinced, my brothers, that you yourselves are full of goodness, complete in knowledge and competent to instruct one another" (Rom. 15:14). Ponder who Paul is addressing with his choice of "brothers." Are these apostles, pastors, elders, deacons, deaconesses, or former Jewish priests? Have they graduated from the exclusive training institutions of Paul's day? Are they the elite philosophers and scholars of Roman society?

No. They are "average, ordinary" Christians in Rome. "Brothers" was the common designation of a believer regardless of gender, status, position, or rank. Based on the context (Rom. 16:1 – 16), Paul is addressing members of small house churches spread throughout the city and dotting the countryside of Rome. These men and women, converted Jews and Greeks, slaves and free, Paul considers competent to counsel.

Based on Paul's language, I conclude that Paul knew that his readers would be skeptical about their ability to counsel one another. I imagine them thinking, "Now, Paul, perhaps you, a super apostle, *you* are competent to counsel. Perhaps the other apostles also. But not us!" Paul is quite emphatic in his language. The NIV accurately translates his emphasis, "I myself." "You yourselves." Paul's addition of the personal pronoun produces emphasis by redundancy. Paul wants no mistakes. He is positive that they are powerful. "I, I myself. Inspired by the Divine Counselor, I am telling you that I am absolutely confident in you, you yourselves. Yes, you yourselves are competent to counsel one another."

Paul is not making an assumption here. He says that he is "convinced." He is confident in them, trusts them, and knows that he can count on them to counsel one another competently. He has faith in their spiritual ability, being inwardly certain *because of* external evidence. The evidence he offers provides the biblical résumé for biblical counselors.

And the Survey Says: The Effectiveness of Paraprofessionals

While I was working on my PhD, an article published in a major counseling journal sent shock waves through the counseling community. Its results called into question the efficacy of professional counseling training, while also distilling basic elements that qualify an individual to be an effective people helper. The article traced the history of modern research into counselor effectiveness beginning with J. Durlak's work examining the results of forty-two studies that compared the effectiveness of professional helpers to paraprofessionals (laypeople helpers). The data from the study indicated that lay helpers equaled or surpassed the effectiveness of the professional therapists.[21]

Hattie, Sharpley, and Rogers attempted to refute those findings by combining the results of forty-six studies. However, their data supported Durlak's conclusions. Clients of lay helpers consistently achieved more positive outcomes than did clients of the professionally educated and experienced counselors.[22] Then Berman and Norton reanalyzed Hattie's study. Their reanalysis indicated that lay counselors were equally effective as professional counselors in promoting positive change. They concluded that no research currently supported the notion that professional training, knowledge, or experience improved therapist effectiveness.[23]

Herman, in his review of these studies, indicated that research suggested that professional training was not the primary means for developing competence in helping people. Rather, the personal characteristics of the helper were the greatest factors leading to competence as a counselor. In other words, the studies demonstrated that maturity, love, genuine concern, empathy, humility, and vulnerability were more important than professional training.[24]

After the appearance of these studies, Tan noted that little research had been done to assess the effectiveness of church-based Christian lay counseling programs. He rectified that through a controlled study of a church-based lay counseling program. His findings indicated that the group counseled by lay counselors reported significantly more improvement on all measures than the control group, and they maintained their gains at significant levels. He concluded that the study supports the effectiveness of Christian lay counseling in a local church context.[25]

Such descriptive research offers valuable support when people raise objections to the effectiveness of equipping biblical counselors for the local church. Of course, 2,000 years earlier the apostle Paul offered all the biblical validation that we need when he affirmed that God's people in Rome were competent to counsel. We return now to our examination of the biblical qualifications that God's Word deems necessary to be considered a competent biblical counselor.

Christlike Character: "Full of Goodness"—Heart/Being

"I myself am convinced, my brothers, that you yourselves are full of goodness, complete in knowledge and competent to instruct one another" (Rom. 15:14). Competent biblical counselors have résumés with "full of goodness" as their first qualification.

"Goodness" is the same word Paul uses in Galatians 5:22 – 23 as one of the nine aspects of the fruit of the Spirit. When I first read Romans 15:14, I wondered why Paul would pick the fruit of goodness. Why not love, joy, peace, or any other fruit of the Spirit? So I explored goodness. The Old Testament highlights the basic confession that God *is* good because his love endures forever (1 Chron. 16:34). It also emphasizes that our good God *does* good (Ex. 18:9). That is, he displays his goodness in active social relationships. Further, I noted Christ's statement that only God is good (Matt. 19:17). Then I noticed the linkage of goodness and godliness with god-like-ness — with *Christlikeness* (Matt. 5:43 – 48; Eph. 2:10; Col. 1:10). In each of these passages, goodness displays itself in active, grace-oriented relationships, as when our good Father causes his sun to shine on and his rain to fall on the righteous and the unrighteous.

William Hendriksen, in his commentary on Galatians, explains that goodness is a virtue that reveals itself in social relationships, in our various contacts and connections with others.[26] Theologian and linguist Walter Gundmann demonstrates that biblical goodness always displays itself in relational contexts through undeserved kindness.[27] Thus, in Romans 15:14, Paul is talking about *Christlike character* that relates with grace. The powerful biblical counselor reflects the ultimate Biblical Counselor — Jesus. We are powerful to the degree that we reflect the loving character of Christ. Paul is teaching us that the competent biblical counselor is the person who relates well, connects deeply, is compassionate, and has the ability to develop intimate grace relationships.

> The powerful biblical counselor reflects the ultimate Biblical Counselor — Jesus.

In discussing goodness, Paul uses the modifier "full." "Full" pictures a net that breaks due to the stress and tension of too much weight and a cup that is so chock-full that its contents spill over. Paul pictures mature love and godly character flowing through Christ to us, then spilling over from us into our counselee's life. In other words, we will be fruitful biblical counselors to the degree that we increasingly reflect Christ and relate increasingly like Christ. The person who is good at relating is the person whose words and actions have deep impact.

Paul's first résumé qualification teaches that knowledge and skill without character is like *one corpse practicing cosmetic surgery on another corpse*. I witnessed this truth in a counseling lab when one of the group members, Amber, shared her deep sorrow over the loss of her mother. As a male group member, Mike, attempted to connect with Amber, it became painfully obvious that it just wasn't working. Mike was trying to "practice skills" instead of relating deeply out of a good heart.

So we asked the question, "Mike, who would you be without your skills?" Mike was dumbfounded — he sincerely wanted to help, but he recognized how truly unable he was to enter into Amber's world. With Amber's and Mike's permission, we shifted our focus to Mike. One group member told his story of slowly learning to relate soul to soul. Another member simply hugged Mike, holding him while the dam of tears burst. A third individual painted a picture of Mike robbed of his toolbox and forced to break into his home to save his wife and children. He asked him, "Mike, what would you do if you did not have your toolbox of techniques?" One year later, Mike shared with us that our interactions with him not only changed how he offers biblical counseling, but transformed how he relates to his wife and children.

We often talk about Christlikeness in ways that are vague and general. The Bible makes it far more practical and realistic. Christlikeness is our inner life increasingly reflecting the inner life of Christ. In *Gospel-Centered Counseling*, I developed a biblical portrait of our inner life as relational, rational, volitional, and emotional.[28] Based on that, here are four marks of Christlike character that every biblical counselor must cultivate and that we will seek to encourage throughout *Gospel Conversations*.

Four Marks of Christlike Character That Every Biblical Counselor Must Cultivate
• Relating Like Christ: Loving God and Others Passionately
• Thinking Like Christ: Renewing My Mind to View Life from God's Eternal Perspective
• Choosing Like Christ: Dying to Self and Living Sacrificially for Others
• Feeling Like Christ: Facing Life Honestly and Managing My Moods Biblically

Biblical Content/Conviction: "Complete in Knowledge" — Head/Knowing

So is Paul implying that the best biblical counselor is the "touchy-feely" person who never dedicates himself or herself to serious study of the Scripture? Not at all. Remember that God calls us to love him with our minds, with our brains (Matt. 22:37). This is why Paul lists "complete in knowledge" as the second qualification on the biblical counselor's résumé.

"Complete" does not suggest that we become walking biblical encyclopedias with absolute knowledge of all theological truth. Only God has encyclopedic knowledge of all things actual and possible. Instead, by "complete" Paul means that we become so filled with God's Word that it claims our entire being and stamps our whole life, conduct, attitude, and relationships. We are captured by God's truth.

What sort of knowledge does Paul emphasize? He could have chosen any of several words that highlight content or factual knowledge alone. However, Paul chooses a word for knowledge that highlights the combination of information and implication. Paul's word focuses on insight and wisdom — the wisdom to relate truth to life. Competent biblical counselors understand how to apply God's Word first to their own life. They also have the insight to see how God's Word relates to their friend's life. Additionally, they have the biblical vision to see how God is relating to their friend. They have discernment to see life from God's perspective.

In Philippians 1:9 – 11, Paul develops his philosophy of ministry, his conviction about what equips us for biblical counseling.

And this is my prayer: that your love may abound more and more in knowledge and depth of insight, so that you may be able to discern what is best and may be pure and blameless until the day of Christ, filled with the fruit of righteousness that comes through Jesus Christ — to the glory and praise of God.

We noticed in chapter 1, Paul's coupling of truth and love. For him, biblical counseling is never either/or — either we are loving, touchy-feely, heart people, or we are scholarly, academic, head people. Rather, ministry is both/and — we unite head and heart, love and truth in our personal ministry of the Word. When our love abounds more and more in knowledge, the result is insight — the ability to help our counselees to discern not simply what is good, but what is best in their life situation — from God's eternal perspective.

At the end of our training, we should be able to say what Paul said to Timothy at the end of his life. "You, however, know all about my teaching, my way of life." (2 Tim. 3:10a). That way we will not be hypocritical when we encourage our counselees the way Paul encouraged Timothy. "Watch your life and doctrine closely." (1 Tim. 4:16a).

In *Gospel-Centered Counseling* and *Gospel Conversations*, we structure our equipping in biblical counseling so that we gain deep insight into people,

> ### Eight Ultimate Life Questions
> ### That Every Biblical Counselor Must Address
>
> - The Word: Where do we find wisdom for life in a broken world?
> - The Trinity/Community: What comes into our mind when we think about God? Whose view of God will we believe—Christ's or Satan's?
> - Creation: Whose are we? In what story do we find ourselves?
> - Fall: What's the root source of our problem? What went wrong?
> - Redemption: How does Christ bring us peace with God? How does Christ change people?
> - Church: Where can we find a place to belong and become?
> - Consummation: How does our future destiny with Christ make a difference in our lives today as saints who struggle against suffering and sin?
> - Sanctification: Why are we here? How do we become like Jesus?

problems, and solutions — from a biblical perspective. Our training seeks to equip biblical counselors with the wisdom to relate those biblical truths to people's daily lives and relationships — changing lives with Christ's changeless truth. In chapter 2, I outlined eight ultimate life questions that every biblical counselor must address. All of our equipping in *Gospel Conversations* builds upon these eight biblical content/conviction categories.

Counseling Competence: "Competent to Instruct" — Hands/Doing

Paul says that the typical Christians in Rome with character and conviction are "competent to instruct." The word "competent" means to have the power to accomplish a mission, the power necessary to fulfill God's call to minister to one another. "Competent" also means to have the ability, capability, resources, and strength to function and relate well. Paul is confident that believers are relationally competent in Christ.

But what are they competent to do? They are powerful to "instruct" (*nouthetein*). Jay Adams, founder of the National Association of Nouthetic Counselors (now the Association of Certified Biblical Counselors), describes nouthetic counseling as confronting for change out of concern.[29] "Instruct" contains this nuance, especially when the proposed change emphasizes inner heart change leading to relational change. The foundational meaning of *noutheteo* comes from the root *noeo*, meaning to direct one's mind, to perceive, and from *nous* — the mind, heart, seat of spiritual, rational, and moral insight and action. The mind is the place of practical reason leading to moral action. The stress is not merely on the intellect but also on the will and disposition. *Noutheteo* means to impart understanding, to set right, to lay on the heart. Nouthetic impartation of truth can take on many forms, such as encouraging, urging, spurring on, teaching, reminding, admonishing, reconciling, guiding, and advising.

Paul uses *noutheteo* in Colossians 1:20–29 to describe one aspect of his multifaceted pastoral ministry. God commissioned him to present Christ's gospel of grace to people (1:20–25), infusing people with the hope of who they are in Christ (1:26–27), with the goal of presenting them mature in Christ (1:28) through personal, passionate, persistent involvement in their lives (1:28–29) by Christ's resurrection power (1:29). Thus Paul is saying in Romans 15:14 that believers who possess Christlike goodness (character) plus Christlike insight (conviction) are competent to disciple one another toward communion with Christ and conformity to Christ through the personal ministry of the Word — biblical counseling.

Paul never intended Romans 15:14 to be the final or only word on the nature of biblical counseling. Nor did he use *noutheteo* as the only or even the primary concept to describe the personal ministry of the Word. For instance, in 1 Thessalonians 5:14, Paul uses five distinct words for biblical counseling. "And we urge (*parakaleo*) you, brothers, warn (*noutheteo*) those who are idle, encourage (*paramutheomai*) the timid, help (*antechomai*) the weak, be patient with (*makrothumeo*) everyone."

Among the many New Testament words for spiritual care, *parakaleo* predominates. Whereas *noutheteo* occurs eleven times in the New Testament, *parakaleo* (comfort, encourage, console) appears 109 times. In 2 Corinthians 1:3–11, Paul informs us that we are competent to comfort (*parakaleo*) one another. Those who have humbly received God's comfort, God equips to offer comfort to others.

The word *parakaleo* emphasizes personal presence (one called alongside to help) and suffering with another person. It seeks to turn desolation into consolation through hope in God. The duty of comfort in Old and New Testament thinking fell not upon professional helpers, but upon close relatives, neighbors, friends, and colleagues. Comforters come alongside to help struggling, suffering people through personal presence coupled with scriptural insight.

When Christ ascended, he sent the Holy Spirit to be our *Parakletos* — our Comforter and Advocate called alongside to encourage and help in times

---

**Four Core Relational Competencies
That Every Biblical Counselor Must Develop**

- Sustaining Biblical Counseling Competencies: Empathize and Embrace—GRACE Relational Competencies
- Healing Biblical Counseling Competencies: Encourage and Enlighten—RESTS Relational Competencies
- Reconciling Biblical Counseling Competencies: Expose and Exhort—PEACEE Relational Competencies
- Guiding Relational Counseling Competencies: Empower and Equip—FAITH Relational Competencies

---

of suffering, trouble, grief, injustice, and hardship. The Spirit performs his ministry by being in us and by revealing truth to us (John 14:16 – 17). As the Spirit of Truth, his ministry is the exact opposite of Satan, who is the father of lies (John 8:44). Satan's name is "the accuser" (Rev. 12:10) and his core strategy is to speak lying words of condemnation to us. The Spirit's name is "Encourager" and "Advocate" and his ministry is to speak the truth in love about our justification and acceptance in Christ.

Think about what Paul is saying to *you*. You don't have to have a PhD in counseling to be a competent counselor. You have the *Resource* planted within you — the *Parakletos*, the Holy Spirit. You also have the *resources* planted within you — the ability to be a competent *parathetic* (combining *parakaleo* and *noutheteo*) biblical counselor.

Throughout *Gospel Conversations*, I have structured our equipping in biblical counseling so that we develop comprehensive biblical counseling relational competencies. Our end goal is to become competent to care like Christ — the Wonderful Counselor. In chapter 4, I will highlight sustaining, healing, reconciling, and guiding as four core relational competencies that every biblical counselor must develop. Chapters 5 – 12 of *Gospel Conversations* will help us to develop these counseling competencies.

Christian Community: "Brothers/One Another"—Home/Loving

Every word Paul has written about competent biblical counselors he has penned in the plural — brothers, one another, you yourselves. The effective biblical counselor is no "Lone Ranger" Christian. Competent biblical counselors live and grow together in community as they commune with Christ and connect with the body of Christ.

Paul sandwiches his words in Romans 15:14 around a one-another community context. In Romans 12:3 – 8, he writes of each member belonging to all the others, and of using gifts in the context of the body of Christ. In Romans 12:9 – 21, the context reflects one-anothering. Be devoted to one another in love. Honor one another. Share with one another. Practice hospitality with one another. Rejoice with one another. Weep with one another. Live in harmony with one another.

In Romans 13, the context is loving one another: "Whatever other commandment there may be, are summed up in this one rule: 'Love your neighbor as yourself.' Love does no harm to its neighbor. Therefore love is the fulfillment of the law" (13:9 – 10). And Paul continues his one-anothering theme in Romans 14:1 – 15:13. Don't judge one another; instead mutually edify each other. Bear with one another. Please one another. Build up one another. Be united with one another. Encourage one another. Accept one another. Worship with one another. Finally, in Romans 16, Paul writes about meeting together with one another in house churches where believers connect intimately. Connecting in community is the context, before and after Romans 15:14.

Effective training in biblical counseling is learned in community. Put another way, growth in character, content, and competence occurs in the context of community. That's why I'm convinced that we become effective biblical counselors by giving and receiving biblical counseling in community — in our small group training labs.

According to Paul, transformed lives occur as we connect together in the body of Christ (Rom. 12:3 – 16:27) *and* as we connect with Christ (Rom. 12:1 – 2). Conformity to Christ is the result of communion with Christ (2 Cor. 3:16 – 18; 4:16 – 18). That's why I'm convinced that growth in grace is a community project. We don't simply launch a biblical counseling ministry. We launch a one-another revolution. Our goal is not simply to become a church *with* a biblical counseling ministry, but a church *of* biblical counseling where every member engages in the effective personal ministry of the Word.

Effective biblical counselors add another important qualification to their résumé: connection in community. We outline it like this:

**Two Kinds of Christian Community
That Every Biblical Counselor Must Participate In**

- Communion with Christ: Our Vertical Relationship
- Communion with the Body of Christ: Our Horizontal Relationship

---

Where We've Been and Where We're Headed

Now we know how the apostle Paul would have responded if Tony had said to him, "If I'm putting my future on the line, I want to know what makes a biblical counselor qualified to help us." Paul's response serves as our tweet-size summary of chapter 3:

+ Every Christian can be an effective biblical counselor by growing in Christlike character, biblical content, counseling competence, and Christian community.

As we've explored the foundations of biblical counseling, we've seen that biblical counselors share Scripture and soul — we speak gospel truth in love. We've also seen that biblical counselors listen to Scripture and the soul — we pivot between God's eternal story and our counselee's earthly story so the whole Bible story impacts the whole person's whole story. And we've just seen the four-dimensional qualifications of the biblical counselor.

There's a fourth cornerstone we must embed in our biblical counseling foundation. It addresses the vital question: Is there a way of thinking about counseling that provides a map or GPS that can guide our gospel-centered counseling journey?

Maturing as a Biblical Counselor

Self-Counsel and Group or Partner Interaction

1. Of Christlike character, biblical content, counseling relational competence, and Christian community, which one do you think you are most inclined to emphasize? To de-emphasize?

2. To become a more effective, competent biblical counselor, what area do you want to develop most? Why? How will you go about growing in this area?

   a. Christlike character

   b. Biblical content

   c. Counseling relational competence

   d. Christian community

3. Dream a bit.

   a. A year from now, what would demonstrate that you had caught God's vision of yourself as a competent biblical counselor?

   b. A year from now, what would demonstrate that your church had caught the vision of the power of the personal ministry of the Word—whether called biblical counseling, one-another ministry, gospel conversations, or spiritual friendship?

Counseling Others

4. How would your counseling be impacted if you overemphasized one of the following? If you de-emphasized one of the following? If you omitted one of the following?

    a. Biblical content

    b. Christlike character

    c. Counseling relational competence

    d. Christian community

5. How would equipping in biblical counseling be impacted if one of the following is overemphasized? De-emphasized? Omitted?

    a. Biblical content

    b. Christlike character

    c. Counseling relational competence

    d. Christian community

6. Picturing biblical counseling as a combination of character, content, competence, and community, rate the relative importance of each component. For instance, is character "worth" 15 percent, content 50 percent, competence 10 percent, and community 25 percent? Are each equal? What is *your* rating and why?

CHAPTER 4

2 Guideposts and 4 Compass Points of Biblical Counseling

Pastor Carl unfolded his story to me layer by layer. He first admitted how exhausted he was in ministry — "burned out." His pastoral ministry, like most, was filled with joys and disappointments, ups and downs. Lately the downs far outweighed the ups. It seemed like no matter what he did, people brutally criticized him. His family felt like they were living in the proverbial pastoral fishbowl. Now people were beginning to leave the church. He even feared a church split. The deacons were focusing the blame entirely on him.

Feeling like he was being heard and respected, Carl was able to open up further. "But here's what's really crushing. Our teenage daughter, Susan, has recently been diagnosed with leukemia. Bob, I feel like Job. I'm waiting for the next messenger to come, the next bearer of bad news. The pastoral issues are hard enough, but my precious daughter ... What am I going to do? Bob, I'm beat up. I'm beat. I just don't know if I can take it anymore."

As we talked further and Carl felt safer, additional layers unfolded. "Bob, the truth is, I'm struggling with doubts. At first it was doubts about the church — I started feeling like the whole idea of church was such a joke. Where are God's people when you need them? I know. I'm a pastor, for goodness sake! But to be brutally honest, I'm having doubts now about prayer, and I'm doing some serious wrestling with God. I mean, why does God let all this continue? Why would he allow this to happen to my daughter? Where is he? I want to believe. To trust."

Maturing as a Biblical Counselor

Self-Counsel and Group or Partner Interaction

1. Describe your typical approach to helping people, your normal way of counseling and discipling.

2. Where were you recruited into your model? Did you learn it officially from a class or training? Did you develop it from your own study? Did it just "happen"?

3. On a scale of 1 to 10, with 1 being unwilling and 10 being very willing, evaluate your willingness to learn a new approach, a new model of gospel-centered counseling. Explain your evaluation.

Counseling Others

4. Thinking about Pastor Carl:

   a. Where should you start with Pastor Carl and why?

   b. How would you minister to Pastor Carl in his *suffering*?

   c. How would you minister to Pastor Carl in his struggle against *sin*?

   d. What "map," "process," "plan," or "model" would guide you as you help Pastor Carl with his suffering and his sinning?

Meeting over the course of the next few weeks, still more details spilled out. "Bob, I'm so empty inside. I feel like such a hypocrite preaching stuff I'm struggling to live out in my life. To make matters worse, I'm not handling my emptiness well at all. My wife and I are distant. And I've been going to the Internet from time to time to look at pornography. I'm not hooked, not addicted. But I know it's wrong — even one time. And I really am trying to fight to be godly. I feel like such a failure, such a sinner. Is there any hope for me?"

Pastor Carl's story forces us to ask some fundamental questions about how a gospel-centered counselor might go about providing the help that Carl is desperate to receive. How do we journey with Pastor Carl, entering his story and connecting his story to Christ's story? How do we engage in gospel conversations where the gospel narrative impacts Carl's life narrative? On our biblical counseling journey with Carl, where do we start? What will our gospel conversation journey with him look like? Where will it take us?

Real-Life Questions for Real-Life Ministry

Our questions about helping Pastor Carl are not merely academic. Anyone who has ever ministered to a hurting person knows the head-spinning feeling when someone unloads a host of messy problems and then looks to us for wisdom.

We know that there are biblical principles that guide our thinking about life issues because God has a take on counseling. His Word is rich, relevant, and robust. In *Gospel-Centered Counseling* and in chapter 2 of this book, we outlined life's eight ultimate questions that provide a comprehensive framework for understanding how Christ changes lives. Yet knowing this framework still leaves us with our real-life question: "How do we move from a biblical understanding of people, problems, and solutions to actually interacting with Carl?"

We know that there are biblical counseling skills and methods that will be a part of our ongoing interactions. *Gospel Conversations* will outline twenty-one biblical counseling relational competencies that provide a comprehensive framework for understanding how to care like Christ. But we don't want our counseling skills to become rote, mechanical, or soulless. We want our counseling competencies to flow naturally and to supernaturally work in gospel conversations so that we're not simply tossing in a "skill" in a way that feels fake, forced, or haphazard. So, learning counseling relational competencies still leaves us with our real-life question: Is there a way of thinking about counseling that provides a map or GPS that can guide our gospel-centered counseling journey?

The Importance of Learning a Biblical Model

Some might counter, "Do we really need a road map? I don't have a counseling model. I just do what comes naturally." Others may state, "I don't follow a model of counseling. I simply use the Bible."

Whether we realize it or not, we all have *some* counseling "model." We all approach the personal ministry of the Word from some perspective, and we practice our approach according to some pattern. We all have a way of thinking about life's ultimate questions (counseling theory), and we all have a way of engaging people when they bring their life issues to us (counseling methodology).

We either develop a biblical approach to counseling theory and practice, or we borrow a secular model of counseling. Speaking about what happens when we lack a well-thought-out Christian model of soul care, William Clebsch and Charles Jaekle explain:

> Faced with an urgency for some system by which to conceptualize the human condition and to deal with the modern grandeurs and terrors of the human spirit, theoreticians of the cure of souls have too readily adopted the leading academic psychologies. Having no pastoral theology to inform our psychology or even to identify the cure of souls as a mode of human helping, we have allowed psychoanalytic thought, for example, to dominate the vocabulary of the spirit.[30]

Urgent concerns plus no Christian model equals acceptance of secular psychology as the only hope. We surrender our approach to the prevailing secular theories and practices unless we follow some road map, some model of Christian care.

Someone says to us, "My daughter has been 'cutting.' You have to help us. Please meet with her tomorrow."

What do we do? Does our Bible concordance have a notation for "cutting and self-harm"? Since it doesn't, you and I are tempted to rush to the self-help shelf of the local bookstore. When faced with the complexity of the human soul, we turn to secular models *if* we have no thought-out Christian model. Without a theological foundation (theory) and a historical Christian model (practice), we reject biblical revelation in favor of human reasoning. In *Gospel Conversations*, we learn an approach to counseling that is based on biblical theology and church history.

The Big Picture

We all want our counseling to be biblical, but what does biblical counseling actually look like in practice? Let's answer that vital question by exploring biblical counseling's *two guideposts* and *four compass points*.

+ The Two Guideposts of Biblical Counseling:

Guidepost #1: Biblical Soul Care for Suffering and Sanctification

Guidepost #2: Biblical Spiritual Direction for Sin and Sanctification

+ The Four Compass Points of Biblical Counseling:

Compass Point #1: Sustaining and the Troubling Story —
          "It's Normal to Hurt."

Compass Point #2: Healing and the Faith Story —
          "It's Possible to Hope."

Compass Point #3: Reconciling and the Redemptive Story —
          "It's Horrible to Sin but Wonderful to Be Forgiven."

Compass Point #4: Guiding and the Growth-in-Grace Story —
          "It's Supernatural to Mature."

In chapter 1, we learned that biblical counseling training can sometimes have an unbalanced focus either on truth or love. The five portraits of a biblical counselor who shares Scripture and soul provide a balanced approach to gospel-centered counseling.

In chapter 2, we learned that biblical counseling training can sometimes swing between listening to God's eternal story *or* listening to our counselee's temporal story. Life's "eight ultimate questions" offer a comprehensive way of uniting God's eternal story and our counselee's earthly story.

In chapter 3, we learned that biblical counseling training can sometimes have a one-dimensional emphasis on character, content, competence, or community. The four-dimensional model from Romans 15:14 provides our comprehensive biblical counseling equipping goals.

Now in chapter 4, we are learning that biblical counseling can sometimes have a one-dimensional focus on either suffering or sin and a one-dimensional focus on one of the four "compass points" — sustaining *or* healing *or* reconciling *or* guiding. That's why in *Gospel Conversations*, we learn a comprehensive biblical counseling map or GPS so that we care like Christ through:

+ Biblical soul care for suffering where we learn how to weep with those who weep by offering *sustaining* care for hurting people — biblical empathy for the *troubling* story.

+ Biblical soul care for suffering where we learn how to give hope to the hurting by offering *healing* comfort for suffering people — biblical encouragement for the *faith* story.

+ Biblical spiritual direction for temptation and sin where we learn how to be a dispenser of grace by offering *reconciling* care-fronting for people struggling with besetting sins — biblical exposure in the *redemptive* story.

+ Biblical spiritual direction for temptation and sin where we learn how to disciple, coach, and mentor by offering *guiding* wisdom for people growing in Christ — biblical equipping in the *growth-in-grace* story.

Figure 4.1 offers the big picture overview. As you read it, first, don't panic! I've had the privilege of using this approach to equip thousands of biblical counselors over the past three decades. People "get it." They learn it. They love it. They use it. So will *you*.

Second, as you view the chart, understand that what looks complicated in chart form ... is *even more complicated in real life*! I'm not presenting figure 4:1 to cloak the complexity of messy, real-life counseling relationships. As vital as it is to build a comprehensive biblical counseling foundation, in real-life ministry, it never looks quite like the linear approach that you'll read on the following pages. As we saw in 1 Thessalonians 2, biblical counseling is a complex, back-and-forth, relational, soulful process.

When I introduce figure 4.1 in seminars and classes, I show one Power-Point slide of a plate of tangled spaghetti and another slide with a toddler at a table covered in spaghetti. I then call counseling "spaghetti relationships" — it is messy, mixed together, twisted, intertwined. In "real life" we might start with Pastor Carl by addressing his struggle with sin, or we might start by comforting him in his suffering over his daughter's leukemia. In reality, we would move back and forth between suffering and sin because counseling is like spaghetti, or like a spider web interwoven with countless links and interconnections. It is real and raw, loving and engaging. So while we will learn a model in a linear way, please understand that biblical counseling is a complex, back-and-forth, relational, soulful process.

Figure 4.1

Comprehensive Biblical Counseling

Biblical Soul Care: Applying the Gospel to the Evils We Have Suffered

"God Is Good Even When Life Is Bad"

Through biblical soul care, counselors compassionately identify with people in pain and redirect them to Christ and the body of Christ to sustain and heal their faith so they experience communion with Christ and conformity to Christ as they love God (exalt God by enjoying and trusting him) and love others.

Sustaining: *"It's Normal to Hurt"*—The Troubling Story and "Climbing in the Casket"

Sensing Your Counselee's Earthly Story of Despair

Empathizing With and Embracing Your Counselee

Healing: *"It's Possible to Hope"*—The Faith Story and "Celebrating the Empty Tomb"

Stretching Your Counselee to God's Eternal Story of Hope

Encouraging Your Counselee to Embrace God

Biblical Spiritual Direction: Applying the Gospel to the Sins We Have Committed

"God Is Gracious Even When I Am Sinful"

Through biblical spiritual direction, counselors understand spiritual dynamics and discern root causes of spiritual conflicts, providing loving wisdom that reconciles and guides people so they experience communion with Christ and conformity to Christ as they love God (exalt God by enjoying and trusting him) and love others.

Reconciling: *"It's Horrible to Sin but Wonderful to Be Forgiven"*— The Redemptive Story and "Dispensing Grace"

Putting Off Your Counselee's Enslaving Story of Death

Exposing Your Counselee's Sin and Christ's Grace

Guiding: *"It's Supernatural to Mature"*—The Growth-in-Grace Story and "Fanning into Flame the Gift of God"

Putting On Your Counselee's Resurrection Story of New Life

Equipping and Empowering Your Counselee to Love Like Christ

Addressing Your Legitimate Questions

I suspect that as you read this chapter, a number of thoughts may be going through your mind. Perhaps you are thinking, "Sounds great! A map or GPS to guide the relational journey of biblical counseling sounds wonderfully helpful!"

Or maybe you are wondering, "Hmm. Sounds nice, but where in the world did you get your guideposts and compass points from? Are those templates biblical?"

Or you may be thinking, "Sounds interesting, but what in the world are biblical soul care, spiritual direction, sustaining, healing, reconciling, and guiding? I'm not familiar with that language, and if it is going to be the format for my training, it sure would help to get a handle on what it all means." I've designed the rest of this chapter and the rest of *Gospel Conversations* to address all of those important questions.

Two Guideposts for Comprehensive, Compassionate Biblical Counseling

It is common in biblical counseling circles to speak of a well-rounded approach to those to whom we minister as sufferer, sinner, and saint.[31] I appreciate that approach greatly, but I suggest we tweak it slightly to saints, sons,[32] sanctification, suffering, and sin.

As a believer, Pastor Carl is a saint — he is a new creation in Christ regenerated or made new in the core of his being and redeemed or freed from slavery to sin's power. Carl is also a son of God — he is justified and forgiven and he is reconciled to his heavenly Father through Christ. Out of his core identity in Christ as a saint and son,[33] Carl lives in a fallen world in which he endures suffering and battles against sin and temptation: the world, the flesh, and the Devil. Counseling with a brother in Christ like Carl is always ultimately about sanctification — growing in Christlikeness as he responds to suffering and battles sin.

In Christ, Carl's *core* identity is *not* sufferer and sinner. His core identity and your core identity in Christ is as a saint and son who endures suffering and battles against sin as you pursue progressive sanctification — increasing Christlikeness.

> Your core identity in Christ is as a saint and son who endures suffering and battles against sin as you pursue progressive sanctification—increasing Christlikeness.

It was while I was in seminary that I became convinced that counseling in the Bible and throughout church history has always been about saints, sons, suffering, sin, and sanctification. During my seminary years, "counseling wars" broke out on our campus. One group supported an approach to counseling that tended more toward a focus on suffering. The other group supported an approach to counseling that tended more toward a focus on sin. I remember thinking, "Surely the church has always been about the business of helping hurting *and* hardened people." That sentence began a three-decade quest to study Scripture and church history — a quest that has resulted in the book you are now reading.

Avoiding Half-Biblical Counseling

Our challenge as counselors is that we tend to gravitate to one or the other of these viewpoints as we respond to people. With Pastor Carl, some of us might have moved immediately to and spent almost all of our time on his battle with Internet temptation, with doubts, and with distance from his wife. Others might be prone to immediately focus on his suffering, especially with his daughter's leukemia, and stay there and not address the sin/heart issues in his life.

However, comprehensive and compassionate biblical counseling seeks to address suffering *and* sin with a focus on sanctification with every counselee rather than to choose an exclusive or predominant orientation to one of the two areas. Counselor and author Frank Lake captures this balance well: "Pastoral care is defective unless it can deal *thoroughly* with these evils we have suffered as well as with the sins we have committed."[34]

A biblical counselor who focuses only on suffering or only on sin is doing counseling that is only half biblical. As Lake noted, "The maladies of the human spirit in its *deprivation* and in its *depravity* are matters of common pastoral concern."[35] God calls every pastor and one-another minister to the comprehensive ministry of dealing with suffering (deprivation and the evils we have suffered) *and* with sin (depravity and the sins we have committed).

A Scriptural and Church History Overview of Biblical Soul Care and Spiritual Direction

In chapter 3, you read that the apostle Paul teaches that Christians can and should become competent *parakaletic* counselors (soul caregivers) who sustain and heal people who are enduring suffering (2 Cor. 1:3 – 11) and competent *nouthetic* counselors (spiritual directors) who reconcile and guide people who are battling sin and temptation (Rom. 15:14). Experts examining the history of Christian spiritual care have consistently identified these twin historical themes of soul care for suffering and spiritual direction for sin.[36]

For example, John McNeil's *A History of the Cure of Souls* traces the art of spiritual care throughout history and various cultures. "Lying deep in the experience and culture of the early Christian communities are the closely related practices of mutual edification and fraternal correction."[37] Speaking of the apostle Paul, McNeil notes, "In such passages we cannot fail to see the Apostle's design to create an atmosphere in which the intimate exchange of spiritual help, the mutual guidance of souls, would be a normal feature of Christian behavior."[38]

Throughout his historical survey, McNeil explains that mutual edification involves *soul care for suffering* through the provision of sustaining (consolation, support, and comfort) and healing (encouragement and enlightenment). Fraternal correction includes *spiritual direction for victory over sin* through the provision of reconciling (discipline, confession, and forgiveness) and guiding (direction and counsel).

Guidepost #1: Hallmarks of Biblical Soul Care for Suffering

A number of years ago, a pastor approached me after one of my "How to Care Like Christ" seminars. "Dr. Kellemen," he began, "you're really making me think. I've always assumed that my focus was to be on confronting sin in my congregation. Frankly, my parishioners *never* come to me with their suffering. We always discuss their sin issues." Having served as a pastor in three churches, I had to pick my jaw up off the table, since many people in those three congregations came to me with their grief and suffering.

Since my flight was not scheduled to depart until much later that evening, I invited my pastor friend to dinner. As we talked, we discovered that the "pastoral culture" of his church had been subtly and not-so-subtly communicating that "pastoral counseling is about the confrontation of sin." In response, his sheep did not feel comfortable approaching their shepherds for comfort. They were much like the people Lake wrote about. "But, like Job, they complain of the comforters whose one-track minds have considered only the seriousness of sin, and not the gravity of grinding affliction."[39]

We need to understand the legitimate concern that can sometimes lead to "half biblical counseling" that focuses only on sin. The world, and sadly also the church, often waters down sin. Therefore, much of church counseling can swing the pendulum so far toward suffering that we are forced to ask,

"Whatever happened to sin?" Or, "Are you saying that our primary problem is our suffering rather than our sin?"

There are biblical responses to these legitimate questions — responses that lead to fully biblical counseling instead of half-biblical counseling. Let's start with what we can agree upon theologically: *Our core problem is sin.* Having said that, we must understand the theological truth that Christ's victory over sin was not only individual and personal but also corporate and cosmic. Christ died to dethrone sin. Christ died to defeat every vestige of sin, to obliterate every effect of sin — individual, personal, corporate, and cosmic — including death, suffering, tears, sorrow, mourning, crying, and pain.

That's why twice in Revelation, John shares the blessed promise that "[God] will wipe every tear from their eyes. There will be no more death or mourning or crying or pain, for the old order of things has passed away" (Rev. 21:4; see also Rev. 7:17). Christ died to defeat every enemy, every evil, including the Devil, who holds the power of death (Heb. 2:14 – 15), and the last enemy — suffering and death (1 Cor. 15:26).

When we invite people in our congregations to come to us with their grief and suffering, rather than ignoring or minimizing sin, we are actually emphasizing and addressing the full impact of sin. That's what Lake meant when he said we must deal thoroughly with the evils we have suffered (biblical soul care) and with the sins we have committed (biblical spiritual direction).

Soul caregivers recognize that not all suffering is due to personal sin (compare Job 1 – 2 and John 9). Therefore, not all counseling focuses on confrontation of the sins we have committed (spiritual direction).

Clearly God calls us to develop the competency to be *parakaletic* comforters who minister to people suffering under the gravity of grinding affliction. "Comfort" is a powerful word both in the English and the Greek. In English, it highlights *co-fortitude*: the idea that we are fortified when we stand together; we are strengthened when others weep with us and grieve with us (Rom. 12:15).

As I noted in chapter 3, in Greek, "comfort" derives from a compound word *para kaletic* or *para klesis*. It means "one called alongside to help a person in need." In John 14, John uses this Greek word when he describes the Holy Spirit as our Comforter/Counselor. He is our encouragement Counselor called not simply alongside, but inside us to help us after Jesus ascends to heaven. In 2 Corinthians 1:3 – 7, Paul uses the same root word nine times in five verses to describe the calling of the body of Christ to come alongside, empathize with, and encourage one another during times of affliction. God calls each of us to be *parakaletic* biblical counselors — biblical soul caregivers.

We live in a fallen world and it often falls on us. Biblical counselors gladly assume the role of encouragers to help a friend crushed by the weight of the world. As the Good Samaritan crossed over to the other side and bloodied himself to care for a stranger's suffering body, so soul caregivers move near to enter the mess and muck of a friend's suffering soul. We *compassionately identify with people in pain.* We reject the shallow pretense that denies suffering. Like Jeremiah, we lament. Like Paul, we groan for home. We're out of the nest. East of Eden. We're not home yet. We join our hurting spiritual friend in admitting that *life is bad.*

We also insist that *God is good.* Therefore, we don't direct people to us. We eschew their becoming dependent on us or needing "lifelong counseling sessions." Instead, we redirect people to Christ and the body of Christ. We point suffering friends to their suffering Savior. We remind them what a friend they have in Jesus. We also equip them to avail themselves of all the resources of the body of Christ through discipleship, worship, fellowship, stewardship, and ambassadorship.

What is the focus of our biblical soul care for suffering with Pastor Carl? We sometimes miss the profound biblical truth that when we minister to a suffering person like Carl, our goal is not only to care, but also to help him to grow. We need to link our ministry to the suffering with the ministry of sanctification — growth in grace. Satan wants Carl to think that when his life is bad, God is bad — those are some of the doubts that Carl is wrestling with. We journey with Carl as he seeks a gospel-centered perspective that *even when life is bad, God is good.* We help suffering people like Carl to *find God even when they can't find relief.*

Guidepost #2: Hallmarks of Biblical Spiritual Direction for Sin

Think about the "spaghetti relationships" as we minister to Pastor Carl. His daughter is suffering with leukemia as a result of living in a fallen body in a fallen world. Carl is suffering at the hands of his deacons who, to use the vernacular of our day, "threw him under the bus." Many of the complaints from members of the congregation related to decisions the deacons pushed through, but when push came to shove, they blamed their pastor. As Carl deals with his external suffering, internally he is now battling doubts about God and temptations toward sin. Carl's sin and suffering are mingled together.

Fortunately, God's road map, our treasure map, provides two directional markers: comforting soul care *and* care-fronting spiritual direction. The absence of either lens would leave our counseling with Carl out of focus, distorted — half biblical.

Before we continue our biblical counseling journey by looking through the lens of biblical spiritual direction, let's have an honest conversation about the phrase "spiritual direction." I recognize that it is a phrase that can have some baggage. Some read "spiritual direction" and think of Eastern mysticism or non-evangelical approaches to helping people. That's certainly not how I will define and use the term.

I use it, as we saw McNeil used it, in its church history sense of *fraternal correction*. Think about that term: brotherly and sisterly wisdom that helps one another to put off an unspiritual way of living and to put on a Christlike, biblical way of living. It is "spiritual" because it is based on scriptural wisdom for living.

Honestly, I'm not hung up on the term. We can call it scriptural direction, spiritual direction, discipleship counseling, fraternal correction, or *nouthetic* biblical counseling. Whatever term you prefer, the important issue is that we understand that fully biblical counseling also addresses the sins we have committed — it deals with sin and sanctification based on a biblical understanding of people, problems, and solutions.

As I noted in chapter 3, *noutheteo* is one Greek word out of many that the Bible uses for one-another ministry. We can translate it as *confronting out of concern for change* — for growth. Because of the emphasis on concern, I like to call it *care-fronting*. Because we care, and because we know that going God's way is right and best, we seek to join with the Holy Spirit in enlightening people when they've veered off track.

The great Reformer Martin Luther helps to illustrate this care-fronting aspect of spiritual direction. Sense his compassion and care in this quote where he confronts — care-fronts — a German prince: "You must be aware that you have become cold, have given your heart to idols.... I am concerned about [y]our ... soul. I cannot permit myself to cease praying for you and being concerned about you, for then I am convinced that I would cease being in the Church."[40]

In biblical soul care with Pastor Carl, we journey together toward the conviction that "*God is good even when life is bad.*" In biblical spiritual direction with Pastor Carl, we journey together toward the conviction that "*God is gracious even when I am sinful.*" God calls us, with folks like Carl, to be disciplers who practice the ancient art of fraternal correction — concerned confrontation and challenge cultivating core change toward Christlikeness through Christ's power.

God calls us to understand spiritual dynamics and to discern root causes of spiritual conflicts. We are to understand *people* biblically — how God originally designed Carl to function so that we know what healthy living looks like. We are to understand *problems* biblically — what heart sin and false cisterns are at the root of Carl's doubts and temptations? We are to understand *solutions* biblically — how does Christ change people like Carl, what will the process of growth in grace look like and involve in Carl's heart, life, relationships, and ministry?

When working with Pastor Carl, we use our biblical discernment to provide loving wisdom that reconciles and guides Carl. Our reconciliation and guiding emphasize the same ultimate purpose of sustaining and healing — communion with Christ and conformity to Christ. We want to empower and equip Carl to fulfill the great commandment of loving God and loving others — even in the midst of the suffering he is facing and the sin he is battling.

Four Compass Points for Comprehensive, Compassionate Gospel Conversations

Three decades ago, when I began my study of the history of biblical counseling, I first saw a "neon light" that continually flashed these words: *Suffering and Sin.* That alone seemed to me like a wonderful treasure trove because it provided a sorely lacking, balanced, comprehensive approach to helping people. Little did I know that there was much more buried treasure to uncover.

While it is vital to know that I need to engage Pastor Carl both in his suffering *and* his sinning, those are like destinations — our guideposts. But how do we get from here to there?

These questions guided my historical search until I found four compass points. Not N-S-E-W, but S-H-R-G: Sustaining, Healing, Reconciling, and Guiding.

It was while reading Clebsch and Jaekle's classic text, *Pastoral Care in Historical Perspective*, that I first came across sustaining, healing, reconciling, and guiding. Clebsch and Jaekle began their study with the *Didascalia Apostolorum* (c. AD 225), which is the earliest description outside of the Bible of the inner life of the Christian congregation. A major portion of this work is a depiction of the office and pastoral function of the pastor-shepherd. The *Didascalia Apostolorum* sets forth four analogies for understanding the character and duty of the chief minister of pastoral care. The pastor is to be

> • a shepherd who sustains by partaking of the suffering of the flock — sustaining.

Maturing as a Biblical Counselor

Self-Counsel and Group or Partner Interaction

1. As you reflect on your ministry to people, what are you more naturally prone to focus on: biblical soul care that offers comfort for suffering *or* biblical spiritual direction that offers care-fronting for sin?

   a. Why do you think you focus there?

   b. How will your awareness of your current focus impact how you approach your training in *Gospel Conversations*?

2. As you reflect on the training you've received in the past, which has it focused on: biblical soul care that offers comfort for suffering *or* biblical spiritual direction that offers care-fronting for sin? How will your awareness of your past training impact how you approach your training in *Gospel Conversations*?

Counseling Others

3. If you are working through this workbook individually, then instead of role-playing, use the space after the next two scenarios to write your response to each situation.

   a. Imagine that Pastor Carl has been sharing his story with you. With a partner, role-play how you would begin to journey with Pastor Carl by offering comforting soul care for his suffering. After you complete your role-play, provide each other with feedback.

   b. Imagine that Pastor Carl has been sharing his story with you. With a partner, role-play how you would begin to journey with Pastor Carl by offering care-fronting spiritual direction for his battle against sin. After you complete your role-play, provide each other with feedback.

- a physician who heals by mending the wounds of the patient — healing.
- a judge who reconciles relationships by providing discerning rulings — reconciling.
- a parent who guides by giving parent-like direction to the young in the faith — guiding.[41]

Reflecting on these four concepts, Clebsch and Jaekle noted:

Thus the pastoral office, even as early as the third century, was seen as consisting of the four functions of guiding, sustaining, reconciling, and healing. The far-reaching influence of this early analysis of pastoral care can be measured by reference to modern writings on the subject.[42]

After reading that, I couldn't put Clebsch and Jaekle's book down. It's so marked up that there are fewer unhighlighted sections than highlighted ones! At first I thought, "I guess no one else has ever seen these four tasks of sustaining, healing, reconciling, and guiding." But my continued historical research showed me just how many *church historians* frequently reference sustaining, healing, reconciling, and guiding.[43]

Notice that in the previous sentence I italicized *church historians*. Here's why: When I began studying the history of Christian spiritual care, I never saw pastors, biblical counselors, Christian counseling educators, or *practitioners* talking about and utilizing sustaining, healing, reconciling, and guiding. The wisdom of the historians remained locked away in the academy. For the past three decades, one of my major ministry missions has been to transport the riches of sustaining, healing, reconciling, and guiding from the academy to the congregation where God's people could embrace it and practice it.

When we combine the two guideposts of soul care for suffering and spiritual direction for sin with the four compass points of sustaining, healing, reconciling, and guiding, we gain a biblical/historical approach that can transform our practice of biblical counseling. There is a beautiful synergy between the two guideposts and the four compass points: We offer biblical soul care for *suffering* through *sustaining* and *healing*, while we offer biblical spiritual direction for *sinning* through *reconciling* and *guiding*. It was like an "Aha!" experience when I first perceived the alliance of:

- *Parakaletic* Soul Care for Suffering through Sustaining and Healing
- *Nouthetic* Spiritual Direction for Sinning through Reconciling and Guiding

Keep reading to understand why these four compass points get me so excited!

Biblical Soul Care for Suffering through Sustaining and Healing

As I learned more about sustaining and healing, I began to uncover the rich history of how men and women *joined with sufferers in their suffering* (sustaining) and *journeyed with sufferers to Christ* (healing). Ponder that sentence. Though simple, it teaches a profoundly compassionate and comprehensive path of ministry to hurting people in their suffering.

Compass Point #1: Hallmarks of Biblical Sustaining for Suffering and the Troubling Story

Some people are great at sustaining. They are able to join with others in their suffering — they weep with those who weep, they grieve, they empathize. They understand and live out the reality that *shared sorrow is endurable sorrow*. They're able to listen compassionately to another person's earthly story of suffering and despair.

I use a rather macabre image to capture the essence of this historical sustaining ministry: *climbing in the casket*. I've developed this picture from 2 Corinthians 1 where Paul says he does not want his brothers and sisters in Christ to be ignorant about the hardships he had suffered. Paul goes on to say, "We were under great pressure, far beyond our ability to endure, so that we despaired even of life. Indeed, in our hearts we felt the sentence of death" (2 Cor. 1:8b – 9a). When Paul despaired of life and felt the sentence of death, he wanted the Corinthians to *climb in his casket* to identify with what felt like a death sentence.

Another way I attempt to translate sustaining from the dusty halls of church history to real-life ministry today is with the phrase you've heard already, "It's normal to hurt." So we communicate to Pastor Carl, "Of course you're going to be in agony when our fallen, messed-up world comes crashing down on you and you hear the doctor say, 'Your daughter has leukemia.'" Together, we face the fact that in this fallen world, *life is bad*. In sustaining, we give Carl permission to grieve — permission to be candid like the psalmists in the lament psalms and like Jesus in the Garden of Gethsemane.

You've just read summaries of some of the wonderful aspects of historical/ biblical sustaining care. As important as sustaining is, imagine if we stopped at sustaining as we ministered to Pastor Carl. He'd feel loved, but he'd be left still wrestling with his doubts about the goodness of God in the badness of life. Worse — we would both be stuck in the casket! If all we are competent at is sustaining, then we're good at hugging but clueless about what to do after the hug. That's why we need to understand the hallmarks of biblical soul care through healing.

Compass Point #2: Hallmarks of Biblical Healing and the Faith Story

Some people are great at healing. They are able to journey with sufferers to Christ — they can explore rich theological truths about the goodness, providence, and affectionate sovereignty of God. They know the importance of *cropping Christ into the picture.* When bad things happen to God's people, Satan attempts to crop Christ out of the picture. He tempts people like Pastor Carl to conclude, "Life is bad, God is sovereign, so God must be bad too!" We have the privilege of journeying with Pastor Carl so that we listen together to God's eternal story of healing hope — cropping Christ back into the picture. We move with Carl to the place where he can say with conviction, "Life is bad, but God is good. He's good *all* the time — which Christ demonstrated on the cross."

To balance the sustaining image of *climbing in the casket*, I capture the essence of historical healing ministry with *celebrating the empty tomb!* Earlier we read 2 Corinthians 1:8b – 9a. I purposely stopped before the end of verse. Paul goes on to say, "But this happened that we might not rely on ourselves but on God, who raises the dead" (2 Cor. 1:9b). Paul does not remain in the casket because Jesus did not remain in the tomb!

I transport healing from the historians' lecture hall to real-life ministry today with another phrase you've read from me before, "It's possible to hope." We communicate to Pastor Carl, "Even in the midst of all of this horrible suffering, you can grow in your faith. God's Spirit, who is the Encourager, en-courages you — places courage within you so that you do not only survive in your suffering. You can actually thrive as you move beyond who you were before your suffering began." In the secular approach to grief and loss, the target is "acceptance" — you face the reality of your loss and move on the best you can. In the biblical approach to suffering, the target is sanctification — comfort from Christ leads to communion with Christ which results in conformity to Christ.

You've just read summaries of a few of the amazing characteristics of historical/biblical healing care. But imagine if the first thing you said after

Pastor Carl stopped talking was, "God works all things together for good." Those are healing truths, but they can feel like spiritual platitudes and clichés if they are preached *at* people. That's especially true if we race to say, "It's possible to hope" (healing) before we've communicated "It's normal to hurt" (sustaining). We'd be insisting that Carl listen to us lecture about God's story before we listened compassionately to Carl sharing his story. We'd be decent preachers, perhaps, but miserable comforters.

Church history fleshes out the brilliance and fullness of biblical soul care for suffering. It is not either/or: either sustaining or healing, either hurting or hoping, either the casket or the empty tomb, either our earthly story or God's eternal story. Church history models what the Bible teaches. Soul care for suffering is Romans 8:17 – 27, where we suffer, groan, grieve, cry out, and admit our weakness and neediness in this broken world. And it is also Romans 28 – 39, where we realize that God truly does work *all* things together for good because he is good, and where we realize that even in all our suffering, in Christ we are more than conquerors because Christ conquered the grave.

Biblical Spiritual Direction for Sinning through Reconciling and Guiding

If we follow our two guideposts, then we know that comforting Carl in his suffering, while so important, is not the end of good counsel. We'd know that we need to address Carl's struggles with sin — his doubts, temptations, distance from his wife …

Through historical/biblical reconciling and guiding, we uncover the rich history of men and women who *exposed the horrors of sin and enlightened people to the wonders of grace* (reconciling) and *empowered saints to apply the supernatural power of Christ's grace to mature them into Christ's likeness.* Again, ponder that sentence. It teaches a profoundly rich and robust path of ministry to people battling against sin.

Compass Point #3: Hallmarks of Biblical Reconciling and the Redemption Story

Some people are great at reconciling. They can expose sin humbly yet firmly — speaking the truth in love. Like the Hebrew Christians, they are aware of the deceitfulness of sin and thus committed to being sure that no one has a sinful, unbelieving heart that turns away from the living God (Heb. 3:7 – 19). Like Nathan with David, they have the ability to paint pictures that say, "You are the man! See your sin in all its horrors! It's horrible to sin." Like the Puritans, they are able, when necessary, to "load the conscience with guilt" so that hard hearts are softened by God's Spirit of truth.

Biblical reconciling does not stop with the exposure of heart sin. God also calls us to be skillful at exposing grace — where we communicate that where sin abounds, grace mega-abounds. Where we not only communicate that "it's horrible to sin" but also convey that "it's wonderful to be forgiven." In historical and biblical reconciling, we say to Pastor Carl, "God is gracious to you, even when you are sinful." We not only load Carl's conscience with guilt; like the Puritans, we lighten Carl's conscience with grace. The real-life image I use to communicate historical reconciling is a painting of every Christian as a *dispenser of grace*. Grace is God's medicine of choice for our sin. Grace is God's prescription for our disgrace.

You've just read summaries of a few of the powerful features of historical/ biblical reconciling care. The balance of exposing sin and grace is an amazing combination. But if we stopped there, Carl would know he was forgiven but still leave the counseling room with a battle on his hands — fighting the world, the flesh, and the Devil. He'd still leave the room wondering, "The next time I'm tempted to turn to Internet pornography, how do I tap into Christ's resurrection power?" That's why we need to understand the spiritual direction compass point of guiding.

Compass Point #4: Hallmarks of Biblical Guiding and the Growth-in-Grace Story

Some people are great at guiding. They can help people to discern how God empowers them to put off the old sinful ways and to put on the new ways of the new person in Christ. They can help Carl to practice the biblical spiritual disciplines that connect him with Christ's resurrection power (Phil. 3:10). They can assist Carl in thinking through the implications of his identity in Christ and what Christ has already done for him (the gospel indicatives), and the implications of commands to obey Christ out of gratitude for grace (the gospel imperatives). They practice what the Hebrew saints practiced in spurring one another on to love and good deeds on the basis of what Christ has already done (Heb. 10:19 – 25).

I've used one phrase and one picture to capture the essence of this type of historical guiding ministry. The phrase: "It's supernatural to mature." The grace that saves us is also the grace that empowers us to grow. Our growth in grace involves responding to and availing ourselves of Christ's resurrection power — the same power that raised Christ from the grave is in us (Eph. 1:15 – 23; Phil. 3:10). The picture I use: *fanning into flame the gift of God*. Our role is not to place power within Pastor Carl. Our role is to stir up and fan into flame the gift of God *already* in Carl, just as Paul stirred up the gift of God in Timothy (2 Tim. 1:6 – 7).

You've just read summaries of some of the central marks of historical/biblical guiding care. But what happens in Carl's heart and life if those "put off and put on" messages are sent to a heart that has not repented of sin and is not filled with the wonders of God's grace? They become legalistic commands that Carl attempts to obey in his own strength, rather than loving wisdom that Carl joyfully responds to in Christ's power out of gratitude for Christ's grace.

Church history fleshes out the brilliance and the fullness of biblical spiritual direction for sin. We engage in spiritual heart surgery with Pastor Carl, using the Word of God to help him, like the prodigal son, to come to his senses, see his sin, and race to Christ's grace. He owns the message, "It's horrible to sin but wonderful to be forgiven." *And* we engage in spiritual heart conditioning with Carl, using God's Word to empower him, like the woman caught in adultery, to go and sin no more. Carl embraces the truth that "it's supernatural to mature."

Where We've Been and Where We're Headed

Here's your tweet-size summary of chapter 4.

+ Fully biblical counseling helps saints and sons who are enduring suffering and battling sin to move toward sanctification through sustaining and healing soul care and reconciling and guiding spiritual direction.

Having laid the foundation of biblical counseling, now throughout the rest of *Gospel Conversations* we'll learn together twenty-one biblical counseling relational competencies of sustaining, healing, reconciling, and guiding. The next two chapters equip us to develop five sustaining counseling competencies that we summarize with the acronym GRACE.

Maturing as a Biblical Counselor

Self-Counsel and Group or Partner Interaction

1. Had you ever heard of sustaining, healing, reconciling, and guiding before? If so, where? If not, why do you think this comprehensive model has remained in "the academy?"

2. Of sustaining, healing, reconciling, and guiding:

   a. Which one do you think you most naturally tend toward? Why?

   b. Which do you think you most need to further develop?

3. What would be missing in your biblical counseling ministry if you omitted either sustaining or healing or reconciling or guiding?

4. What would your counseling approach be like if you focused almost exclusively on either sustaining or healing or reconciling or guiding?

5. Share about a person who has helped you to sense that *it's normal to hurt*. Who has climbed in the casket with you?

6. Share about a person who has helped you to realize that *it's possible to hope*. Who has helped you to celebrate the empty tomb?

7. Share about a person who has helped you to sense that *it's horrible to sin but wonderful to be forgiven*. Who has been a dispenser of Christ's grace in your life?

8. Share about a person who has helped you to sense that *it's supernatural to mature*. Who has fanned into flame the gift of God in you?

Counseling Others

9. If you are working through this material individually, then instead of role-playing, use the space below each scenario to summarize what some of your interactions might sound like.

   a. With a partner, role-play *sustaining* interactions with Pastor Carl.

   b. With a partner, role-play *healing* interactions with Pastor Carl.

   c. With a partner, role-play *reconciling* interactions with Pastor Carl.

   d. With a partner, role-play *guiding* interactions with Pastor Carl.

Counseling One Another

10. Recall our primary premise: *we learn to be effective biblical counselors by giving and receiving biblical counseling in community.* With that in mind, a group member can share a personal concern related to an area of suffering and/or a battle with sin and temptation and receive biblical sustaining, healing, reconciling, and/or guiding from the entire group or from a lab partner or from the lab facilitator or from another member of the lab.

5 SUSTAINING BIBLICAL COUNSELING COMPETENCIES: GRACE

GRACE

Here's what we've seen so far in preparing to be a biblical counselor through the foundations of biblical counseling. Before we ever step foot in a counseling office or sit down to minister to a hurting friend at our favorite restaurant:

- We need to be the type of person who shares Scripture and soul. We don't sit down with our hurting friend just to hug them. And we don't sit down with them just to preach at them. We're more than just the UPS delivery guy. We're a brother, mother, father, child, and mentor committed to living truth in love.

- We need to be the type of person who listens to the Scriptures about the soul. We derive our foundational understanding of the person sitting across from us from God's Word. We listen well and wisely, comprehensively and compassionately to our counselee by listening to the Bible's grand story and our friend's earthly story.

- We need to be the type of person who is growing in Christlike character, biblical content, counseling competence, and Christian community. Every believer can be competent to counsel, but every believer needs to be committed to growth in being, knowing, doing, and loving in order to be an effective counselor.

- We need to be the type of person who offers compassionate and comprehensive soul care for suffering through sustaining and healing. And we need to be the type of person who offers compassionate and comprehensive spiritual direction for sin through reconciling and guiding.

Competent to begin counseling, we now have someone sitting in front of us whose world has caved in on them. In their suffering, how do we help? What do we do after the hug? How do we care like Christ?

In chapters 5 and 6 we learn and practice the five skills of sustaining biblical counseling. Here are the student-oriented learning objectives (SOLOs) that will be our target in the sustaining process.

Active participants in the reading and application of chapters 5–6 will be able to:

- Develop four character qualities of effective sustainers (chapter 5).
- Define relational competencies and distinguish between them and skills, techniques, and methods (chapter 5).

- Engage in grace relationships that sustain faith in the goodness of God during the badness of life (chapter 5).
- Develop the sustaining relational competency of grace connecting — counseling incarnationally (chapter 5).
- Develop the sustaining relational competency of rich soul empathizing — climbing in the casket (chapter 5).
- Develop the sustaining relational competency of attuned gospel listening — hearing life redemptively (chapter 6).
- Develop the sustaining relational competency of comforting spiritual conversations — sustaining theological trialogues (chapter 6).
- Develop the sustaining relational competency of empathetic scriptural explorations — sustaining biblical trialogues (chapter 6).

If you are working through *Gospel Conversations* with a group of people, then to meet these learning objectives, you will want to do the following prior to meeting with your small group training lab:

- Chapter 5: Sustaining through Climbing in the Casket
  - Read pages 123 to 150.
  - Respond to all questions on pages 125, 130 – 31, 134 – 35, 142 – 44, and 149 – 50.
  - Read, meditate on, and study Job 4 – 6; Proverbs 27:6; John 11; Romans 12:15; Galatians 6:1 – 3; Hebrews 2:14 – 18; and 4:14 – 16.
  - Optional: Read chapter 10 of *Gospel-Centered Counseling*.
- Chapter 6: Sustaining through Grace Relationships
  - Read pages 151 to 176.
  - Respond to all questions on pages 152, 162 – 63, 170 – 71, and 176.
  - Read, meditate on, and study 2 Samuel 13; Proverbs 18:4, 13, 21; 20:5; Jeremiah 17:9 – 10; Matthew 12:33 – 37; John 2 – 4; Ephesians 4:29; Hebrews 10:19 – 25; and James 3:1 – 6.
  - Optional: Read chapter 13 of *Gospel-Centered Counseling*.

CHAPTER 5

Sustaining through Climbing in the Casket

Soul physicians of the past have described sustaining as *a line drawn in the sand of spiritual retreat*. To understand this imagery, ponder any significant suffering you have faced or loss that you have endured. Often in the midst of our suffering, Satan whispers to us, "Life is bad, so God must be bad too. Either he's not loving enough to care about you in your pain, or he's not powerful enough to do anything about your suffering."

At that moment, we enter a faith point. Our world has come crashing down around us. Now the question is, "Will my faith come crashing down within me?" If we start believing Satan's lie that our suffering means that God has turned his back on us and is getting back at us, then we're tempted to turn our back on God — spiritual retreat. Our retreat from God doesn't have to be overt — becoming the rebellious prodigal son or the angry atheist. It is often much more subtle — an inch-by-inch relational distance from God creeps in as we battle doubts about his good heart. Slowly, almost imperceptibly, our trust in our heavenly Father grows lukewarm.

Sustaining biblical counseling doesn't deny spiritual temptations, subtle doubts, and creeping distance. It does the opposite because denial only feeds spiritual retreat. Sustaining draws a line in the sand of retreat by encouraging people to *face suffering face-to-face with Christ and the body of Christ*. We've started to turn away from God in doubt but begin to turn back to God — to face God — so we can face our suffering and disappointment *with* God instead of *without* God.

As biblical counselors, we join with our suffering friends in their suffering

Sustaining

Maturing as a Biblical Counselor

Self-Counsel and Group or Partner Interaction

1. What was one of your more difficult casket experiences—a time of despair like Paul in 2 Corinthians 1:3–10?

2. Read Psalm 13 and Psalm 88. During your casket time, if you had written your own Psalm 13 or Psalm 88, how would you have worded it?

3. What is it like for you to invite God into your casket? Do you find it hard or easy to share honestly with God your pain, anger, disappointment, and doubts? Why do you suppose that is?

4. During your "casket time," did anyone, trying to be helpful, dismiss your pain, not really listen to your inner struggles, and quickly share how God would work it all together for good?

    a. What did that feel like? How did it short-circuit your face-to-face grieving with God?

    b. What would you have wanted instead?

healing

(sustaining) and journey with them to Christ (healing). In sustaining, we meet them on their road to retreat, acknowledging that their life right now is bad. We listen compassionately to their candid doubts and their painful laments, but we draw a line in the sand of their spiritual retreat and help their faith to *survive* by encouraging them to wrestle *with* God. "You may be turning slowly away from God, but God has not turned his back on you, and he is not getting back at you. Instead, he is drawing you and inviting you back to himself. Whatever is happening to you and everything that is going on inside you — tell it to Jesus."

Sustaining is weeping with those who weep, but it is much more than just a *tearful hug*. It is an *inviting tug*. As ambassadors of reconciliation for Christ, we speak on behalf of Christ, inviting our suffering spiritual friends not simply to weep with *us*, but to weep with *God*. We remind them that in all their distress, God says "he too was distressed" (Isa. 63:9a). Their faith may not be ready to *thrive*, but it can *survive*. Sustaining faith is a faith that perceives the presence of God in the presence of suffering.

The Christlike Character of a Sustaining Comforter

Over the course of the next two chapters, we'll learn and practice five biblical counseling competencies for sustaining — helping people to face their suffering face-to-face with Christ. However, before we learn new competencies, we have to remember that competencies apart from Christlike character are like working on the outside of the cup and ignoring the more important matters of the inside (see Matt. 23:25 – 26). That's why we each need to prayerfully ponder the question What type of person do I need to be in order to offer Christ's sustaining comfort to others?

Powerful Sustainers See God as Their Sustaining Father

Paul uses the Greek word for "comfort" ten times in 2 Corinthians 1:3 – 7 — do you think this may be the theme of these verses? He begins developing his theme by presenting a crystal clear image of God. "Praise be to the God and Father of our Lord Jesus Christ, the Father of compassion and the God of all comfort, who comforts us in all our troubles" (2 Cor. 1:3 – 4a). All comfort is ultimately sourced in God. The flip side of that is to say that worldly comfort — comfort not sourced in God — is ultimately empty, vain, hollow comfort.

The Greek word for "compassion" means to feel another person's agony. People in Paul's day used the word to signify sympathetic lament. God laments our pain; God aches when we ache; he weeps when we weep. He is the Father of compassion. Is that our image of God when life is bad?

The word for "comfort" pictures God fortifying us — he gives us his strength to draw a line in the sand of retreat. Paul and others used the word to picture a lawyer advocating for a client, a mother wrapping her arms of protection around her child, a soldier standing back to back with a comrade in danger. Even when I am tempted to turn my back on God, he stands back-to-back with me, fortifying me in my suffering. He is the God of all comfort. In the midst of our suffering, is that our image of God?

Powerful Sustainers Admit Their Own Helplessness

Sustaining comfort always starts with the person in need being willing to call out for aid, summoning help, beseeching rescue. Paul alerts us to our neediness when he tells us that God comforts us in all our *troubles* (2 Cor. 1:4). "Troubles" literally means to press, squash, squeeze. It's used of the pressures of life that squeeze the life out of us, that crush us — that bring us to a faith point — either we cry out to God or we retreat from God.

In a similar way, Psalm 34:17 – 18 tells us, "The righteous cry out, and the LORD hears them; he delivers them from all their troubles. The LORD is close to the brokenhearted and saves those who are crushed in spirit." The world says, "God helps those who help themselves." The psalmist and Paul say, "God helps those who admit they can't help themselves. He comforts those who humbly cry out, 'I can't handle my suffering on my own. I need your help, Father.'" God invites us to verbalize our suffering, our neediness.

Notice how facing our helplessness relates to comforting others: "… who comforts us in all our troubles, *so that* we can comfort those in any trouble with the comfort we ourselves have received from God" (2 Cor. 1:4, emphasis added). When we are weak — admitting our powerlessness to God, crying out for his comfort — then we are strong — empowered to empower others. God comforts and empowers us in our weakness so that we can comfort and empower others in their weakness.

Powerful Sustainers Face Their Own Suffering Face-to-Face with Christ

There's a third important sustaining principle tucked away in verse 4. We tend to think, "For me to help another person, I must have gone through *the same* situation or *the identical* trial." For instance, we think, "For me to help someone struggling with alcoholism, I must have battled alcoholism in my life." That's not what this verse teaches. Notice it again: "... who comforts us in *all* our troubles, so that we can comfort those in *any* trouble with the comfort we ourselves have *received* from God" (2 Cor. 1:4, emphasis added).

Whatever my trouble is, if I've taken *that* trouble *to Christ*, then *his infinite* comfort in *my* life supplies me with the power to comfort *you* with *any* trouble in *your* life. My ability to help you is not based on what I've gone through; it is based on my going through suffering face-to-face *with Christ*. Because God is infinite, I do not need to experience the same situation or soul pain as you; I need to have experienced the same comforting Father in my suffering.

Paul develops his thinking further in verse 5 when he says, "For just as the sufferings of Christ flow over into our lives, so also through Christ our comfort overflows." Only comfort-receivers spill over and overflow into comfort-givers. When we're the type of person who turns humbly to God in our suffering, then we become the type of person who tunes in to others. We become Jesus with skin on. Then we offer small tastes of what it is like to be comforted by Christ. Of course, as we do this, we don't point people to ourselves, we point people to Christ, who is the Ultimate Comforter.

Powerful Sustainers Apply the Truth that Shared Sorrow Is Endurable Sorrow

Notice what happens when the body of Christ offers Christ's comfort to one another.

> *For just as the sufferings of Christ flow over into our lives, so also through Christ our comfort overflows. If we are distressed, it is for your comfort and salvation; if we are comforted, it is for your comfort, which produces in you patient endurance of the same sufferings we suffer. And our hope for you is firm, because we know that just as you share in our sufferings, so also you share in our comfort.* (2 Corinthians 1:5 – 7)

Together we are empowered by the fellowship of Christian endurance. Or, as we saw in chapter 4, *shared sorrow is endurable sorrow.* Do we believe that for *others* but not for *ourselves?* Do we encourage others to be open with the body of Christ about their struggles, but we keep our battles and wounds hidden from others? Powerful sustainers not only turn to Christ, they turn to the body of Christ to stop their own retreat.

Paul describes the result as *patient endurance.* It is the Greek compound word, *hupomeno*, meaning "remaining under." We can remain under pressure without giving in to pressure. The word has the sense of resilience — the ability to turn setbacks into comebacks. It is more than just patience as we think of it. It is courageous endurance. It has the active significance of energetic successful resistance. It is spiritual heroism in the face of pain, the firm refusal to give in or give up, the brave determination to stop retreating and to start forging forward.

The heroic Christian is not the person who never asks for help. Instead, the heroic Christian and the effective sustaining comforter is the person who knows that they can endure sorrow only by inviting others to share in their sorrows.

Our "Bedside Manner" and "Relational Competencies"

You sit silently at Emilio's bedside. He doesn't even know you're there. His wife, Maria, just called you with the news concerning his liver biopsy — cancer. Anesthetized in the recovery room, within the hour he'll awake with groggy head and blurry eyes to see you and his wife.

Waiting, you picture his "firstborn," Stefan, the always energized nine-year-old who loves Daddy's fist bumps and hugs. You picture "the middle child," Isabel, a six-year-old bundle of joy who's always holding Daddy's hand in church. You picture "the baby of the family," Carlos, just three, who has Daddy's eyes and smile.

You silently pray, "Lord, what do I say? Keep me from trite platitudes. How do I help? Help me to be here for Emilio, Maria, and the kids. What would Jesus do? What would Jesus say? How would he relate?"

Jesus Loved and Jesus Wept

Your mind drifts to Jesus and Lazarus. "Jesus loved Martha and her sister and Lazarus" (John 11:5), you recall. "Jesus loved ... Help me to love, Lord."

"This sickness will not end in death. No, it is for God's glory so that God's Son may be glorified through it" (John 11:4). You know that you don't have a promise that *this* sickness will not end in *physical* death. You do know that Emilio's sickness will not end in spiritual death. You smile, remembering burly, bike-riding Emilio reluctantly attending Carlos's baptism two years ago. Who would have thought that two months later, Emilio would be baptized, publicly expressing his newfound faith in Jesus. "Lord, be glorified."

"A short while ago the Jews tried to stone you, and yet you are going back there?" (John 11:8). Pondering the ever-impetuous disciples and their warning to their Master, you pray again. "Father, this death and dying stuff terrifies me. I hate it. I loathe hospitals. I despise funerals. Give me a nice chair, a functional computer, a terrific biblical library, and let me prepare sermons. Bedside manners? How do you learn this stuff? Help me to face my fears so I can help Emilio to face his."

"Our friend Lazarus has fallen asleep; but I am going there to wake him up" (John 11:11). "Let me be Emilio's *friend*, Lord. His spiritual friend. His Jesus-like friend. What does that mean? Look like?"

"When Jesus saw her weeping, and the Jews who had come along with her also weeping, he was deeply moved in spirit and troubled" (John 11:33). Interesting, you think to yourself. Jesus knew the outcome. "Your brother will rise again" (John 11:23). He knew God would be glorified. Yet he was still deeply moved and troubled. "Father, help me to feel before I talk. To sustain before I heal. Don't let my awareness of your final victory minimize my hatred of the final enemy — Death! Don't let my confidence in your capability to weave all things together for good depreciate my groaning in this messed-up world."

"Jesus wept" (John 11:35). And your tears flow. Unashamed. Unbridled.

"See how he loved him!" (John 11:36). "Help me to love Emilio," you pray.

Maria enters. Seeing your tears, she hugs you as you stand. "Thank you for being here. Thank you for loving Emilio," she says.

Relational Competencies

Perhaps now it becomes clear why words like "skills," "techniques," and "methods" are far too shallow for what biblical counseling and gospel conversations are all about. "Relational competence" still doesn't fully grab me, but it's a better phrase, especially when carefully defined. Relational competence is our ability — given by grace and cultivated by our dependence on the Spirit — to express the character of Christ in our relationships with people so they experience our love as a small taste of Christ's grace and are changed by his grace.

> Relational competence is our ability—given by grace and cultivated by our dependence on the Spirit—to express the character of Christ in our relationships with people so they experience our love as a small taste of Christ's grace and are changed by his grace.

Maturing as a Biblical Counselor

Self-Counsel and Group or Partner Interaction

1. On a scale of 1 to 10, with 1 being low/needing growth and 10 being high/very mature, rate yourself in each of the four character areas necessary for powerful sustaining comfort.

    a. In the midst of my suffering, I see God as my sustaining Father of compassion and comfort.

    5

    b. In the midst of my suffering, I admit my own helplessness—crying out to God for his sustaining care.

    6

    c. In the midst of my suffering, I face my suffering face-to-face with Christ—turning back to Christ and receiving his care so I can tune in to others in their suffering.

    4

    d. In the midst of my suffering, I apply the truth that shared sorrow is endurable sorrow—I turn to the body of Christ to sustain me in my suffering.

    1

Counseling One Another

2. Respond to the following questions in writing if you are working through this material alone. If you are working in a small group, then in your lab discuss with a partner:

    a. Possible reasons for lower "scores" on 1 a, b, c, or d.

    b. Ways that you can grow more mature in each of 1 a, b, c, and d.

    Being mindful of 2 Cor 1:3-4

Counseling Others

3. How would it impact your counseling of someone who was suffering if you were low in each of the character areas in 1 a, b, c, and d?

We relate deeply to others only when we are already relating deeply to Christ. Paul expresses it like this in Philippians 2:1 – 2: "If you have any encouragement from being united with Christ, if any comfort from his love, if any fellowship with the Spirit, if any tenderness and compassion, *then* make my joy complete by being like-minded, having the same love, being one in spirit and purpose" (emphasis added). When we nourish our souls in Christ, then our souls spill over to others.

Then, like Christ, we will be other-centered in our relationships. "Do nothing out of selfish ambition or vain conceit, but in humility consider others better than yourselves. Each of you should look not only to your own interests, but also to the interests of others" (Phil. 2:3 – 4). Our attitude will then be like Christ, "Who, being in very nature God, did not consider equality with God something to be grasped, but made himself nothing, taking the very nature of a servant, being made in human likeness" (Phil. 2:6 – 7). Like Paul, who was like Christ, we pour our souls into those we minister to. And like Paul, we followed a lifestyle of spiritual formation that empowers us as we connect to Christ so that Christ's goodness flows out of us into others.

We proclaim him, admonishing and teaching everyone with all wisdom, so that we may present everyone perfect in Christ. To this end I labor, struggling with all his energy, which so powerfully works in me. I want you to know how much I am struggling for you and for those at Laodicea, and for all who have not met me personally. My purpose is that they may be encouraged in heart and united in love, so that they may have the full riches of complete understanding, in order that they may know the mystery of God, namely, Christ. (Colossians 1:28 – 2:2)

Biblical counseling is grueling. Agonizing. Exhausting. It's work that results in the release of grace. Biblical counseling requires biblical content, Christlike character, *and* relational competence in the context of Christian community. Let's not simply become more skillful. Let's be empowered by grace to give tastes of grace. I call these tastes of grace "relational competencies."

Sustaining Relational Competencies: GRACE

I define sustaining relational competencies in several overlapping ways:

+ Climbing in the casket: joining sufferers in their troubling story.
+ Helping people to know that it's normal to hurt.
+ Drawing a line in the sand of retreat.
+ Empathizing with people when our fallen world falls on them.
+ Encouraging people to face their suffering face-to-face with Christ.
+ Engaging in grace relationships that sustain faith in the goodness of God during the badness of life.

> Biblical sustaining engages in grace relationships that sustain faith in the goodness of God during the badness of life.

While defining sustaining relational competencies is pretty easy, they take a lifetime to develop. Over the course of the next two chapters, we'll learn and practice five biblical counseling competencies for sustaining — competencies that I summarize using the acronym *GRACE*:

+ **G** Grace Connecting
+ **R** Rich Soul Empathizing
+ **A** Attuned Gospel Listening
+ **C** Comforting Spiritual Conversations
+ **E** Empathetic Scriptural Explorations

Whenever you think of the essence of sustaining, think "grace." Picture grace that helps others in their time of need.

Therefore, since we have a great high priest who has gone through the heavens, Jesus the Son of God, let us hold firmly to the faith we profess. For we do not have a high priest who is unable to sympathize with our weakness, but we have one who has been tempted in every way, just as we are — yet was without sin.

Let us then approach the throne of grace with confidence, so that we may receive mercy and find grace to help us in our time of need. (Hebrews 4:14 – 16)

What a perfect picture of sustaining relational competency, of grace relating. Jesus is not aloof, distant, or removed. In his incarnation, he went through the heavens to earth, sharing in our humanity, becoming like us, so that he might help us (Heb. 2:14 – 18). Jesus is not unsympathetic. He is touched with the feelings of our infirmities. He's able to suffer with and be affected similarly to us. He has the same pathos, shares the same experience, has fellow feelings, endures a mutual participation, and partakes of a full acquaintance with us.[44] He offers grace to help in our time of need — well-timed help, help in the nick of time, words aptly spoken in season and seasoned with grace.[45]

We can become Jesus with skin on. In sustaining, we do so by expressing GRACE relational competencies. The first of which is aptly called "Grace Connecting."

Grace Connecting: Counseling Incarnationally

Throughout *Gospel Conversations*, you'll read many current/modern counseling scenarios. You'll also read numerous examples of one-another ministry throughout church history. We have much to learn from our brothers and sisters from the past — that great cloud of witnesses and one-another ministers. Olaudah Equiano leads the way.

Equiano was born free in 1745 in Benin and then kidnapped at age ten along with his older sister. Sold and separated from one another several times during their trek to the slave ships, years later Equiano described one of their reunions. "The only comfort we had was in *being in one another's arms* all that night, and *bathing each other with our tears.*"[46] Ponder that: being in one another's arms, bathed in comforting tears. People need our presence, not our platitudes; they need our connection, not our simplistic solutions.

In his life story, Equiano included words of confrontation to the slavers who continually separated him and his sister. "Are the dearest friends and relations still to be parted from each other, and thus prevented from cheering the gloom of slavery with the small comfort of being together, and mingling their *sufferings* and *sorrows?*"[47]

Equiano beautifully portrays the truth we've written about: *shared sorrow is endurable sorrow.* God never intends for us to suffer alone. As we mingle our sufferings and sorrows, two become stronger than one, and the one is empowered to endure.

Maturing as a Biblical Counselor

Self-Counsel and Group or Partner Interaction

1. Describe how someone has ministered to you through grace relationships (listening, compassion, comforting, caring, empathy, connecting deeply, climbing in the casket).

2. Share how God has helped you to minister to someone through grace relationships (listening, compassion, comforting, caring, empathy, connecting deeply, climbing in the casket).

Counseling Others

3. Assess your "bedside manner." Not simply how well or how poorly you handle a crisis situation in a hospital, but how well or poorly you connect with suffering people. Use the following 1–10 scale to evaluate and explain your "CCQ: Compassion and Comfort Quotient." One: "I believe in pulling myself up by my bootstraps. Wipe your nose. Don't navel gaze, don't whine." Ten: "I weep with those who weep, I make their pain my pain. Like God the Father, I have compassion and share comfort."

   7

4. How would you minister to Emilio? To his wife, Maria? Before lab, write out some trialogues. In lab, be prepared to role-play ministering to this family.

   #1 Try to empathize. #2 Listen #3 Ps 34:18 The Lord is near to the broken hea
   #4 Pray for family members reminding them that God is near in their pain.
   #5 Commit to be with them in this. #6 How are you thinking about God
   right now? What is the most important thing to you.

Counseling One Another

5. Be prepared to share an area of suffering in your life—a casket experience—with your group or a lab partner so they can offer you sustaining biblical counseling. What happened *to* you? What happened *in* you (doubts, confusion, grief, pain, etc.)?

Our calling from God as soul caregivers gets more and more intense. We are to enter our spiritual friend's earthly story. Equiano illustrates this for us in these words to his long-lost sister. "Happy should I have ever esteemed myself to encounter every misery for you, and to procure your freedom by the sacrifice of my own!"[48] Do we understand what he is implying? It is like what Paul said in Romans 9:2–3 when he was willing to trade places with his unsaved Jewish friends and willing to suffer being accursed — suffer hell — if it meant their salvation.

It is *incarnational suffering* — suffering that enters into the world of another person. Suffering that cares so much that, if possible, it would endure substitutionary suffering. It is what Jesus did. Seeing our earthly story, empathizing with our earthly story, he left heaven, left the Father, came to earth, was born in our likeness, and then suffered *on our behalf*. That's incarnational suffering (see Heb. 2:14–18).

This seems to be the hardest part — volunteering to suffer along with another

Entering Our Counselee's Story

Grace connecting is more of a heart attitude than simply a counseling intervention. It is the mind-set of personal involvement with a deep commitment to another person's maturity, evidenced by incarnational participation in their suffering. Grace connecting is a heart commitment to love another person. It is not a technique to be mastered, but a way of life to be nurtured by personal communion with Christ — who embodies grace connecting.

Recall the biblical counseling "meta-competency": listening well and wisely to Scripture and listening competently and compassionately to the soul. We hear God's eternal story, Emilio's earthly story, and we journey together to link both stories. This relational competency can degrade into a non-relational technique if we are not grace connectors who enter our suffering friend's story through incarnational counseling.

Christ calls us to *participate in the suffering of others* to the point of experiencing their pain (1 Cor. 12:26). We don't listen to Emilio's story from an aloof distance. We enter his story as one of the main characters in his story. It's not just "Emilio, I understand your pain." It's "Emilio, I connect with you in your pain — the pain of wondering whether you will ever see your children graduate, get married, have children of their own. The pain of wondering why in the world a good God would allow this to happen to you and your family."

Christ also calls us to *give others permission to grieve.* Our grace connection with Emilio communicates that "I will grieve for you first, my friend, so you can then allow yourself to grieve."

> Grace connecting is the mind-set of personal involvement with a deep commitment to another person's maturity, evidenced by incarnational participation in their suffering.

And Christ calls us, in the sustaining *and* healing process, to *point others to the Person to turn to* in their suffering. Psalm 120:1 teaches this well: "In my distress I cried unto the LORD, and he heard me" (KJV). Martin Luther powerfully captures the implication of this verse:

> The first verse teaches us where we should turn when misfortune comes upon us — not to the emperor, not to the sword, not to our own devices and wisdom, but to the LORD, who is our only real help in time of need. "I cried unto the LORD in my distress," he says. That we should do this confidently, cheerfully, and without fail he makes clear when he says, "And he heard me." It is as if he would say, "The LORD is pleased to have us turn to him in our distress and is glad to hear and help us."[49]

We tune in to Emilio's earthly story of suffering, embracing him in his pain, so he can courageously embrace his pain, faithfully embrace God in his pain, and be embraced by the God who feels his pain. Our committed connection with Emilio encourages him to connect with God rather than to retreat from communion with God.

Refusing to Race through Our Counselee's Story

I often learn best by opposites, by poor examples. Grace connecting does not race through our counselee's story, speed reading it as a surface letter. It is not:

+ *A Warm Feeling:* "I feel neat when I'm with you." Climbing in the casket is rarely a pleasant experience.

+ *Sweetness:* It is not stereotypical Rogerian counseling where we merely reflect and mirror whatever our counselee says. It is not the nondirective acceptance of everything, including retreating from God.

+ *A Counseling Technique:* "Crying 101," or "Three steps to really caring."

+ *A Stage in Counseling:* "We'll do connecting today and then drop it. I can check it off my counseling to-do list."

We don't race through Emilio's story because his story is his soul — it's him. Proverbs 27:6a captures the essence of grace connecting. "Faithful are the wounds of a friend" (KJV). Grace connecting is not a stage in counseling that is appropriate only for sustaining — it is appropriate all the time, including for reconciling — care-fronting sin.

"Wounds" are a splitting apart as a doctor does for surgery, an exposure. You enter the ER and say, "Doctor, my chest and the right side of my body are killing me!" You don't want your doctor simply to be sweet: "That must be really hard for you." You want your physician to be skillful, competent — able to diagnose and treat your ailment. So too with biblical counseling. We want to be able to compassionately diagnose heart issues, pulling open the soul and peering deep inside — with suffering and with sin. Emilio wants to know that we will use all our resources to help him in his time of need. Connection means that we are committed to Emilio's growth even when it hurts him and us.

"Faithful" means to support, to bear, and to be trustworthy. Emilio, facing the diagnosis of liver cancer, wants to be able to say about us, "I trust you with my soul." "Faithful" also means to be strong, stable. Emilio wants to know that his words will not overwhelm us. Touch us deeply, yes. Overwhelm us, no. As his wounds are opened, he wants to know that they will not make us faint, that we will not think less of him.

"Friend" literally means "one who loves you, lover." The Scriptures use the same word in 2 Chronicles 20:7, calling Abraham God's "friend." Think of God's grace relationship with Abraham — encounter, intimacy, fellowship, accountability, fidelity, stability — and you will picture grace connecting.

Building a Connected Grace Relationship

Again, we can learn how not to build a connected grace relationship from bad examples — such as Job's "miserable comforters" (Job 16:2) "Miserable" means troublesome, vexing, and sorrow-causing. They were the opposite of "comforters" — a word that means consoling, sympathetic, feeling deeply the hurt of others.

Instead of grace connecting, Job's miserable comforters practiced *condemning distancing*. When we combine their bad theology (Job 42:7) with their cold hearts (Job 16:2), it is not at all surprising that they lacked relational competency. They communicated *superiority*. "We're better than you. You're inferior to us" (see Job 5:8; 8:2; 11:2 – 12; 12:1 – 3; 15:7 – 17). They communicated *judgmentalism*. "It's *not* normal to hurt! Your suffering is due to your sinning!" (see Job 4:4 – 9; 15:2 – 6). They offered *advice without insight and discernment*. "Here's what I would do if I were you." "Do this and life's complexities will melt away." "I have the secret that will fix your feelings and change your circumstances" (see Job 5:8; 8:5 – 6; 11:13 – 20).

Galatians 6:1 – 3, in the context of Paul's discussion of the fruit of the Spirit in Galatians 5, models how to build a grace connection. First, grace connection requires *intimate family relationship*. Paul begins with the profound word "brothers" (6:1). We saw in chapter 1 how Paul uses "brothers" to highlight family closeness, equality, and protection — a band of brothers who have each other's backs. Paul's word reminds us of the wisdom of Solomon. "A friend loves at all times, and a brother is born for adversity" (Prov. 17:17). "A man of many companions may come to ruin, but there is a friend who sticks closer than a brother" (Prov. 18:24).

Evaluation forms from people who have been counseled by lay encouragers express this sense of intimate friendship. "Even though we had never met before, our times were like two friends walking together." "I could feel your concern; we were on the same level." "You accepted me. You didn't scold me like a mom but were honest like a friend."

Second, grace connection involves *spiritual maturity leading to Spirit-like comforting*. Paul continues, "… you who are spiritual …" (Gal. 6:1). The Holy Spirit is the Comforter who comes alongside to help in time of need. In the Spirit's power, we are a friend acting in the best interests of our friend. We're an encourager standing up for, standing behind, standing with, and standing back-to-back and alongside our spiritual friend.

Third, grace connection requires *gentle persistence* — two words we don't always equate. Paul counsels counselors to "restore … gently" (Gal. 6:1). Gentleness looks like a tamed stallion, strength under control, firm compassion, mature self-control, and power and love mingled through wisdom. Christ labels himself "gentle" in Matthew 11:29, saying that unlike the Pharisees, who were sin-spotters and burden-givers, he was the rest-giver and sin-bearer.

Paul places "restore" in the present, continual tense. Biblical counselors maintain a patient persistence in mending, furnishing, equipping, and setting the dislocated member of the body back in place. Picture the physical therapist who brings a patient back to the place of health by pushing without being pushy. Picture the marathon runner. "I love you for the long haul. I'm in this relationship for a lifetime." That's grace connection.

Fourth, grace connection conveys _humility._ Paul further counsels the counselor: "But watch yourself, or you also may be tempted" (Gal. 6:1). "Watch" is the Greek word _skopon,_ from which we gain our word "scope." We put ourselves under the microscope before examining our spiritual friend. As a grace connector, we maintain a strong mental attention to our own potential temptability. We remain humble in spirit, knowing that we are also susceptible to Satan's lies about God's good heart.

Fifth, Paul describes the spiritual friend as a _committed burden-bearer._ "Carry each other's burdens" (Gal. 6:2a). God calls us to pick up and help carry the weight that overwhelms our friend. "Weight" means anything pressing on people physically, emotionally, or spiritually that makes a demand on their resources. When our friend's platelets are low, we become a spiritual blood transfusion of grace.

Verbal Grace Connecting

The preceding narratives and principles focus on our _attitude_ as we interact. The following trialogues and principles focus on our _actual interactions_ — what we say and how we communicate — verbal grace connecting, gospel conversations. "Works conversations" are the opposite of gospel conversations. Pharisaical counselors communicate works, not grace.

- _"Shoulds":_ Pharisaical counselors put heavy burdens on others but refuse to lift a finger or say a word to help carry that load (Matt. 23:1 – 4).

- _Self-Centered Words:_ Pharisaical counselors engage in interactions designed to make them look good and to make the other person look bad. It's all about them instead of being all about Christ (Matt. 23:5 – 12).

- _External Focus:_ Pharisaical counselors focus on external actions while avoiding issues of the heart, avoiding intimacy, and maintaining a safe distance (Matt. 23:13 – 29).

Biblical counselors communicate grace, not works, by highlighting nurturing words of wisdom. "Friends mean well even when they confront you. But when enemies put their arm around your shoulder — watch out!" (Prov. 27:6, author's paraphrase). In interacting with Emilio, a week after he received his diagnosis, verbal grace connection could include:

- *Acceptance and Reflection*: Putting His Words into Our Own
  - Emilio says, "This is too much. I have no idea what to do next."
  - We respond, "With everything you've been hit with, Emilio, it's understandable that you'd feel overwhelmed and confused."
- *Clarification and Exploration*: An Implied Question or Open-Ended Question Designed to Elicit More Detail
  - Emilio says, "That captures it well — overwhelmed and confused!"
  - We respond, "Those seem like pretty normal responses, Emilio. Could you tell me more about those times when you feel most overwhelmed and confused?"
- *Intimate Interaction*: Conveying the Courage to Talk Seriously and Offering to Go Further/Deeper
  - Emilio says, "It's not so much about my own death — I have peace. On one level, it's about the real practical stuff of how we pay for this now and what happens to Maria and the kids when I'm gone. On another level, it's about the spiritual stuff and why God would let this happen — especially right after I just came to know him ..."
  - We respond, "All *three* of those issues are really important: your peace with God, the 'practical stuff,' and the 'spiritual stuff.' I'm here to talk about all three of those. Where would you like to start?"
- *Personal Presence*: Mingled Suffering
  - Emilio says, "You have no idea how much it means to me to have someone to talk to. It seems like everyone treats me like I'm fragile, and they're afraid to have an honest conversation with me. I may be weak, but I'm not fragile. I'd love to talk about all three. Could we start by talking about Maria ... and the ... kids?" Emilio can barely finish his sentence. He weeps.
  - We respond: Silence. Lean forward. Hand on his shoulder. Waiting. Weeping ...

[handwritten margin note: Really Important – Gold]

Our grace connecting with Emilio has just begun. It will continue through our entire relationship. While it is especially important in sustaining, we connect with grace also in the healing, reconciling, and guiding process. And remember: this is *not* a linear process. There's no "order" in which we engaged in any of the twenty-one biblical counseling relational competencies. This is spaghetti relationships — real and raw soul-to-soul connecting.

Rich Soul Empathizing: Climbing in the Casket

Like Olaudah Equiano, Octavia Albert knew something about suffering and about comforting others in their suffering. Albert was a college-educated, ex-enslaved African American pastor's wife living in Louisiana. In the 1870s, she ministered to many other ex-enslaved men and women by recording their stories of suffering. One of those individuals was Charlotte Brooks. Of Brooks, Albert writes, "It was in the fall of 1879 that I met Charlotte Brooks.... I have spent hours with her listening to her telling of her sad life of bondage in the cane-fields of Louisiana."[50]

If we would do what Albert did, then we would be miles ahead in our biblical counseling: *spend hours listening to sad stories.* Rather than rescuing and compulsively fixing, we need the courage and compassion to listen to stories of suffering. As we listen to our spiritual friends' earthly stories, we need to empathize with them in their story. Empathy is not some secular Trojan horse. It is a biblical word and a scriptural concept. Think of the word *em-pathos*: to enter the pathos, or the passion, of another, to allow another person's agony to become your agony, to weep with those who weep (see Rom. 12:15).

Notice how Octavia Albert allowed Charlotte Brooks's agony to become her own. "Poor Charlotte Brooks! I can never forget how her eyes were filled with tears when she would speak of all her children: 'Gone, and no one to care for me!'"[51] Albert pictures for us the essence of sustaining empathy: climbing in the casket.

Not only must we feel what another person feels, we need to express and communicate that we "get it," we feel it, we hurt too. Consider how Albert does so with Brooks. "Aunt Charlotte, my heart throbs with sympathy, and my eyes are filled with tears, whenever I hear you tell of the trials of yourself and others."[52] What Albert modeled in 1879, the church has long called "compassionate commiseration." Don't let these two beautiful, powerful words intimidate you. *Co-passion*: to share the passionate feelings of another. *Co-misery*: to partner in the misery of your spiritual friend.

Maturing as a Biblical Counselor

Self-Counsel and Group or Partner Interaction

1. Who has been an Olaudah Equiano for you? How have they been present with you in your pain, mingled your suffering and sorrows with theirs, and offered incarnational suffering? How has their grace connection ministered to you?

   Matt Woodley He helped me grow in my faith for a year after coming to Christ

2. Share examples of how you have provided grace connection to others by:

   a. Participating in their suffering.

   Customers sometimes

   b. Giving them permission to grieve.

   c. Pointing them to the person (Christ) to turn to in their suffering.

Counseling Others

- If you are working through this material individually, then instead of role-playing, use the space after each scenario to write your responses to each situation.

3. Emilio says, "This is too much. I have no idea what to do next."

   a. Role-play doing it wrong by being like Job's miserable counselors. Use condemning distance, communicating superiority, and offering advice without insight and discernment.

   Just quit whining and think about your wife + kids

b. Role-play doing it wrong by being like pharisaical counselors. Use works conversations, "shoulds," self-centered words, and an external focus.

4. Emilio says, "This is too much. I have no idea what to do next." Role-play grace connecting through:

a. Acceptance and Reflection

"I completely would have the same feelings and thoughts"

b. Clarification and Exploration

Is there something specific that you are struggling with?

c. Intimate Interaction

Can we start by looking to God for help together in prayer?

d. Personal Presence

I am here to help in whatever way that I can. Could I help you with...?

Counseling One Another

- If you are working through this material individually, then respond to this question in writing.

- If you are working through this material in a lab small group, then with the entire group, or with a lab partner, or with the lab facilitator counseling one group member, or with a lab member counseling another lab member, use this question as a starting place for giving and receiving biblical counsel.

---

5. Grace connection is a mind-set of personal involvement with a deep commitment to another person's maturity, evidenced by <u>incarnational participation in their suffering.</u> If this competency is foreign to you or difficult for you, explore why this is so. What life experiences or heart issues might you want to work through to grow in this area?

    Really hard suffering is foreign to me in my life.

Aunt Charlotte describes the result of Octavia Albert's ministry in her life. "La, me, child! I never thought anybody would care enough for me to tell of my trials and sorrows in this world! None but Jesus knows what I have passed through."[53] Octavia Albert was *Jesus with skin on.* Her care gave Aunt Charlotte a human taste of Jesus' care — a taste Charlotte thought she would never receive this side of heaven.

With grace connecting, we talked about entering another person's story and becoming a main character in their life narrative. Empathy goes deeper. Continuing the "story" idea, in empathy we seek to enter into the character's soul and experience their suffering as they experience it. It is rejoicing with those who rejoice, mourning with those who mourn (Rom. 12:15) and suffering along with those who suffer (1 Cor. 12:26). We suffer in the soul of another person, feeling with and participating in their inner world while remaining ourselves. We seek to understand their outer story and their inner story from their perspective.

Slamming the Casket Shut: How Not to Empathize

Consider "Job's Miserable Counselors, Part II." If empathy is climbing in the casket, then slamming the casket shut pictures its opposite. Eliphaz (Job 4 – 5, 15, and 22) is the master of discouragement and dismay. He provides Job with conditional love and curses God. Eliphaz teaches that God is good to the good, but bad to the bad. He does not know grace. He does know works: "You can manipulate God into being good to you by being good to him." What a petty God Eliphaz worships. Eliphaz says to Job, "Don't live *coram Deo.* Don't tell God your heart. Be surface." He misinterprets Job's words as venting rage at God rather than soul-sharing with God. Bildad (Job 8, 18, and 25) has a somewhat right theology with a very wrong application. "The issue is your sin!" Seeing only sin, he is wrong in Job's case. For God, the issue was Job's response to him in his suffering. The issue was Job's privileged opportunity to be a universal witness to God's goodness. The issue was not Job's sinfulness. Bildad does not know the man he calls "friend." He labels (and libels) Job "an evil man … who knows not God" (Job 18:21). Zophar (Job 11 and 20) also presents a works righteousness. He believes that good works can cover shame.

How does Job view their counsel? He longs for the devotion of his friends (Job 6:14), which they aren't. He calls them undependable brothers (Job 6:15), which they are. They can't handle Job's doubts, treating the words of a despairing man as wind (Job 6:26). He feels they say, "Forget it! Smile!" His dread remains. "If I say, 'I will forget my complaint, I will change my expression, and smile,' I still dread all my sufferings, for I know you will not hold me innocent" (Job 9:27 – 28). He experiences their total lack of empathy. "Men at ease have contempt for misfortune" (Job 12:5).

Miserable comforters they are. Rather than communicating that "it's normal to hurt," they increase Job's hurt. Having no compassionate discernment, they claim that his wounds are self-inflicted. They crush Job's spirit through their long-winded speeches, argumentative nature, lack of empathy and encouragement, failure to bring relief/comfort, and their closed-minded and arrogant, superior, hostile attitudes based on wrong motives and a condemning spirit (Job 17:1 – 5).

Of them, Job concludes, "These men turn night into day; in the face of darkness they say, 'Light is near'" (Job 17:12). They are like the counselor who says, "Don't talk about your problems, don't think about your suffering, and don't remember your past hurts. Forget those things that are behind!" They have no dark-night-of-the-soul vision, no 20/20 spiritual vision, and no long-distance vision; so they have to call the darkness light. Job, however, has long-distance vision. His heart yearns for God, and he knows he will see God (Job 19:25 – 27).

Job feels no rapport with them. "They torment me, crush me with words. I sense their reproach as they shame me. They exalt themselves. I feel so alone when I am with them. So alienated and forgotten. Here's how my 'spiritual friends' make me feel: estranged, offensive, loathsome. My friends detest me; they have turned against me, having no pity on me" (author's paraphrase of Job 19).

Job's three friends are unwise. They offer nonsense answers because they're not paying attention to life, not learning life's lessons. "You have not wisely paid attention to how things work in the real world. Your academic

[handwritten margin note:] Lots of "men at ease" at FCC God will do a work to change us

knowledge, your theologizing, is out to lunch. How can you console/comfort me with your vain nonsense, since your answers are falsehood? You are wrong about life, about me, and about God!" (author's paraphrase of Job 21). They are "sin-spotters." They know only confrontation. Thus, they become coconspirators with Satan the accuser, who condemns men and curses God.

What was God's view of their counsel? After speaking to Job, Yahweh said to Eliphaz, "I am angry with you and your two friends, because you have not spoken of me what is right, as my servant Job has" (Job 42:7). They failed to speak of God's generous goodness and grace. Their God was a tit-for-tat God who could be easily manipulated by and impressed with works. *Our greatest failure in counseling arises when we speak wrongly of God while we speak to one another.*

Climbing in the Casket

Rich soul empathy involves our capacity for "as if" relating. The church father Ambrose wrote, "Show compassion for those who suffer. Suffer with those who are in trouble *as if* being in trouble with them."[54]

Soul empathy requires *compassionate imagination*. We need to imagine what it is like for our friends to experience their life stories. To understand others with intimate knowledge, we must read into their experiences, asking, "What is it like to experience and perceive the world through their stories, their eyes, their feelings?" Hebrews 2:14 – 18 and 4:14 – 16 teach that empathy is more than intellectual. It is also experiential. Biblical Christlike empathy shares the experiences of another, connecting through common inner experiences. Such soul sharing occurs by way of incarnation — entering another's world and worldview.

As a biblical counselor, the more human we are, the more real, the more fully alive and passionate, the more we will tune in to others. Then we'll experience a sympathetic resonance no matter the melody, dirge, minor or major key, or discordant note.

When our soul is attuned to others, then we "pick up their radio waves, the vibes of their inner reactions." Having accomplished this, we need to go the distance. We need to communicate to our spiritual friends in a way that helps them to "have empathy with our empathy." They need to feel that we feel with them. Otherwise, their sorrow is not shared, it is simply "understood." When both our "soul radios" are tuned to the same frequency, then we can share our soul friends' experiences. We share their sorrows by climbing in the casket with them, and they know we are there.

While death is separation; shared sorrow is connection, the stitch closing the wound. It is the healing balm. However, shared sorrow must never be a healing replacement. It must not replace grief. Shared sorrow does not purpose to eliminate sorrow, to rescue, or to cheer up. Shared sorrow purposes to help another to face and embrace sorrow.

Effective soul empathy includes several "levels."

1. *Level One Empathy:* "How would that affect an image bearer?" Here we seek to understand Emilio through God's eyes. A foundational level of empathy, it builds upon a *universal* biblical understanding of people.

2. *Level Two Empathy:* "How would that affect an image bearer like me?" Here we seek to understand Emilio through our eyes. A filtering level, we use our life as a filter through which we relate God's truth to our friend's life. We prayerfully ponder what it would be like for us if we were facing our own death, never to see our children grow up ...

3. *Level Three Empathy:* "How would that affect an image bearer like Emilio?" Here we understand Emilio through his eyes. We move from *universal* to *unique* empathy. In this final, deepest level of soul empathy, we need to: ___ *Brother/Freind*

   a. *Adopt Our Counselee's Soul Experience:* We replace our internal frame of reference with Emilio's. We seek to sense what it is like to be him — to be his character through his longings, perspective, motivations, feelings.

   b. *Express Our Counselee's Soul Experience:* We express in our own words what we sense Emilio has communicated about his longings, perspective, motivations, and feelings about the situation.

   c. *Encourage Our Counselee to Accept His/Her Soul Experience:* We nudge Emilio to acknowledge his own inner responses to his outer situation. We help him to verbalize how he is responding internally.

   d. *Help Our Counselee to Evaluate His/Her Soul Experience:* We want to help Emilio to begin to assess how he is responding to his unmet longings (hope deferred), how near or far his perspective on his situation is from God's perspective, how near or far the motivations of his heart are from God's will, and how well or poorly he is facing his feelings face-to-face with God.

I'm sure you've detected that empathy is much more than a hug. It also is more than trying to sense how someone feels. It is a *comprehensive* sensing of what the whole person longs for in their situation (relational being), what they think about their situation (rational being), what their goals are in their situation (volitional being), *and* then how they feel about their situation (emotional being).

Rich soul empathy like this not only helps us to better understand how Emilio is responding to his suffering. It also helps Emilio to better understand and honestly face his inner responses. We become a mirror reflecting back to Emilio what is going on in his soul. The more clearly he understands his inner responses, the more powerfully and profitably he can take his soul to the Shepherd of his soul.

Where We've Been and Where We're Headed

Here's our tweet-size summary of chapter 5.

+ Sustaining offers people GRACE to help in their time of need by encouraging people to face suffering face-to-face with Christ and the body of Christ.

Through grace connecting and rich soul empathy, we give people permission to grieve by grieving with them. In a sense, this is "the hug." But what do we do after the hug? We learn that in chapter 6 through attuned gospel listening, comforting spiritual conversations, and empathetic scriptural explorations.

Maturing as a Biblical Counselor

Self-Counsel and Group or Partner Interaction

1. Who has been an Octavia Albert for you, spending hours listening to your sad story of suffering, engaging in co-passion and co-misery, and helping you to know by their care that Jesus cares?

2. Share examples of how you have provided rich soul empathy by spending hours listening to someone's sad story of suffering, engaging in co-passion and co-misery, and helping others to know by your care that Jesus cares.

Counseling Others

- If you are working through this material individually, then instead of role-playing, use the space after each scenario to write your response to each situation.

3. Emilio says, "This is too much. I have no idea what to do next." Role-play doing it wrong by being like Job's miserable counselors. Use discouragement, conditional love. Teach that God is good to the good, but bad to the bad. Ignore grace. Be a sin-spotter and focus on works righteousness. Crush his spirit through long-winded speeches.

4. With an encouragement partner, role-play rich soul empathy. Each of you share a recent real-life event. Interact, with the goal of trying to understand how your encouragement partner experienced this event—their longings, thoughts, reactions/actions/motivations, and feelings. When you're done, share with one another your honest evaluation/feedback of each other's level of empathy and understanding—where you "climbed in the casket well" and where you could have been more empathetic and understanding.

Counseling One Another

*   If you are working through this material individually, then respond to this question in writing.

*   If you are working through this material in a lab small group, then with the entire group, or with a lab partner, or with the lab facilitator counseling one group member, or with a lab member counseling another lab member, use this question as a starting place for giving and receiving biblical counsel.

5. Rich soul empathizing is entering into another person's soul and experiencing their suffering as they experience it. If this competency is foreign to you or difficult for you, explore why this is so. What life experiences or heart issues might you want to work through in order to grow in this area?

CHAPTER 6

Sustaining through Grace Relationships

I've detected a common theme as I've equipped hundreds of biblical counselors. Counselors want to know how to move from caring connection to competent intervention. "I'm not too bad at caring, if caring means connecting and empathizing with my counselee. However, I'm not always sure what to do next. I can nod, hug, and listen. Yet even with listening, what do I listen for and why? Once I'm done listening, then what? What do we interact about? Where do the Scriptures enter? What difference does Christ make for my suffering friend?"

As caring counselors, we want to know how to care biblically — how to care like Christ. We seek guidance that addresses our core sustaining question: How do I engage in grace relationships that sustain faith in the goodness of God during the badness of life?

Consider how our five sustaining *GRACE* biblical counseling competencies work together toward this goal.

- *G* Grace Connecting
- *R* Rich Soul Empathizing
- *A* Attuned Gospel Listening
- *C* Comforting Spiritual Conversations
- *E* Empathetic Scriptural Explorations

Maturing as a Biblical Counselor

Self-Counsel and Group or Partner Interaction

1. Ponder a current area of suffering/loss.

   a. What is this loss like for you? What are you feeling right now?

   b. What has been robbed from your life due to this loss? What is missing? What are you grieving over the most?

   c. What do you wish were happening instead of what you're experiencing?

   d. What do you fear the most in this situation? What's the worst-case scenario? What if that happened?

2. While pondering this area of suffering/loss, face your suffering face-to-face with Christ.

   a. What are you doing with God in your suffering?

   b. Where is God in all of this? What might God be up to?

   c. Have you been able to share your heart with Christ? What have you said?

Grace connecting and rich soul empathizing help us to communicate and convey the compassion that we feel for Emilio. We care like Christ by giving Emilio a small taste of Christ's compassionate commiseration. By being Jesus with skin on, we encourage Emilio to face his suffering face-to-face with Christ as Emilio sees and believes that Christ suffers with him.

We realize that for Emilio, and for all of us, *when life stinks, our perspective shrinks*. And our perspective shrinks because Satan attempts to crop Christ out of the picture. Through comforting spiritual conversations and empathetic scriptural explorations, we join Emilio in his earthly story of suffering. As we do, we encourage Emilio to invite Christ to join him in his earthly journey.

Observant readers are likely thinking, "Bob, you've skipped *attuned gospel listening*." Good catch. Listening — biblical, theological, relational listening — is the bridge between joining people by caring like Christ and encouraging people to invite Christ into their journey. Without wise listening, our spiritual conversations and scriptural explorations become preaching at the crowd. With wise listening, we engage in the *personal* ministry of the Word — relating Christ's gospel of grace relevantly and richly to the specific person and their particular situation and unique story.

Attuned Gospel Listening: Hearing Life Redemptively

In chapter 5, we witnessed the power of listening as modeled by Octavia Albert, who listened for hours to Charlotte Brooks's telling of her sad life of bondage. Such sustaining listening is a constant theme in the history of African American soul care. Solomon Northrup (his life was the basis of the movie *12 Years a Slave*) had lived free for thirty-three years before he was kidnapped and enslaved for a dozen years in Louisiana. When he was first stolen, he spent two weeks in a slave pen, where he met an enslaved woman named Eliza, her daughter Emmy, and her son Randall. His account of their interactions offers insight into the need for hearing one another's stories. His summary of their mutual spiritual friendship captures well the nature of spiritual listening in suffering. "We were thus learning the history of each other's wretchedness."[55] They participated in "Spiritual Friendship 101" by practicing the art of story sharing and story listening.

What Solomon and Eliza shared one-to-one, the black church also practiced communally. Pastor Peter Randolph describes the "invisible institution" — the secret worship services held by the slaves, often assembling in the swamps, out of reach of the patrols. Randolph outlines the initial component of those worship services. "They first ask each other how they feel, the state of their minds, etc."[56] Given their hardships and hard times, it is not surprising that African American Christians began their worship services with lengthy spiritual conversations where they listened to one another's feelings and thoughts. They cared enough to seek to understand each other's emotional life and mental state. This mutual story-listening was a natural part of every worship service.

What we learn from black church history about how to care like Christ we learn also from Christ himself. In John 2, John places a narrative marker just before Christ's encounters with Nicodemus and the Samaritan woman. "He did not need man's testimony about man, for he knew what was in a man" (John 2:25). Jesus knew the scriptural, universal nature of human nature. And he used that knowledge as he also listened to and tuned in to the unique nature of individuals. Jesus remained attuned to two stories simultaneously: God's universal story and the individual's unique story.

In John 3 and 4, Jesus could not have encountered two people more different from each other than the Jewish male religious leader Nicodemus and the Samaritan female irreligious woman at the well. His approach to ministering to them was idiosyncratic — uniquely fitting the gospel need they each had. Jesus listened to their souls, understood their individual stories, and personally applied the gospel remedy to their hearts.

He did so by listening to their "cues." Nicodemus talked *about* God, but Jesus heard his need to *know* God by being born again. The Samaritan woman talked about *physical* water, but Jesus heard her need to know God by drinking from *the spring of living* water. She spoke at length about her earthly needs without reference to God, when in fact her words cried out for God the entire time. Jesus knew that her heart, like all hearts, craved God even when she suppressed and misdirected her thirst.

We who have the greatest message in the world — the death and resurrection of Jesus Christ — ought to be the most compelling communicators. But we fail to communicate the gospel message when we fail to listen carefully and theologically. As Chris Castaldo explains, "Every physician knows that attentive listening is a powerful requisite for healing, without which there is no diagnosis, and without a diagnosis there can be no personalized application of the remedy."[57] Jesus — the Great Physician — understood this when he listened to Nicodemus and the Samaritan woman and with keen attention diagnosed their true need and prescribed the gospel remedy. His ministry helps us to define our ministry of gospel listening. Attuned gospel listening tunes our ears to God's redemptive story so that we hear our counselee's story with theologically informed ears and compassionate hearts.

> Attuned gospel listening tunes our ears to God's redemptive story so that we hear our counselee's story with theologically informed ears and compassionate hearts.

Listening with Biblical Attentiveness: Theologically Informed Listening

We all understand the value of listening. The more important question is, "What do we listen for?" To answer that question, think back to chapter 2 and the meta-competency of listening to Scripture and the soul. I call this theory-guided or theologically informed listening — the Bible tells us what to listen to, how to listen, and how to interpret what we hear.

Listen to Soul Messages

Since the Bible teaches that our counselees are relational, rational, volitional, and emotional beings, we fine-tune our listening for soul messages in each of these areas.

1. Listening to Relational Beings: Sacrificial Love or Self-Protective Separation?

As a relational being, God designed Emilio to love passionately. Passion relates not just to Emilio's intense feelings, but to his *selfless sacrifices*. Even in the midst of his suffering, if Emilio is failing to give generously and sacrificially in relationships, then something is out of whack in his soul.

So we listen for separating narratives. How is Satan duping Emilio? Where is he backing away from life, refusing to long, and quenching his thirsts apart from Christ? We listen also to how God's grace is enlivening Emilio even in the midst of his soul's suffering. Where do we see signs of biblical groaning, awakened longings, thirsts directed toward Jesus, and sacrificial love directed toward others?

2. Listening to Rational Beings: Spiritual Eyes or Eyeballs Only?

As a rational being, God designed Emilio to think imaginatively, with 20/20 spiritual vision. Imagination is not simply thinking in 3-D or thinking creatively. Imagination is Emilio's capacity to make sense of his world *from*

God's perspective. When Emilio is failing to interpret his story through *grace eyes,* then something is amiss.

So we listen for works narratives where Emilio's being deluded by Satan to think small. Where is Emilio handling life on his own, where is he thinking foolishly, and where are his mind-sets rooted in the ruts of the flesh? We also listen for grace narratives where Christ is freeing Emilio to think as big as God, for he is able to do abundantly above all that Emilio could ever think, dream, or imagine (Eph. 3:20). We're also listening to hear how Emilio is perceiving his need for God, where we see signs of wise interpretations, and where we detect his mind-sets being led by the Spirit.

3. Listening to Volitional Beings: Courageous Risk or Compulsive Self-Preservation?

As a volitional being, God designed Emilio to choose courageously. Courage includes Emilio's freedom to be responsible and his awareness of his ability to choose how to live an epic life in Christ. When Emilio is failing to see himself as an *active agent,* when he sees life controlling him, then something is wrong.

So we listen for controlling narratives where Emilio is being conned by Satan to surrender. Where do we hear Emilio acting "choiceless," purposeless, and hopeless? What aimless purposes/pathways does he appear to be following? We listen also for freeing narratives where Emilio is being led by the Spirit to persevere. Where do we hear him acting responsibly, purposefully, and hopefully? What focused and selfless purposes is he pursuing?

4. Listening to Emotional Beings: Psalmist or Stoic?

As an emotional being, God designed Emilio to experience life deeply. Psalmist-like living is not simply his ability to cry or sob, laugh or jump for joy, though it might include that. Emotional depth is Emilio's awareness, acknowledgment, and acceptance of his emotional state, which he uses to strengthen his relationships to God and others. Emilio can cry to keep you far from him by making you see him as too fragile to approach. This is not depth. On the other hand, he can cry as a courageous invitation for you to draw near to him. This is depth. It is an *aliveness that invites.* When Emilio is failing to feel alive, when he's in denial, when he's bland, then something is missing.

So we listen for deadened, despairing emotions used by Satan to deceive Emilio into drying up. When he comes alive, then he faces life fully, in living color. We listen also for laments motivated by a groaning desire for deeper relationships. We listen for the mood state that is predominant in Emilio.

Listen to Storied Messages

While listening to soul messages, we keep our ears tuned also to "storied" messages. Remember that life is a story, a narrative. Job's miserable comforters told one story of his suffering; Job told another. All the while, behind the curtain, Satan and God each had their stories to tell — one full of works and lies, the other full of grace and truth.

Emilio's soul story requires soul listening. We start by *joining his journey* as *a participant* — incarnational listening. We feel, connect, and empathize. As we journey, we *listen for Emilio's protagonist — God.* Where do we hear God's grace, acceptance, forgiveness, faith, love, goodness, and new covenant story as Emilio tells his story? Perhaps we hear it as we sense that Emilio, though confused and much afraid, is still clinging.

He clings while in conflict. Therefore, we *listen for Emilio's antagonist.* Certainly his diagnosis itself fits that bill. Perhaps there are discouraging friends or family members who are antagonistic to Emilio's faith journey (like Job's wife). However, his ultimate antagonist is none other than Satan. Do we hear his works, condemnation, rejection, old covenant, law, hate, fear, run-and-hide narrative when Emilio talks about dreading the thought of talking openly with Maria about his fears *and* her fears?

Since Emilio's wife and children are lead actors in his story, we *listen for the identity of these significant characters.* How does Emilio see them, describe them, and relate to them? How do they relate to him? How does Emilio see himself? We *listen for his self-identity.* We hear his suffering identities when we sense his desire to give up. We hear his sustaining identity when we sense his desire to look up. Also, we *listen for our identity in Emilio's story.* After all, we are a vital player now. How does Emilio relate to us — as a rescuer, peer, friend, hero, distant helper, or perhaps another potential betrayer?

As with any good story, we need to *listen for the setting.* What are the details of his story? What is his background, his history? When is Emilio worse, better? In all of this, we *listen for core story themes and threads.* Perhaps we hear in Emilio's story the shame moral of "You must have been a very bad person for God to allow this to happen to you." Or the grace theme of "God is good even when life is bad — God can be trusted even when our fallen world falls on us."

In *sustaining,* we *listen for life's losses and crosses.* What death/separation events do we hear? What are the external losses (the situations and suffering he is facing) and what are the internal losses (faith battles going on within Emilio)?

Listening to Biblical Principles of Gospel Listening: God's Word about Human Words

Sometimes in the biblical counseling world, we have the idea that if a secular system of counseling utilizes a given skill, technique, or competency, then it must be unbiblical and we should shun it. At times we think that about listening. However, God's Word has much to say about our need to listen well to one another's words.

Our Words Are Powerful: Proverbs 18:21

"The tongue has the power of life and death" (Prov. 18:21). The tongue, says James, is a small body part with power far beyond its size (James 3:1 – 5a). "Consider what a great forest is set on fire by a small spark. The tongue also is a fire, a world of evil among the parts of the body. It corrupts the whole person, sets the whole course of his life on fire" (James 3:5b – 6). God's Word calls biblical counselors to listen carefully to the powerful life-and-death words of our counselees.

Our Words Are Meaningful: Proverbs 18:4; 20:5

"The words of a man's mouth are deep waters" (Prov. 18:4). "The purposes of a man's heart are deep waters, but a man of understanding draws them out" (Prov. 20:5). Words carry the soul's longings, beliefs, purposes, and feelings. Through careful, caring listening, we can perceive the depth of the soul. Through active, accurate listening, we can draw out the motivations of the heart — the hidden desires, convictions, goals, and emotions.

Some may counter, "But doesn't Jeremiah 17:9 teach that we can't know the heart?" "The heart is deceitful above all things and beyond cure. Who can understand it?" (Jer. 17:9). But we stop too soon when we ignore the next verse. "I the LORD search the heart and examine the mind" (Jer. 17:10a). In the New Testament we read, "For the word of God is living and active. Sharper than any double-edged sword, it penetrates even to dividing soul and spirit, joints and marrow; it judges the thoughts and attitudes of the heart" (Heb. 4:12).

Jeremiah 17:9 – 10 teaches us that apart from the Spirit of God and the Word of God, we can't understand the motives of the heart. It is a warning against any self-attempt or secular attempt to understand the soul apart from the Creator of the soul. Hebrews 4:12 along with Proverbs 18:4 and 20:5 teach the biblical counselor that through the Word of God, the Spirit of God, and relationships among the people of God, we can and should listen to and draw out the issues of the heart.

Our Words Convey Soul Messages: Psalm 39:1–3; Matthew 12:33–37

"Out of the overflow of the heart, the mouth speaks" (Matt. 12:34b). Spoken words flow out of the depths of the heart, revealing the content of the heart (Ps. 39:1–3). The good heart bears nourishing fruit conveyed by wholesome words, while the evil heart bears poisonous fruit conveyed by unwholesome words. If we want to know our counselees, then we must listen skillfully to their words.

Our Words Are Worthy of Soulful Attentiveness: Proverbs 18:13; James 1:19

"He who answers before listening — that is his folly and his shame" (Prov. 18:13). "My dear brothers, take note of this: Everyone should be quick to listen, slow to speak and slow to become angry" (James 1:19). The caring soul carefully listens to words spoken from the soul.

Our Words Reflect One of Two Life Interpretations: Job 42:7

"After the Lord had said these things to Job, he said to Eliphaz the Temanite, 'I am angry with you and your two friends, because you have not spoken of me what is right, as my servant Job has'" (Job 42:7). Job and his friends witnessed one situation but derived two vastly different interpretations. The set of information involved Job's life experiences. The first interpretation consisted of the works, condemnation, cursing, and shame narrative inspired by Satan. The second consisted of the grace, faith, openness, and acceptance narrative inspired by God. According to God, Job got him right; Job's friends got God all wrong.

Whenever we listen, we listen for three sets of stories. We listen for our counselee's life stories: listening attentively to what they're saying about what they're experiencing. Then we listen to two possible interpretations of their stories. We listen attentively for signs of Satan's narrative creeping in. And we listen attentively to God's narrative gaining dominance. These competing interpretive frameworks are at work in every life story.

Listening with Relational Competence: LISTEN

We can use the following acrostic to remind ourselves of basic components of competent gospel listening.

- ⋄ *L* Loving Motivation: Proverbs 21:13
- ⋄ *I* Intimate Concern: Galatians 6:1–3; Colossians 4:6; James 3:17–18
- ⋄ *S* Slow to Speak: Proverbs 18:13; James 1:19

- *T* Timely Listening and Speaking: Proverbs 15:23; 25:11
- *E* Exploratory Listening and Encouraging Speaking: Hebrews 3:7 – 19; 10:24 – 25
- *N* Need-Focused Hearing: Ephesians 4:29

L   Loving Motivation

"If a man shuts his ears to the cry of the poor, he too will cry and not be answered" (Prov. 21:13). Relationally competent biblical counselors are motivated, like God, to listen for, hear, care about, empathize with, and respond to the hurts of the wounded. Neither secular theory nor human curiosity drives careful listening. Care does. Concern does. Compassion does.

I   Intimate Concern

Paul (Gal. 6:1 – 3; Col. 4:6) emphasizes the humble, spiritual, gentle, and gracious concern that ought to accompany spiritual listening. James (James 3:17 – 18), in a context sandwiched between the use of the tongue and the cause of quarrels, explains that true wisdom for living flows from a heart that loves people and peace, a heart that is considerate and submissive, impartial and sincere.

S   Slow to Speak

James is quite emphatic. "My dear brothers, take note of this: Everyone should be quick to listen, slow to speak and slow to become angry" (James 1:19). Solomon explains why: "He who answers before listening — that is his folly and his shame" (Prov. 18:13). Relationally competent biblical counselors hear Emilio's story so they can relate God's story relevantly to Emilio.

T   Timely Listening and Speaking

"A man finds joy in giving an apt reply — and how good is a timely word!" (Prov. 15:23). "A word aptly spoken is like apples of gold in settings of silver" (Prov. 25:11). "Apt" means fitting, timely, given in due season — words said at the right time, in the right way, for the right reason because of right listening.

E   Exploratory Listening and Encouraging Speaking

The author of Hebrews (Heb. 3:7 – 19; 10:24 – 25) exhorts us to know and listen to our brothers and sisters so well that we can perceive their doubting, hardening, deceived heart. Then our powerful words of encouragement will flow from accurate exploratory listening.

N   Need-Focused Hearing

To benefit others, biblical counselors listen for specific needs. "Do not let any unwholesome talk come out of your mouths, but only what is helpful for building others up according to their needs, that it may benefit those who listen" (Eph. 4:29). Biblical counselors ask, as they listen, "What is it that Emilio most needs? What are his hurts and wounds? His fears and scars? What wholesome words relate to Emilio's specific situation? Specifically, given his situation, what words will benefit him?"

Comforting Spiritual Conversations: Sustaining Theological Trialogues

This book is called *Gospel Conversations* for a reason. The gospel — Christ's victory narrative, the story of our redemption from sin through Christ's grace — is the meta-narrative, the grand story, that shapes every conversation. That ought to be true not simply during a formal hour of counseling, but 24/7 in every informal family, work, and leisure conversation we ever have.

"Gospel" is vital to biblical counseling and "conversation" is vital also. We've previously seen the difference between the pulpit ministry of the Word (preaching/teaching) and the personal ministry of the Word (counseling). In preaching, the communication from the Word is primarily one-way: from the speaker to/at the hearer. In counseling, the communication about the Word ought to be at least two-way: back and forth between the counselor and the counselee — it's a conversation.

We've also previously seen the difference between a monologue, a dialogue, and a trialogue. Counseling is not a monologue — one-way teaching *at*. It's not even just a dialogue. It is a trialogue, a three-way communication between the counselor, the counselee, and the Divine Counselor through God's Spirit and God's Word. In comforting spiritual conversations, we use biblical wisdom principles to engage Emilio in interactions that help him to think through his external situation and his internal soul responses. We accomplish this through trialogues where we seek to make the presence of Christ our Redeemer the central dynamic in our conversation. We interact in Jesus' name, helping Emilio to face his personal issues on a personal level. Our personal relationship with Christ and with Emilio helps him to deepen his personal relationship with Christ.

Maturing as a Biblical Counselor

Self-Counsel and Group or Partner Interaction

1. In black church history, one of the primary and regular aspects of their worship services was listening to one another share about how they feel and their state of mind—emotions and beliefs, emotional health and mental health. How would church services, church relationships, and Christian lives be different if we all followed their model?

   A lot healthier (but not on time)

Counseling One Another: Constructive Feedback

2. You're into the sixth chapter together. By now you are getting to know one another, including your biblical counseling strengths and weaknesses. Using the categories below, provide one another with feedback on your listening competency. If you are working through this material alone, assess yourself and/or ask someone who knows you well to assess your listening competency.

   a. *L:* I listen with loving motivation—not as a technique, but because I truly care about you and want to know you well.

      Good at caring
      Working on listening

   b. *I:* I listen with intimate concern—my listening conveys a humble, gentle, and gracious concern for you.

      Good - mostly body language

   c. *S:* I am slow to speak when I am listening to you and others.

      Getting better

   d. *T:* My listening and speaking are timely and apt—right speaking at the right time because of right listening.

      Getting better

---

e. *E:* I tune in to and explore what is going on inside you—relationally, rationally, volitionally, emotionally—your longings, thoughts, motivations, and feelings.

A beginner but with potential

f. *N:* While I listen, I am asking myself what it is that you most need—need-focused hearing.

A beginner but with potential

In spiritual conversations, we invite Emilio into a robust experience of grace narratives (applying the gospel story to his story) through grace relationships (caring for Emilio like Christ cares for him). In Hebrews 10:19–25, it is in the context of our bold access to God because of Christ's grace that we receive a clear command to engage in gospel conversations.

> *Therefore, brothers, since we have confidence to enter the Most Holy Place by the blood of Jesus … let us draw near to God with a sincere heart in full assurance of faith.… And let us consider how we may spur one another on toward love and good deeds. Let us not give up meeting together, as some are in the habit of doing, but let us encourage one another—and all the more as you see the Day approaching. (Hebrews 10:19, 22, 24–25)*

Gospel conversations are the intersection of two types of speech: God's grace story and our need-for-grace stories. We always keep both ears open to both stories, pivoting between both worlds. When we read the Bible well and read people well, then we can effectively communicate gospel-centered, personally relevant application of Scripture.

The Nature of Spiritual Conversations

Spiritual conversations involve good talk about our good God in the midst of our bad life. "Do not let any unwholesome talk come out of your mouths, but only what is helpful for building others up according to their needs, that it may benefit those who listen" (Eph. 4:29). Spiritual conversations are grace conversations. Law conversations crush people and destroy relationships (compare

Matt. 23). Grace conversations edify people and build relationships — with Christ and the body of Christ.

"Unwholesome" words are corrupt and rotten like decaying fruit. They're putrid, defiling, and injuring words. They're toxic speech — words that poison others, making their spirit sick. Paul's emphasis on words is clear in the original language of Ephesians 4:29: "All words of rottenness, do not let come out of your mouth." Biblical counselors restrain themselves, refusing to speak until they understand what words will be:

+ *Helpful*: Good because they flow from moral character and promote beautiful living.

+ *Strengthening/Building Up Others*: Edifying words that bring improvement and promote maturity.

+ *According to Their Need*: Carefully chosen words that specifically fill up a need, meet a lack, minister to a want, or express care in a difficulty, where it is most necessary.

+ *Beneficial/Ministering Grace*: Attractive speech that helps others to perceive and receive God's grace narrative. They are gift words — generously given, freely granted words that accept, that free, that empower, and that give hope.

To the Colossians, Paul writes, "Let your conversation be always full of grace, seasoned with salt, so that you may know how to answer everyone" (Col. 4:6). Grace words are words of connection, giving, affirming, accepting, freeing, and justifying. They are seasoned with salt — they preserve relationships with God, others, and self.

The Careful Use of Spiritual Conversations

Throughout *Gospel Conversations*, you will read hundreds of sample spiritual conversations. Because of the nature of the printed word, you will not be able to hear the inflection and tone of these sentences. You also will not be able to fully sense the spontaneity and individuality necessary in the skillful use of spiritual conversations. If we simply mimic these samples, then we will come across wooden, generic, academic, and out of touch. The samples are meant to stir our imagination, not to limit our creative, individual, personal interaction with our counselees.

Additionally, we need to be careful in the use of questions. I put many of the trialogues in question form because they need to be generic. However, we can think of spiritual conversations more as a quest to invite Jesus in, not as questions that push Jesus out and people away. It is wise to question the use of questions, especially the poor use of questions. A few principles can help.

- As biblical counselors we're not interrogators. "Just the facts, ma'am. Just the facts." Biblical counseling is a conversation, not a cross-examination.
- We need to be aware that questions can cause our counselee to feel like an object to be diagnosed or a lab specimen to be dissected.
- We never use questions as an excuse to avoid intimacy.
- We don't use questions as filler because we're unsure what to say.

When we do use questions, we can use them effectively by:

- Always asking ourselves, "Will this question further or inhibit the flow of our relationship, of our conversation?"
- Normally asking open-ended questions: ones that can't be answered with a "Yes" or "No."

I wonder what your feeling?

- Using indirect questions that imply a desire for further exploration, without having a question mark at the end of our sentence. "Emilio, that had to have been incredibly hard when your wife left the room ..."

The Practice of Spiritual Conversations

Our desire in spiritual conversations is to help our counselees to live *coram Deo* — face-to-face with God in Christ. In sustaining, our quest is to help our counselees to find God in the midst of their suffering. We want to send them on a God-quest where they bring God back into the center of their life journey. Comforting spiritual conversations in *sustaining* are a quest to encourage our counselees to invite God into their casket.

> Comforting spiritual conversations in sustaining are a quest to encourage our counselees to invite God into their casket.

Spiritual Conversations and Giving People Permission to Grieve

Before Emilio can invite God into his casket, he has to candidly face his own suffering. He needs to be given permission to groan and grieve through probing interactions like these:

+ I'm so sorry you're going through this.

+ I can only begin to imagine what you might be feeling ...

+ If I were going through this, I think I might be feeling _____ . How does that compare to what you are feeling now?

+ Who has wept with you in your weeping? What has that been like for you?

+ What is your understanding of the Bible's teaching about sharing our thoughts and feelings honestly with God?

+ Jesus in the garden was brutally honest with his Father. What would it be like for you to follow his example?

+ If you were to write a Psalm 13 (or any psalm of lament) to God, what would you write?

Spiritual Conversations and a Quest to Face What Was Lost

Once Emilio understands and receives the Bible's invitation to grieve, he will likely need help putting words to his grief. So you want to engage Emilio in conversations that help him to face what was lost. We might call these "casket conversations" that help counselees to muster the integrity and courage to explore honestly their hurts, fears, and disappointments. *Bedside response*

1 + What is this loss like for you?

2 + What are you feeling and going through right now?

3 + What do you wish were happening instead of what you're going through? *Go away*

4 + What has been robbed from your life due to this? What is missing? *Get out*

5 + In 2 Corinthians 1, Paul said he despaired even of life. How do his feelings compare to yours? *Not quite as bad*

6 + What are you grieving over the most? What hurts the most in this situation? *Thank you, thats a good question*

7 + What's the worst-case scenario? What if that happened? *A scary but helpful question*

Spiritual Conversations and a Quest to Face God in Loss

First, we trialogue about how bad life is. Next, we trialogue about bringing God into the center of our losses and crosses.

+ You've shared a lot. There's obviously so much going on inside. Rightly so. Yet, so far we've not talked much about where God fits in your picture . . .

+ I'm curious what your conversations with God have been like in light of all of this . . .

+ What are you doing with God in your suffering?

+ What might God be up to in all of this?

+ Have you been able to share your heart with God? What have you said?

+ What are you sensing from God as you go through this?

+ If you painted a picture of how you sense God right now, what would you paint?

+ Has your loss made any difference in your feelings about God? Your relationship to God? Your view of God?

Spiritual Conversations and a Quest to Wrestle with God

People in the Bible like Jacob, Job, David, Paul, and Jesus, among many others, not only knew that life was bad. They not only knew that God was good. They wrestled with the tension between a good God who allows evil and suffering. As biblical counselors, we encourage our counselees to do the same.

+ How would you compare your response to your suffering to Jacob's response to God in his suffering? To Job's response? To David's response? To Paul's response?

+ Jesus in the garden was brutally honest with his Father. What would it sound like for you to follow Jesus' example of sharing your heart with your heavenly Father? *A good question for consideration*

+ If you were to write a Psalm 88 (a psalm of the dark night of the soul) to God, how would it sound? What would you write?

+ What Scriptures could we look at that illustrate how God's people have talked to God when they felt that he was not hearing their cry?

Ps 73

Spiritual Conversations and a Quest to Cling to God

As our counselees, like Emilio, wrestle with God, they also need our encouragement to cling to God.

+ What is your suffering teaching you about God's power and your weakness? *He comes near to the brokenhearted and saves the crushed in spirit*

- How could your agony cause you to cry out to God for help, love, strength, joy, peace, or deliverance?

- What passages have you found helpful in gaining a new perspective on your suffering? To find comfort as you go through your suffering? *Ps 34:18*

- When else have you experienced suffering similar to this? How did *I Jn 2:1* you respond? What did you learn about God in that situation? What would you repeat and what would you change about your response to that situation? *What to change: I want to consider what God may be teaching me and how He might want me to respond: rather than just working to solve the problem myself*

Spiritual Conversations and a Quest to Sustain Faith

Recall that one of the main roles of sustaining is to help believers to draw a line in the sand of retreat. To say, "My faith has been shaken, doubts have arisen, but I will not give up. I will not surrender to despair. My hope will remain. My faith is sustained."

- You feel like your faith is fading. That frightens you, and you'd like to find your way to deepened faith in Christ.

- It's hard to feel anything but sadness because of your loss, but some part of you would welcome genuine faith and consolation.

- How does your faith in Christ fit into your feeling and thinking about your loss? *My faith reminds me that I have lost nothing of eternal value*

- What Scriptures give you hope in the midst of your hurt? *Is 41:10*

- Isaiah 63:9 teaches us that in all our distress, God too is distressed. How does it impact you to know that God is suffering with you in your suffering? *It gives me courage and hope*

I understand that some of us get nervous at the thought of candid conversations with God about our grief. Martin Luther did not share such nervous concern. Luther was convinced that God knew all that the sufferer felt and thought; therefore all feelings and thoughts could be expressed openly to God. One of the Reformer's table talks reflected this viewpoint. The recorder, Veit Dietrich, wrote of a conversation he and Luther had concerning what a Christian was free to share with Christ.

> When I asked him about the passage in which Jeremiah cursed the day in which he had been born and suggested that such impatience was a sin, he (Martin Luther) replied, "Sometimes one has to wake up our Lord God with such words. Otherwise he doesn't hear. It is a case of real murmuring on the

part of Jeremiah. Christ spoke in this way. 'How long am I to be with you?'
(Mark 9:19). Moses went so far as to throw his keys at our Lord God's feet
when he asked, 'Did I conceive all this people?'[58] *(Numbers 11:12)*

Luther continued by saying that everyone feels and thinks such things; so
those who say that Christians should not express them to God are unrealistic.
"Accordingly it is only speculative theologians who condemn such impatience
and recommend patience. If they get down to the realm of practice, they will
be aware of this."[59] An open, honest relationship with God was important to
Luther's soul care because it prevented retreat in the midst of suffering. He felt
that speaking directly and openly to God helped hurting people to maintain
their faith in God.

Empathetic Scriptural Explorations: Sustaining Biblical Trialogues

Spiritual conversations use broad theological concepts to prompt people to
ponder more deeply their walk with God. *Scriptural explorations* use specific
applicable Bible passages to help people to relate God's truth to their circumstances. Specific sustaining, empathetic scriptural explorations relate God's
truth to our counselee's life to promote comfort from Christ through communion with Christ.

> Empathetic scriptural explorations relate God's truth to our counselee's life to
> promote comfort from Christ through communion with Christ.

Imagine that you've connected with Emilio. He senses that you're in his
casket with him. You sense that you understand something of what he's going
through both in his external suffering (what's happening to him) and his internal suffering (what's happening in him). Having heard some of the depths of
his soul through listening to his words, you're praying silently for opportunities for the two of you to listen together to God's Word.

In a natural, friend-to-friend manner, you long to help Emilio to invite
Christ into the casket with him. Your quest requires a loving understanding of
Emilio, biblical wisdom about the character and purposes of God, and biblical
knowledge of Scripture. It also requires a wise, humble, and bold commitment
to help Emilio to connect with God — his ultimate Spiritual Friend.

Maturing as a Biblical Counselor

Self-Counsel and Group or Partner Interaction

1. Reflect on a casket experience in your life (distant past, recent past, or current). Select a few of the trialogues under "Spiritual Conversations and a Quest to Face What Was Lost" on page 166 to help you to explore your responses.

   A difficult experience: My daughter Faith. What I am greiving the most: the happiness and health of my daughter, for her, my wife and myself

2. Reflect on a casket experience in your life (distant past, recent past, or current). Select a few of the trialogues under "Spiritual Conversations and a Quest to Face God in Loss" on pages 166–67 to help you to explore your responses.

   A difficult experience: Working with and relying on coworkers that I can't trust. What might God be up to in all of this? He wants me to learn to love my enemies, trust Him and have patience.

3. Reflect on a casket experience in your life (distant past, recent past, or current). Select a few of the trialogues under "Spiritual Conversations and a Quest to Wrestle with God" on page 167 to help you to explore your responses.

   A difficult experience: My daughter-in-laws decision to take my son and 4 grandchildren and move to Georgia. Compared to Job. My loss does not involve death so its not as final. I can pray for their return to the area

4. Reflect on a casket experience in your life (distant past, recent past, or current). Select a few of the trialogues under "Spiritual Conversations and a Quest to Cling to God" on pages 167–68 to help you to explore your responses.

   I'd like to learn to trust God with the solution to my problems/suffering rather than just trying to solve them myself.

5. Reflect on a casket experience in your life (distant past, recent past, or current). Select a few of the trialogues under "Spiritual Conversations and a Quest to Sustain Faith" on page 168 to help you to explore your responses.

   Ps 34:18 is a powerful promise to look to when going through any suffering. Also Is 41:10

Counseling One Another

6. If you are working through this material in a lab small group, then be prepared to work through questions 1, 2, 3, 4, and 5 with the entire group, or with a lab partner, or with the lab facilitator counseling one group member, or with a lab member counseling another lab member.

A Sample Pattern for Scriptural Explorations

But how do we do that? Do we preach a thirty-minute sermon on suffering and the affectionate sovereignty of God? But that would be the pulpit ministry of the Word and a monologue, not the personal ministry of the Word and a trialogue. While we would certainly exhort Emilio to be in the Word — his own personal quiet time and Bible study along with hearing the preaching of the Word — we don't preach at Emilio in counseling. Instead, we invite him to explore the Scriptures with us as we relate God's Word to his suffering. You can use the following trialogues as a basic pattern for exploring biblical narratives/stories, psalms, or passages together.

Gold

- How do you react to this biblical story/psalm/passage?
  - How is it different from your situation? How is it similar?
  - How have you been responding differently? Similarly?
  - What in this story/psalm/passage would you like to add to your story? How do you think you could do that?
- Imagine writing your own story, somewhat like this biblical story/psalm/passage.
  - What role would God play in your story?
  - What would your relationship to God be like?
  - What role would you play in your story?
  - Who else might be in your story?
  - Are there any characters in this story who remind you of any people in your life?

- What would the theme of your story be?
- How would God work out your story for good?
- How would God give you strength in your story?

A Biblical Sampler for Empathetic Scriptural Explorations

Imagine that you're counseling Ashley. It's the day after her twin sons' eleventh birthday. With tears streaming down her face, Ashley says that twenty-five years earlier, not long after *her* eleventh birthday, a relative began sexually abusing her.

Ashley's self-description was poignant. "Yes, I'm the good girl from the good home. The good mom; the good wife. But nobody knows the ugliness I feel inside. Nobody knows how I've pretended and denied all these years. I just can't keep faking it any longer. I'm a mess — depressed to the point that at times I've thought of suicide. Always fearful and anxious — terrified I'll displease someone. Terrified someone will find out what an empty but evil thing I am …"[60]

Now, imagine that you've met several times with Ashley. You've been addressing, in a comprehensive way, the crisis issues of depression and suicide. You've also been climbing in the casket with Ashley regarding her sexual abuse. Then last week, you began interacting with Ashley about 2 Samuel 13 and the rape of Tamar by her half-brother Amnon. Consider just a sampler of the trialogues you could engage in with Ashley. First, some general trialogues about the passage:

- Ashley, as you read Tamar's story, what is similar in what happened to her compared to what you experienced?
- What is different in Tamar's story from what happened to you?
- Ashley, as we read about Tamar's response in verses 12 – 20, what is similar and what is different in her response from your response?

Because the Bible is real and raw, this passage allows Ashley and you to explore aspects of Tamar's rape that are potentially comparable to the abuse Ashley experienced. The fact that the Bible talks about these experiences can free Ashley to talk about her experiences.

- Ashley, as we read about the "setup" in 2 Samuel 13:5 – 10, what feelings does that stir in you? How were you set up by your abuser?

+ What do you feel when you read Amnon saying he was "in love with" his sister?

+ The Bible is raw and honest. We're told in 2 Samuel 13:12 – 16 that Amnon forced Tamar, refused to listen to her, overpowered her, and raped her. What is it like for you to read those words? How do those descriptions compare to your abuse?

+ What was it like for Tamar to experience her brother's betrayal? Brutality? Hatred? How does her experience compare to yours?

+ Amnon later acted as if Tamar was the guilty party — treating her like a "thing" and a dangerous woman (13:15 – 17). Did you experience this victimizing of the victim? Being treated like a nonperson? What was this like for you?

+ Tamar's beauty, femininity, and servant's heart are all used against her (13:1 – 2, 5 – 11). How do you think this impacted Tamar? How did this impact you?

The Bible is not only real about the external abuse, it realistically depicts the internal struggles. Thus you can explore with Ashley trialogues such as:

+ In 2 Samuel 13:12 – 16, we see Tamar's battles with powerlessness and voicelessness. How do her struggles compare to yours?

+ We're told that Tamar struggled with feelings of disgrace, desolation, and shame (13:13, 20). Have you battled any of these feelings? Other feelings? What are you doing with those feelings? How do you see yourself?

+ Words like "sister" and "brother" are used repeatedly in this passage — highlighting the pain of incestuous abuse. What do you feel when you read those words?

+ Tamar grieves deeply. She tore her richly ornamented robe, put ashes on her head, and wept aloud (13:18 – 19). How does Tamar's grief response compare to yours? Have you given yourself permission to grieve like Tamar?

The Bible also depicts realistically how other family members often revictimize the victim. You can explore these common dynamics with Ashley.

+ Tamar's other brother, Absalom, responds in a horribly hurtful way by telling her to be quiet and not take the rape to heart (2 Sam.

13:20 – 22). Who has responded to you in similarly hurtful ways? What has that felt like?

+ Tamar's father, King David, was angry but inactive (13:21). Who has responded to you in a similarly hurtful way? What did that feel like?

+ David grieves the death of Amnon (13:37), but we're never told he grieves the rape of Tamar. Honestly, that makes me furious. What feelings does that bring up for you?

God's Word never leaves us without hope, even in a passage like 2 Samuel 13. So you can explore hope-giving, God-facing trialogues like these with Ashley.

+ Given the culture of her day, it is remarkable that Tamar somehow found the strength to speak forcefully about the foolish, wicked nature of Amnon's sin (13:12 – 13). Where do you think Tamar found the courage to overcome her feelings of powerlessness and voicelessness and speak out like this? Through Christ's strength, how are you finding the strength to do the same?

+ In 2 Samuel 13, we find an inspired account of a wicked event. God speaks through the narrator and through Tamar to voice his view of this abuse. God calls sexual abuse "wicked" (13:12) and sexual abusers "wicked fools" (13:13). How does it impact you to know that God is on the side of the abused and stands against your abuser?

+ Just two chapters earlier, we read of David's great sin (2 Sam. 11). In this section of Scripture, how is God directing our gaze to focus on our fallen condition? How is God directing our gaze to our desperate need for the greater David — for Jesus? Our need for shame?

+ In 2 Samuel 14:27, we learn that a daughter was born to Absalom. "The daughter's name was Tamar, and she became a beautiful woman." Where sin abounds, grace super-abounds. Could 2 Samuel 14:27 be a subtle portrayal of the gospel hope that is available for all the Tamars and all the Ashleys of the world?

The examples could go on for pages. They model how to view and use God's Word in a trialogue manner rather than in a monologue.

You can also use scriptural explorations as powerful homework assignments. For instance, between now and the next time you meet, Ashley could write her responses to some of the trialogues you did not discuss during your meeting. Or she could write her own psalm to God. Or she could write the next chapter in Tamar's story and in her own story — factoring God into the equation.

Where We've Been and Where We're Headed

Here's our tweet-size summary of chapter 6.

• Through gospel listening and gospel conversations, we relate Christ's grace relevantly and richly to the specific person and their particular situation and unique story.

Sustaining empathy helps faith to survive because shared sorrow is endurable sorrow. Healing encouragement helps faith to thrive because God is good even when life is bad. In chapters 7 – 8, we learn five healing relational competencies that help people to rest in Christ's grace.

Maturing as a Biblical Counselor
Self-Counsel and Group or Partner Interaction

1. Ponder an area of suffering in your life. What passage of Scripture relevantly relates to your loss and grief? From that passage, craft empathetic scriptural exploration trialogues for yourself. Then write out your responses. Be prepared to interact about them in lab. *Distrust of some of my coworkers*

    Pr. 3:5-6 Trust in the Lord with all your heart and lean not on your own understanding. In all your ways acknowledge Him and He will make your paths straight. Do not be wise in your own eyes but fear the Lord and turn away from evil. It will be healing to your

Counseling Others

2. Read 2 Samuel 13 and create additional empathetic scriptural exploration trialogues that you could use in counseling with Ashley.

3. Use Psalm 13 or Psalm 23 or Psalm 88 to craft empathetic scriptural exploration trialogues that you could use in counseling with Emilio.

Counseling One Another

4. You've worked through the five sustaining relational competencies for suffering. In lab, be prepared to share an area of suffering, loss, or grief that you are facing. And be prepared to receive biblical counsel either from the entire group, or from a member of the lab in front of the group, or from your lab facilitator in front of the group, or privately with your lab partner.

5 HEALING BIBLICAL COUNSELING COMPETENCIES: RESTS

RESTS

Having climbed in the casket in the sustaining process, now it is time to celebrate the empty tomb through the healing process. Sustaining emphasized grace relationships and now healing will build on that by emphasizing grace narratives. In chapters 7 and 8 we learn and practice the five skills of healing biblical counseling. Here are the student-oriented learning objectives (SOLOs) that will be our target in the healing process.

Active participants in the reading and application of chapters 7–8 will be able to:

- Engage in grace narratives that heal faith in the good heart of God by offering hope that *rests* in Christ alone (chapter 7).
- Develop the healing relational competency of redemptive, relational mind and soul renewal — cropping Christ back into the picture (chapter 7).
- Develop the healing relational competency of encouraging communication — celebrating the empty tomb (chapter 8).
- Develop the healing relational competency of scriptural treatment planning — pursuing Christlikeness (chapter 8).
- Develop the healing relational competency of theo-dramatic spiritual conversations — healing theological trialogues (chapter 8).
- Develop the healing relational competency of stretching scriptural explorations — healing biblical trialogues (chapter 8).

If you are working through *Gospel Conversations* with a group of people, then to meet these learning objectives, you will want to do the following prior to meeting with your small group training lab:

- Chapter 7: Healing through Celebrating the Empty Tomb
  - Read pages 181 to 203.
  - Respond to all questions on pages 182–83, 189–90, and 202–3.
  - Read, meditate on, and study John 13–16; Romans 8 and 12:1–2.
  - Optional: Read chapter 5 of *Gospel-Centered Counseling*.
- Chapter 8: Healing through Grace Narratives
  - Read pages 205 to 232.

- Respond to all questions on pages 207, 214 – 15, 221, 227 – 28, and 232.
- Read, meditate on, and study Genesis 50:20; 2 Kings 6:15 – 17; Isaiah 61; Ephesians 3:8 – 11; Hebrews 3:12 – 19 and 10:19 – 25.
- Optional: Read chapter 14 of *Gospel-Centered Counseling.*

CHAPTER 7

Healing through Celebrating the Empty Tomb

Imagine yourself having ministered to Emilio and Maria over the last few weeks. At first it was at Emilio's hospital bedside. Receiving chemotherapy now, he's home, attending church, and active in his small group. You, Emilio, and Maria have had some candid conversations — they're certainly not pretending. They readily admit that "life is bad!" As you've climbed in the casket with both of them, your sustaining care has helped them to draw a line in the sand of retreat. Rather than their suffering moving them far from God, they've been clinging to God like never before.

But they still have questions. "Where is God in all of this? What is God up to in allowing this diagnosis of liver cancer? How can I find God and his healing hope even if I don't find physical healing? What would it look like for me to handle this *with* Christ and *like* Christ?"

Emilio and Maria also face temptations from Satan. He hisses, "Where are God's great and precious promises now? You say, 'God is good all the time,' but from where I'm standing, he doesn't look so good to me!"

You have questions too. You're thankful that the Father's compassion has flowed into and out of your life so you can empathize with Emilio and Maria. Still, you're asking yourself, "But now what? What do I do after the hug?" While you're ready to flow from empathy to encouragement, you want to know, "Just what is biblical encouragement? And what are the 'how-tos' of encouragement?"

Maturing as a Biblical Counselor

Self-Counsel and Group or Partner Interaction

1. The apostle Paul talks about his "casket experience" in 2 Corinthians 1:8–9—great pressure far beyond his ability to endure, despairing of life, feeling the sentence of death. However, he does not stop there. He also clings to the God who raises the dead—he celebrates the empty tomb (2 Cor. 1:9).

   a. When has God rescued you from an emotional, spiritual, mental casket?

   When I was saved in 1982. I was so dead in my sins - alcohol and drug abuse were my masters.

   b. How did God draw you out of the casket of despair into the rarified air of resurrected hope?

   A freind introduced me to Jesus and the Gospel

   c. Whom did God use to help you to hope in God again? How did this person(s) minister to you? *Julie + Matt Woodley*

Counseling Others

2. As you assess your personality and your style of ministry, do you tend more toward climbing in the casket, empathy, and listening to the earthly story (sustaining and the troubling story), or more toward celebrating the resurrection, infusing hope, and helping others to listen to God's eternal story (healing and the faith story)?

   a. Why do you think you tend toward one emphasis over the other?

   I don't like to suffer someone elses pain

---

b. What impact might it have on your counselees that you tend toward this one emphasis over the other? *I will not be able to fully enter into another persons pain*

The purpose of this chapter and the next is to answer your legitimate questions and to help you to minister well and wisely to folks like Emilio and Maria as they face their own questions and temptations related to suffering. Suffering has brought them each to a faith point: "I'll trust God; I'll trust him not." In the crisis and crucible of suffering, Satan has been tempting them to turn their backs on God. Through sustaining, you've fortified them to face their suffering face-to-face with God.

During times of suffering, we each wrestle against Satan's lies and his attempts to crop Christ out of the picture. Through healing, we learn to wrestle *with* God like Jacob did. In healing, by cropping Christ back into the picture, we point people to the Christ of the cross as the ultimate demonstration of the good heart of God.

So what is your role in bringing God's healing hope to Emilio and Maria? Sustaining is *drawing a line in the sand of retreat;* healing is *driving a stake in the heart of Satan's lies* and *clinging by faith to the good heart of God.* Sustaining is *joining with sufferers in their suffering;* healing is *journeying with sufferers to Christ.*

In sustaining, we've listened well to Emilio's earthly story. Now in healing, we encourage Emilio to listen well to Christ's eternal story *and* to cling humbly to God by faith. Healing involves mind renewal, but even more than that, it involves *relationship* renewal — knowing Christ and the power of his resurrection and the fellowship of his suffering so we become like Christ (Phil. 3:10). The Confessional Statement of the Biblical Counseling Coalition powerfully captures the truth that we point people to a relationship with Christ.

> We point people to a person, Jesus our Redeemer, and not to a program, theory, or experience. We place our trust in the transforming power of the Redeemer as the only hope to change people's hearts, not in any human system of change. People need a personal and dynamic relationship with Jesus, not a system of self-salvation, self-management, or self-actualization

(John 14:6). Wise counselors seek to lead struggling, hurting, sinning, and confused people to the hope, resources, strength, and life that are available only in Christ.[61]

As we become adept at sustaining and healing, we will become known for our biblical *parakaletic* counseling — coming alongside suffering brothers and sisters and offering them biblical comfort and encouragement *in Christ*. Much more important than becoming known for something is the fact that when we care for the hurting, we become counselors who care like Christ.

God: The Ultimate *Parakaletic* Counselor

When we offer each other sustaining comfort and healing encouragement, we follow in the path of our triune God. God the Father is the God of all comfort (2 Cor. 1:3). God the Son and God the Spirit are each divine Comforters. Jesus tells his suffering and grieving disciples that he will ask the Father, who will send them *another* Comforter (from the Greek word *paraklaton* — comforter, encourager, counselor) (John 14:16 KJV). Jesus is thus indicating that his current ministry is characterized by comforting and that the Spirit's ongoing ministry will likewise personify a ministry of encouragement.

Our triune God's soul caregiving provides the perfect example of the seamless uniting of sustaining (it's normal to hurt/climbing in the casket) and healing (it's possible to hope/celebrating the empty tomb). We are witnesses to this amazing ministry in John 13 – 16.

Jesus, Sustaining, and Our Troubling Story

Put yourself in the disciples' souls. They've surrendered everything to follow Jesus, and now he tells them, "My children, I will be with you only a little longer. You will look for me, and just as I told the Jews, so I tell you now: Where I am going, you cannot come" (John 13:33). Jesus, who likely was younger than many of his disciples, still calls them "my children." Truly, he was a spiritual father to them. Jesus, empathizing with them, puts words to their emotions. They feel bereaved like orphans (John 14:18).

Jesus, who understands everything about every one of his disciples (John 2:23 – 25), sustains them by addressing their *troubling* story. In fact, Jesus "bookends" his counseling ministry to them with spiritual conversations that candidly address both their external suffering (what is happening to them) and their internal suffering (what is happening in them). He concludes his trialogue in John 16:33 by facing the fact that life is bad (their external troubling story). "In this world you will have trouble." His word for "trouble" communicates hemmed in, harassed, distressed, oppressed, vexed, persecuted, afflicted — squashed by a fallen world that falls on them!

Jesus begins his trialogue in John 14:1 by meeting head-on the reality that when life stinks, our perspective shrinks (their internal troubling story). "Do not let your hearts be troubled." Here Jesus uses a different word for "troubled" than he chose in John 16:33. This word pictures a sea stirred up and a soul agitated. It is a heart that is disturbed, confused, and perplexed.

Knowing that climbing in the casket once would not be enough, Jesus adds in John 14:27, "Do not let your hearts be troubled and do not be afraid" (fearful, trembling, timid). And then he climbs in a third time, as he acknowledges that they are "filled with grief" (John 16:6). And then a fourth time: "I tell you the truth, you will weep and mourn" (John 16:20). And a fifth: "Now is your time of grief" (John 16:22). If we're ever tempted to think that this "sustaining stuff" is a little much, a little too touchy-feely, we should remind ourselves how Jesus gives his disciples permission to grieve by *repeatedly* climbing in their casket.

Jesus, Healing, and Our Faith Story

As vital as sustaining is, we also notice throughout Jesus' soul care ministry his continuous mingling of sustaining *and* healing. Talk about "spaghetti relationships" — in the very sentence where Jesus talks about their troubled hearts, he also says, "Trust in God; trust also in me" (John 14:1). In the sentence where Jesus talks about their troubling world, he also says, "I have told you these things, so that in me you may have peace. In this world you will have trouble. But take heart! I have overcome the world" (John 16:33).

Jesus knows how to relate and what to do *after the hug*. In John 14 – 16, he heals his suffering disciples by addressing their *faith* story. We can translate the Greek tense and form of John 14:1 as, "Keep on trusting in God and in me. Let your faith find in me one on whom it can rest." Jesus senses, draws out, stirs up, and fans into flame the mustard seed of his disciples' faith.

He also takes them to the end of the story. "In my Father's house are many rooms. . . . And . . . I go [to] prepare a place for you" (John 14:2 – 3). His counsel is so heavenly minded, it is of great earthly good because Jesus does not ignore their earthly story, but weaves it together with God's eternal story. He will not leave them as orphans in this life, just waiting aimlessly and alone for the next life. He promises that the Father will give them another Counselor to be with them *forever* (John 14:16 – 18).

Notice that our sustaining, comforting Counselor is also our healing, encouraging Counselor. He is the Spirit of truth (John 14:17) who teaches them all things (John 14:25 – 26), testifies about Christ (John 15:26), guides them into all truth (John 16:13), and leads them to glorify God (John 16:13 – 15).

Jesus and the Spirit bring the troubled but faith-clinging disciples to healing hope not by directing them to a principle, but to a Person — to communion with God. When Philip asks to see the Father, Jesus directs him to himself with these incredibly personal words, "Don't you know me, Philip, even after I have been among you such a long time?" (John 14:9). As if that was not personal enough, Jesus tells them twice, "You are my friends." "I have called you friends" (John 15:14, 15).

The disciples have communion with the Son and with the Spirit. The Spirit will be with them forever; they will know him because he is with them and *in* them (John 14:16 – 17). And they have communion with the Father. They will be loved by the Father who will make his home with them (John 14:21 – 23). It's possible to hope because we have the assurance of communion with God the Father, God the Son, and God the Holy Spirit.

When life is bad, Satan whispers or shouts that God is bad too. "He's mad at you and getting back at you! He's left you!" Our Divine *Parakaletic* Counselors trialogue with us, reminding us, "This world is not your home. We're preparing a home for you. The Father is not getting back at you; he's getting you back to himself. You are loved children and friends of God!" That's hope. That's cropping Christ back into the picture.

Through sustaining and healing, we gain comfort from Christ through communion with Christ. That's a lot, but it's not the ultimate goal of Jesus' counsel for suffering. Jesus makes the intention of his counsel crystal clear. In the midst of his disciples' inner and outer troubles, Jesus says, "All this I have told you so that you will not go astray" (John 16:1).

Rather than going astray, and thus moving far from God and becoming less like Christ, Christ's prayer for us in our suffering is that we would conform to his image. As his suffering in the garden led him to cling to his Father (Matt. 26:36 – 46), so our suffering can lead us to abide in Christ (John 15:1 – 8). Our suffering can bring us to the humble realization that without Christ we can do nothing (15:5). As we abide in Christ (15:1 – 4), we become like Christ (17:17 – 19), and we produce much fruit through Christ (15:5 – 8) for the glory of the Father (15:8).

Conformity to Christ means that we live for the same purpose Christ lives for — celebrating and glorifying the Father. "And I will do whatever you ask in my name, so that the Son may bring glory to the Father" (John 14:13). "This is to my Father's glory, that you bear much fruit" (John 15:8).

The ultimate purpose of soul care is to help the sufferer to glorify God. You'll not find that purpose in any secular counseling training manuals. The endgame of much counseling in suffering is just the hug — to empathize with feelings. Or just to help the sufferer to survive. Or even to help the sufferer to thrive — but defined as the sufferer feeling better and moving on with life. But the scriptural purpose of biblical counseling for suffering is much richer. The Son and the Spirit model robust biblical sustaining and healing: *candor about suffering that longs for comfort in Christ and journeys toward communion with Christ, leading to conformity to Christ that results in celebrating Christ.*

People often talk about "suffering well," but at times they seem to imply that it means not feeling any hurt or sorrow. Jesus models in his counseling ministry (John 13 – 16) and in his life (Matt. 26) that suffering well involves candidly facing and deeply feeling the pain of life in a fallen world (candor), which drives us to cling desperately to the Father of all compassion and the God of all comfort (comfort), which produces an increased depth of connection to and abiding in Christ (communion), which leads to becoming more like Christ (conformity), which results in glorifying the Father (celebration).

In sustaining and healing, we journey with our suffering friends from their casket to Christ's empty tomb. As their travel companions and guides, we help them to move from despairing of life and feeling the sentence of death to not relying on themselves, but on God, who raises the dead (2 Cor. 1:8 – 9). Their suffering this side of heaven may not be removed, but their souls can move closer to their great Soul Physician.

Biblical counselors care deeply about and suffer with sufferers. That care extends all the way to the cross — we seek to launch people on a mission of finding and celebrating Christ in the midst of their suffering. The heart of healing involves journeying with people back to the heart of God.

Healing Relational Competencies: RESTS

Five healing relational competencies are instrumental in helping people find Christ's healing hope. I define these healing relational competencies in several overlapping ways:

- Celebrating the empty tomb/celebrating the resurrection: journeying with sufferers to Christ in their faith story.
- Helping people to know that it's possible to hope.

[handwritten margin note: to trust God and thereby glorify God]

[handwritten margin note: Romans 5:2-5]

?????

- Driving a stake in the heart of Satan's lies and clinging by faith to the good heart of God.
- Enlightening people to see the presence of God in the presence of suffering.
- Encouraging people to interpret life and to know God through the Christ of the cross: cropping Christ back into the picture.
- Engaging in grace narratives that heal faith in the good heart of God by offering hope that rests in Christ alone.

As with sustaining, it is relatively easy to define healing relational competencies, but it takes a lifetime to cultivate them. Over the course of the next two chapters, we'll learn and practice five biblical counseling competencies for healing — competencies that I summarize using the acronym *RESTS*:

- *R* Redemptive, Relational Mind and Soul Renewal
- *E* Encouraging Communication
- *S* Scriptural Treatment Planning
- *T* Theo-Dramatic Spiritual Conversations
- *S* Stretching Scriptural Explorations

Since the Bible is a grand narrative of redemption, then the core of biblical counseling involves compassionately relating that grace narrative to our suffering friends so that by faith they rest in Christ alone. Grace is God's prescription for our disgrace. It is God's medicine of choice for our suffering and sin. Grace is not simply a label for a theoretical concept. Grace is the essence of God's holy and loving heart. God *so loved* that *he gave his Son* — that's grace.

Grace is a Person and rest is found in that Person. To the weary and burdened, Jesus says, "Come to *me* ... and I will give you rest" (Matt. 11:28, emphasis added). We come to him when we believe that he has a good heart: "... for I am gentle and humble in heart, and you will find rest for your souls" (Matt. 11:29). That's biblical healing: engaging in grace narratives that heal faith in the good heart of God by offering hope that *rests* in Christ alone. When you think healing relational competencies, think RESTS.

> Biblical healing engages in grace narratives that heal faith in the good heart of God by offering hope that *rests* in Christ alone.

Maturing as a Biblical Counselor

Self-Counsel and Group or Partner Interaction

1. Think through an issue in your life where you are experiencing trouble from the outside (John 16:33) that is leading to trouble on the inside—in your heart (John 14:1).

   a. With a partner or your entire lab, use John 14–16 to work through the issue in your life—facing it with candor, face-to-face with Christ, seeking his comfort (sustaining in the troubling story). *My coworkers (some) seem to be either untrustworthy or incompetent or both. It is very upsetting to work with people that sometimes seem to be working against me.*

   b. With a partner or your entire lab, use John 14–16 to work through the issue in your life—journeying toward communion with Christ, conformity to Christ, and celebrating Christ (healing in the faith story).
   "You know Him, for He dwells with you and will be in you" Jn 14:17C

Counseling Others

2. Imagine that you are counseling one of the disciples—Peter, Philip, John …

   a. What could you do to follow Jesus' model of entering their troubling story (sustaining)?

   b. What could you do to follow Jesus' model of stretching their faith story (healing)?

3. How could the following definition impact how you minister to people who are suffering?

> *Parakaletic* biblical counseling for suffering moves toward candor about suffering that longs for comfort in Christ and journeys toward communion with Christ leading to conformity to Christ that results in celebrating Christ.

Redemptive, Relational Mind and Soul Renewal: Cropping Christ Back into the Picture

The author of Hebrews encourages us to approach the throne of grace with confidence so that we may receive mercy and grace to help us in our time of need (Heb. 4:16). He introduces his words of encouragement with "therefore" (Heb. 4:14), which takes us back to Hebrews 3:1. "Fix your thoughts on Jesus, the apostle and high priest whom we confess." In our time of need, there's only one thing that gives us confidence to approach God. And that "thing" is a Person — Christ our High Priest. Biblical mind and soul renewal involves a new way of thinking about *and* a new way of relating to God in Christ.

It is because we have a great High Priest, Jesus the Son of God, that we can hold firmly to our faith in God (Heb. 4:14). It is because we have a High Priest who sympathizes with our weaknesses, who has been tempted in every way we are tempted, and who is without sin that we have confidence in God's good heart (Heb. 4:15 – 16).

The classic Bible passage on mind and soul renewal (Rom. 12:1 – 2) also unites the redemptive and the relational. Before Paul exhorts us to no longer conform to the pattern of this world (putting off) and to be transformed by the renewing of our minds (putting on), he writes, "Therefore, I urge you, brothers, in view of God's mercy, to offer your bodies as living sacrifices, holy and pleasing to God — this is your spiritual act of worship" (Rom. 12:1).

Mind and soul renewal is redemptive — it is *in view of and in light of God's salvation mercies*, which Paul described in Romans 1 – 11, that we renew our minds. And mind and soul renewal is relational — Christ's grand redemptive narrative changes how we see God and relate to God so that we live to please and worship God.

Redemptive, relational mind and soul renewal is necessary because since the Fall, life is not just *one* grand narrative. It is a competition between *two grand narratives* that each vie for our attention and commitment. Satan's grand narrative is filled with *lies, self* (self-sufficiency, selfishness, self-effort), *works,* and *condemnation,* while Christ's grand narrative is filled with *truth,* God (Christ-sufficiency), *others* (other-centered), *faith, grace,* and *forgiveness.*

2 narratives of life

Confronted by these two competing narratives of life and God, we're forced to face questions like, "Whose interpretation of the story will I believe — Christ's or Satan's? Whose view of God will I accept — Christ's or Satan's?" Ever since Genesis 3, *life is a battle for our love* that raises the ageless question, "Who captures my mind and captivates my heart — Christ or Satan?"

What is our role when Emilio and Maria face this battle? What does mind and soul renewal look like in our biblical counseling interactions? When Emilio and Maria come to us, we don't shout, "Gospel!" as if it's some magic wand. Instead, we first understand the gospel story, then we seek to understand their story, and then we journey together to *intersect* God's eternal story and their temporal story. We pivot back and forth with Emilio and Maria between the larger story of the gospel and the smaller (but real and meaningful) story of their lives. We earn the right to bring God's perspective to bear on their lives by first listening well to their life story. Redemptive, relational mind and soul renewal is journeying together to intersect Christ's gospel story and our counselee's troubling story so the Christ of the cross is cropped back into their heart and their story.

this is the place that I want to get to

> Redemptive, relational mind and soul renewal is journeying together to intersect Christ's gospel story and our counselee's troubling story so the Christ of the cross is cropped back into their heart and their story.

Gospel-centered counseling means that together with our counselees, we derive our understanding of earthly life from heaven's viewpoint. Mind and soul renewal means that we look at life not with eyeballs only, but with spiritual eyes; we live under the Son, not under the sun. We do so through:

Discipleship

+ Taking Our Imagination Captive to God's Grand Purpose
+ Putting Off Satan's Lying, Works Narrative
+ Putting On Christ's Grace and Truth Narrative

Taking Our Imagination Captive to God's Grand Purpose

Maria's battle to trust God was almost more difficult than Emilio's. She simply could not fathom why a good Father might take away the father of her children. As my wife (Shirley) and I ministered to Maria, we did not start by racing in with cliché words about how God works everything together for good (Rom. 8:28). We didn't start there because the apostle Paul doesn't start there. He starts with groaning: suffering, frustration, bondage, decay, pain, waiting, weakness (Rom. 8:18 – 27).

Before Paul talks about our calling, he follows the ancient path of lament, as in Psalms 13 and 88 (examples of scores of lament psalms). As Paul invites us to groan and lament to God, so Shirley and I invited Maria to groan and lament; we gave her permission to grieve.

Maria, like most us when we're facing suffering, had two main goals, "Change my circumstances and fix my feelings!" Shirley and I could identify with those goals, and we joined Maria in humbly and fervently praying for Emilio's physical healing. And, while we didn't exactly pray that her feelings would be fixed, we did take Maria's feelings seriously and encouraged her to take those feelings to God — to soothe her soul in her Savior.

"Why, God?"

Because Maria felt free (and safe) to be honest with us about her emotions, she then felt free to verbalize her deepest spiritual questions. Like most of us, Maria had one main question as she faced Emilio's cancer prognosis. "Why, God?" Some of us get very nervous when people ask God "Why?" Yet the psalmists model asking that question all the time. "Why, God?" is our gateway into healing. Just as "How do you feel?" is a gateway into the sustaining process, so "What are you doing with God in your suffering?" is a gateway into the healing process.

"Why, God?" is actually a great question. The problem is that we typically ask it not truly wanting or really waiting for an answer. Or we ask it, not looking to the Bible's grand redemptive narrative for the ultimate answer. Our role as gospel-centered counselors is to stretch people's shrunken perspective. We do that by compassionately and comprehensively addressing their "Why, God?" questions.

Explore Christ's Grand Gospel Narrative: In What Story Do We Find Ourselves?

"Maria, we're so glad you have the freedom to approach God's throne of grace boldly and ask God, 'Why?' Before we can even begin to grasp why God might be allowing this into your family, we have to ponder why God does *anything*.

We promise you, we'll come back to your specific question about why God might be allowing Emilio's cancer, but would it be okay if we first took a look together at God's larger purposes?"

Because we had listened well to her story, Maria was eager to listen with us to God's story. Since the Bible is a redemption-centered book, we could have turned anywhere in God's Word to trialogue with Maria about the question, "In what story do we find ourselves?" Since our pastor had been preaching on Hosea, we turned there, exploring God's grand plan. Out of the overflow of his Trinitarian love, God created a perfect paradise for his perfect bride. But she committed adultery, giving her heart to another lover. *But God* pursued his adulterous spouse tenaciously and tenderly. Her drama of redemption concludes with the calling to return to the Lover of her soul, to seek forgiveness, to receive grace, to be healed, *and* to become a fruitful witness to God's great grace (Hosea 14).

"Why does God do anything, Maria? Every single thing God does is designed to fulfill the same purpose — to accomplish his original and eternal purpose of a world created for and enjoying fellowship with the Father, Son, and Holy Spirit.

"And your role, Maria? To be a fruitful witness to God's great grace. Ephesians 2:10 reminds us that we are God's *masterpiece* — his opus, his poem, main characters in his drama of redemption. Maria, your life is a lived sermon. A couple of months ago, after years of your faithful prayers and Christlike witness, Emilio the prodigal became Emilio the son of God.

"Now, *together*, you and Emilio are lead actors in God's drama, and your script is to enlarge the community of the Trinity by inviting others to join. As you and Emilio respond to his cancer diagnosis by clinging to Christ, people are watching the sermon that is your life. As you imitate Christ, your life is inviting others to return home to the Father's good heart — just like Emilio returned home a few months ago ..."

What we shared with Maria is exactly what Paul shared with the believers in Rome after he talked about their suffering and groaning (Rom. 8:18 – 27). "And we know that in all things God works for the good of those who love him, who have been called according to *his purpose*" (Rom. 8:28, emphasis added). We frequently quote that verse out of the context of God's redemptive purposes. *Romans 8:28 isn't a Band-Aid over a surface wound. It's a heart transplant for a sin-sick world.* God's redemptive purpose is for us "to be conformed to the likeness of his Son" (Rom. 8:29) so that our lives will attract others to Christ. That's the truth that must capture our imaginations when suffering and Satan seek to shrink our perspective.

Keep the Vision Vibrant: What Are God's Redemptive Purposes in This?

The drama of redemption, like all redemptive dramas, ends with everyone on stage at the wedding banquet (Rev. 19). As gospel-centered counselors, we work to keep that vision vibrant. The vision is a distinct view of the purpose for which God created us. When our imaginations become captive to the grand narrative of the Bible, then we will entrust our hearts — *no matter what is happening to us* — to God's good heart and his larger purposes, redemptive plans, and eternal perspective. Then we will see our world and our place in it, even in suffering, from God's redemptive perspective.

We cannot keep that vision vibrant by ourselves. As Kevin VanHoozer notes, the church is the theater of the gospel because we can only exhibit our in-Christness in community.[62] That's why we should always be talking about and pursuing a church *of* gospel-centered counseling and not simply a church *with* a gospel-centered counseling ministry. The entire church — Sunday sermons, children's church, small group meetings, fellowship picnics — all must live out Hebrews 10:19 – 25. On the basis of the gospel (Heb. 10:19 – 22) we spur one another on to love and good deeds — the good deeds of imitating Christ and inviting others to the wedding banquet. Every church ministry and meeting has as its ultimate purpose considering how we can provoke one another to fulfill our calling of being witnesses to Christ's gospel of grace.

When a congregation is saturated with a Christ-centered mind-set, then in our biblical counseling meetings, we don't necessarily have to "teach" these concepts. More productively, we can trialogue about how God's larger faith story of redemption relates to our smaller troubling story of suffering.

- What do you think God's purposes might include in allowing you to experience this?
- In what ways is God drawing you nearer to himself through your suffering?
- How is God making you more like his Son through your suffering?
- As hard as this is, what lessons is it teaching you about your desperate need for God?
- Christians are not only people of the Book, but people of the Cross. In what ways are your responses to your suffering attracting others to the cross? How is your worshipful clinging to God drawing others toward Christ?
- What testimony of hope might spring from your suffering?

Putting Off Satan's Lying, Works Narrative

We rightfully talk about putting off lies and putting on truth. But putting off lies about what? Putting on truth about what? We put off lies and put on truth about who God is, what his purposes are, and what our role is in God's eternal plan. Then Christ's grand gospel narrative and our role in the drama of redemption can become the governing framework for how we live out the truth in love. In the putting off process, we join with our counselee in driving a stake in the heart of Satan's lies that cause us to doubt God's good heart.

[handwritten:] pg 188]

And remember, this is not just mind renewal, but also heart/soul renewal — renewal of our relationship with God. The Bible's drama forces us to address the question, "Who do you say that I am?" Behind all of Scripture is not simply the question, "Will you agree?" but rather the more personal, "Will you join up?" The meta-narrative of Scripture is divine address: "Will I or will I not respond? Will I acknowledge God for who he is and myself for who I am?"[63]

[handwritten: will I agree? will I join up? submit?]

The relational battle to win our heart is won or lost in the rational battle regarding the heart of God. Puritan Pastor Richard Sibbes explains the root source of our battle. "It was Satan's art from the beginning to discredit God with man, by calling God's love into question with our first father Adam. His success then makes him ready at the weapon still."[64]

It was also Martin Luther's conviction that attacks on God's holy love were a staple of the Devil. "This, then, is the most furious and sudden of all attacks, in which the devil exerts to the full extent all his powers and arts, and transforms himself into the likeness of the angry and ungracious God."[65]

How are we to help Maria when Satan attempts to crop Christ and the cross out of her picture? How do we care like Christ when Satan parades before Maria the troubling circumstances of her life and shouts, "You see, God does not care about you!"

Assess the Dominant Doubting-God Theme in Satan's Story

Every story has a plot, a thread, a theme. Counseling can be endlessly confusing and complex if we fail to listen carefully for patterns as our counselees talk about their situation. So, as we've illustrated previously, we start by inviting Maria to tell her God story with probing questions such as: "Where is God in your suffering? How do you see God? What are your thoughts about God as you go through this? If you were to pen a psalm of lament right now, what would it sound like?"

[handwritten: What might you imagine could be God's purpose in allowing you to suffer through this?]

As we listen to Maria's God story, we ask *ourselves* theology-guided questions that seek to discern patterns so we can assess the dominant theme of Satan's lie (2 Tim. 2:26). As Maria tells her story, what hopeless, doubting theme is driving her interpretation of her life story? What is the unique lie that Maria is believing about God? Herself? Her role in God's story? In what consistent ways is the cross being belittled, demeaned, or dismissed? What patterns reflect the replacement of grace, justification, and Christ-sufficiency with works, condemnation, and self-sufficiency?

Label the Dominant Doubting-God Lie

Once we've latched onto the dominant doubting story that Maria is believing, then we help her to challenge that old narrative and replace it with a narrative of hope-in-Christ. As we sense a theme developing in our mind, we give it a metaphor — one compressed picture with power. We state Maria's doubt-saturated plot in a nutshell — in one picture, label, or image that captures the essence of Satan's lie.

[handwritten note in margin: Seems dangerous.]

The more we can label it according to a person's language, lingo, or realm of experience, the better. For example, to Maria, who works for the local newspaper, you might say, "Maria, if your view of your life were a front-page headline, it seems like it would be screaming, 'Extra! Extra! Read All About It. Woman Buried in Avalanche of Problems.' And the body of the article makes it clear that you are on your own. No one, especially God, is going to lift a finger to rescue you."

Or, to a lawyer you might say, "May I share a picture of what I sense as I hear you discuss your situation? It's like you're on trial, and God is the Prosecutor who has stacked the jury against you. He's also the Judge who objects to every statement you make."

Or to a teenage high school wrestler you could say, "It seems like you see yourself pinned before you ever step on the mat. It's like Satan is the defending heavyweight state champ, and you're a first-year JV lightweight. And God is the referee, but for some reason he has a vendetta against you and keeps giving your opponent every advantage."

Expose the Root Source of the Doubting-God Story

Often we are unaware of the source of the lies we believe. That's the deceitfulness of sin and the cunning of Satan. So after we have labeled Satan's lie, it can be very powerful to challenge our counselees to ponder the true source of their beliefs. With Maria, after sharing the newspaper imagery, we might ask, "Who do you think wrote that headline and the article that goes with it?"

With the lawyer, we might ask, "Where do you suppose you came to see God, yourself, and your situation like that?" With the high school wrestler, we might say, "I'm wondering where you were recruited into this view of yourself, your situation, and God?"

Acts 26:17 – 18; 2 Corinthians 10:3 – 7; Ephesians 5:6 – 14; and Colossians 1:13 all model exposing the works of darkness. Christ calls gospel-centered counselors to give light to those blinded by Satan's deceptive darkness. Paul commands believers in Ephesians 6:10 – 14 to stand guard, while Peter exhorts Christians to stand watch in 1 Peter 5:8 – 10. Our job is to name Satan's scheme, label the counterplot, and expose its author. So we probe, "Who do you suppose is behind your way of thinking about your life?" Or "Are there any passages we could explore that might expose the true source of this viewpoint?" Or "Who is the real enemy who is energizing this?"

Why do you suppose you believe that?

Putting On Christ's Grace and Truth Narrative

Shirley and I had climbed in the casket with Maria in our sustaining journey. In our overlapping healing journey, we had helped Maria to ponder God's grand purpose and her role in it. That foundation made it easier for Maria to drive a stake in the heart of Satan's lies that were causing her to doubt God's good heart. We were more than ready to celebrate the empty tomb so Maria could cling by faith to the good heart of God.

Coauthor Cross Narratives

Since the Christ of the cross is the ultimate demonstration of the love of God, when Maria, Emilio, you, or I doubt God's good heart, we need our brothers and sister to stretch us to Christ's outstretched arms on the cross. When Martin Luther counseled people struggling with doubts about God, he emphasized the importance of a biblical perspective. "The Holy Spirit knows that a thing has only such value and meaning to a man as he assigns to it in his thoughts."[66]

Luther understood that sometimes human reason, difficult experiences, and Satan shout that God cannot be trusted. In response, Luther dispensed the medicine of reason redeemed by grace.

> Therefore, whenever anyone is assailed by temptation of any sort whatever, the very best that he can do in the case is either to read something in the Holy

Scriptures, or think about the Word of God, and apply it to his heart. The
Word of God heals and restores again to health the mind and heart of man
when wounded by the arrows of the devil.[67]

When assailed by doubts about God's good heart, Luther counseled his
sheep to turn to gospel self-counsel.

> Whatever thoughts the devil awakens within us in temptation we should
> put away from us and cast out of our minds, so that we can see and hear
> nothing else than the kind, comforting word of the promise of Christ, and
> of the gracious will of the heavenly Father, who has given his own Son for
> us, as Christ, our dear Lord, declares in John iii. 16: "God so loved the world
> that he gave his only begotten Son, that whosoever believeth on him should
> not perish, but have everlasting life." Everything else, now, which the devil
> may suggest to us beyond this, that God the Father is reconciled to us, and
> graciously inclined to us, and merciful and powerful for the sake of his
> dear Son, we should cast out of our minds as wandering and unprofitable
> thoughts.[68]

We coauthor these cross narratives with trialogues such as:

- What difference could it make in your view of God if every time Satan
  tempted you to doubt God, you reflected on passages about the cross
  of Christ, such as John 3:16; Romans 5; Romans 8; Ephesians 1; or
  Colossians 1? *Col 1:24-29*
- When everything seems darkest and your doubts the strongest, what
  passages could you turn to regarding the cross of Christ and God's
  grace and love for you? *Ps 34:18*

Coauthor Repentance-unto-Life and Weakness-into-Strength Narratives

Maria was suffering. Her fallen world was falling on her in the form of Emilio's
cancer diagnosis. She was not at fault or responsible for his cancer — only
Job's miserable counselors would say such a thing.

However, like all of us, Maria could *respond to* the evils she suffered either
with Christlike trust in God or with Satan-inspired doubts about God. So,
while soul care for suffering highlights being sinned against, in the "spaghetti
relationships" of counseling, it was important that we interacted with possible
areas of sinful responses.

Maria was actually the first to bring it up. "Bob and Shirley, the psalmists are brutally honest with God. Job was ferociously honest with God.

God seems to invite that intense frankness. But isn't there a line somewhere between temptation to doubt and sinfully giving in to that temptation?"

Shirley responded first. "That takes a *lot* of integrity and spiritual maturity, Maria, to ask that question in the midst of your struggle." After wholeheartedly agreeing with Shirley's affirmation, I said, "It's a great question and it is one of the reasons Christ put us into community — we need one another to sort through where temptation begins and where it crosses the line to sin."

With God's searching, searing Word (Heb. 4:12 – 13), together we examined Maria's heart responses. Infusing grace at each step (Heb. 4:14 – 16), God's Spirit convicted Maria that at times she had given in to and acted upon Satan's lies about God. We returned to the Hosea 14 passage and applied the words, "Take words with you and return to the LORD" (Hosea 14:2). The implication being that we are to be specific about our sins of the heart, which Maria was.

We didn't stop at the first third of Hosea 14:2 and repentance, but also applied the next part of the verse. "Say to him: 'Forgive all our sins and receive us graciously,'" which is exactly what Maria did and exactly how God responded.

Then we moved to the final third of Hosea 14:2: "That we may offer the fruit of our lips." This is "repentance unto life." Freed from doubt and forgiven for sin, Maria was energized by hope and grace to serve God in Christ's strength.

Notice that the header also says "Weakness-into-Strength Narratives." It certainly is possible that Maria or others could face temptation to doubt, candidly share laments, and *not* sin. In such cases, we work with people not in terms of repentance unto life, but in terms of weakness into strength. As Christ says, "My grace is sufficient for you, for my power is made perfect in weakness" (2 Cor. 12:9). And as Paul says, "For when I am weak, then I am strong" (2 Cor. 12:10). Whether in sin or in weakness, we work with counselees to move toward surrender to Christ and dependence on his resurrection power.

Coauthor Resurrection Narratives

Paul's words from 2 Corinthians 1 reflect strength into weakness and dependence on Christ's resurrection narrative. After candidly admitting that he despaired of life and felt the sentence of death, Paul cropped in the resurrection narrative. "But this happened that we might not rely on ourselves but on God, who raises the dead" (2 Cor. 1:9). God's mission statement is, *I Am Indispensable!* Our mission statement is to be, *I Need Christ!*

"Resurrection narratives" unite both our helplessness in ourselves and God's power at work within us in Christ. We coauthor these using trialogues such as:

+ In your suffering, how has Christ's strength been made perfect in weakness?
+ Paul says that the same power that raised Christ from the dead is in *you* (Eph. 1:15 – 23). What difference does it make in your response to your suffering when you live according to Christ's resurrection power?
+ Paul says in Philippians 3:10 that he wants to know the power of Christ's resurrection. How can you avail yourself of that power at work in you?
+ Paul says in Romans 8:17 – 25 that the sure hope of our final victory gives him Christ's strength to keep serving the Lord even in the midst of suffering. What would it be like for you to apply Romans 8:17 – 25 to your life?

Coauthor Heroic-in-Christ Narratives

Satan not only lies to us about God, he lies to us about who we are *in Christ*. In Christ's drama of redemption, we are lead characters — heroes in Christ. God calls us to encourage one another to live out our new identity in Christ. So we trialogue with one another, "As you face this suffering, what difference could it make if you saw yourself the way Christ sees you and has made you: forgiven and reconciled sons and daughters (Rom. 5) and as empowered and victorious saints and spiritual conquerors (Rom. 8:31 – 39)?"

Satan attempts to blind us from Christ's past and current work in our lives. Helping one another to see Christ at work in us gives us confidence of his ongoing and future work on our behalf. So we trialogue with one another:

+ How has Christ already been giving you some victory in this area?
+ Tell me about some times when, through Christ's strength, you're already defeating some of these problems?
+ Have you ever struggled with anything like this before? How did you overcome it through Christ then? What could you take from that past victory and use now?
+ Who else in the body of Christ is on your side and in your corner as you work to overcome these struggles?

Gaining Christ-focused perspective like this helps people to gain hope. We need to see that we are not trying to solve our problems from a dead stop.

Sometimes in counseling it is not only our counselees who are "defeat-and-doubt focused." We can fall into the same snare of Satan. People share a time of victory, and we are clueless how to celebrate with them. Instead of missing great opportunities to expand about these victory narratives, we could respond with:

+ Wow! After all you've faced, you're still facing life with Christ. What does that say about who you really are in Christ?

+ What do these recent times of victory say about you and Christ?

Gospel-centered counselors should be more *opportunity-minded* than *problem-focused*. We want to help people to see that their future hope is greater than their past suffering, that God's healing is greater than their hurts, and that Christ's redemption is greater than their sins.

+ If you applied what you learned from those victorious times this past week, what would you do to work through this issue?

+ In light of that time of victory, what will you do differently this week?

As hope-focused counselors, we want to provoke ongoing action empowered by and glorifying to Christ.

Where We've Been and Where We're Headed

Here's our tweet-size summary of chapter 7.

+ The heart of healing involves journeying with people back to the heart of God.

We've started our healing journey through redemptive, relational mind and soul renewal where we've helped people to crop Christ back into the picture. We continue to help people to find *rest* in Christ through the healing relational competencies of encouraging communication, scriptural treatment planning, theo-dramatic spiritual conversations, and stretching scriptural explorations.

Maturing as a Biblical Counselor

Self-Counsel and Group or Partner Interaction

- If you are working through this material individually, then record your answers below.
- Think through an issue in your life where you desire to crop Christ back into the picture—where you need redemptive, relational mind and soul renewal. With a partner or your entire lab, use the outline below to work through the issue in your life through redemptive, relational mind and soul renewal.

1. With this issue, what would be involved in *taking your imagination captive to God's grand purpose?* A memorized scripture —

   a. With this issue, explore Christ's grand gospel narrative: *in what story do I find myself?* Martha and Mary

   b. With this issue, keep the vision vibrant by pondering: *what are God's redemptive purposes in this?* Rest in His care and purposes

2. With this issue, what would be involved in *putting off Satan's lying, works narrative?* It's not I that can make this happen as I want

   a. With this issue, *assess the dominant doubting-God theme in Satan's story.*

b. With this issue, *label the dominant doubting-God lie.*

He does not care about this, or your efforts

c. With this issue, *expose the root source of the doubting-God story.*

Zero attendance

3. With this issue, what would be involved in *putting on Christ's grace and truth narrative?*

Looking into the promises of God for encouragement + strength

a. With this issue, *coauthor cross narratives.*

Col 1:24-29

b. With this issue, *coauthor repentance-unto-life and weakness-into-strength narratives.*

II Cor 12:9
My grace is sufficient for you, for my power is made perfect in weakness

c. With this issue, *coauthor resurrection narratives.*

d. With this issue, *coauthor heroic-in-Christ narratives.*

who else in the body of Christ is on your side and in your corner as you work to overcome these struggles?

CHAPTER 8

Healing through Grace Narratives

In biblical healing, we are exploring the question, "How do we engage in grace narratives that heal faith in the good heart of God by offering hope that rests in Christ alone?" Martin Luther understood the importance of this question. Luther knew that the absence of faith in God during the presence of suffering leads to a terrified conscience that perceives God to be angry and evil instead of loving and good. He addressed these pangs of doubt with these words of counsel:

> It is not as reason and Satan argue: "See there God flings you into prison, endangers your life. Surely he hates you. He is angry with you; for if he did not hate you, He would not allow this thing to happen." In this way Satan turns the rod of a Father into the rope of a hangman and the most salutary remedy into the deadliest poison.[69]

For Luther, suffering was God's medicine of choice to wake us from our slumbering self-sufficiency and turn us to heightened Christ-sufficiency. Satan seeks to turn God's medicine into poison by causing us to doubt God's goodness and thus create a hemorrhage in our relationship with God. The Bible tells us that what people intend for evil, God weaves together for good (Gen. 50:20). Satan twists that around and tempts us to believe that what God intends for good is really evil — God is getting back at us instead of getting us back to him.

If Luther were counseling Emilio, he would be convinced that Emilio's core questions were, "Where is God in my suffering? Is he for me or against me?

Maturing as a Biblical Counselor

Self-Counsel and Group or Partner Interaction

1. Martin Luther believed that the absence of faith in God during the presence of suffering leads to a terrified conscience that perceives God to be angry and evil instead of loving and good.

   a. In what situation(s) in your life has Satan tempted you to believe that God was against you?

   b. How did you fight and overcome that temptation through Christ?

2. In counseling people who struggled to see the good hand and good heart of God, Luther wrote:

   > Oh, if we could only see the heart of Christ as he was suspended from the cross, anguishing to make death contemptible and dead for us.... If only a man could see his God in such a light of love ... how happy, how calm, how safe he would be! He would then truly have a God from whom he would know with certainty that all his fortunes—whatever they might be—had come to him and were still coming to him under the guidance of God's most gracious will.[70]

   a. How could this quote impact you as you face suffering in your life?

   b. What Scriptures come to mind that reflect, deepen, and further develop Luther's thoughts? How could you apply these passages to your life as you face suffering?

Has he abandoned me?" And Luther would be certain that only one relational reality could ever adequately answer Emilio's questions: *the Christ of the cross.* Listen to Luther's spiritual conversation with Frederick the Wise when Frederick was stricken with a terminal illness. Luther is teaching us a primary lesson of healing: *we care like Christ by journeying with people to the Christ of the cross.*

> Oh, if we could only see the heart of Christ as he was suspended from the cross, anguishing to make death contemptible and dead for us.... If only a man could see his God in such a light of love ... how happy, how calm, how safe he would be! He would then truly have a God from whom he would know with certainty that all his fortunes — whatever they might be — had come to him and were still coming to him under the guidance of God's most gracious will.[71]

T. G. Tappert in his work *Luther's Letters of Spiritual Counsel* proposed that Luther's soul care for suffering always sought to move people toward a gospel-centered, Christ-focused faith in God.

> In Luther's eyes, therefore, spiritual counsel is always concerned, above all else, with faith — nurturing, strengthening, establishing, practicing faith — because "faith cometh by hearing," the Word of God (or the Gospel) occupies a central place in it. The ministry to troubled souls is a ministry of the gospel. It is a ministry to those who have or who lack faith.[72]

We heal (nurture, strengthen, establish, practice) faith by pointing people to the cross of Christ. We care like Christ by pointing people to Christ. We bring healing hope through RESTS relational competencies:

- *R* Redemptive, Relational Mind and Soul Renewal
- *E* Encouraging Communication
- *S* Scriptural Treatment Planning
- *T* Theo-Dramatic Spiritual Conversations
- *S* Stretching Scriptural Explorations

In chapter 7, we introduced redemptive, relational mind and soul renewal, where we crop Christ back into the picture. We continue the healing journey with encouraging communication where together we celebrate the empty tomb.

Encouraging Communication:
Celebrating the Empty Tomb!

In our modern culture, our concept of "encouragement" is often decidedly shallow. "Buck up, you can get through this!" Or "Think positive thoughts and you can achieve your dreams!" Biblical encouragement is much deeper and richer, much more Christ-centered and other-focused.

I introduced redemptive, relational mind and soul renewal by exploring Hebrews 3 – 4. It is instructive to note that the entire discussion in Hebrews 3 – 4 revolves around unbelief or faith. "See to it, brothers, that none of you has a sinful, unbelieving heart that turns away from the living God. But encourage one another daily, as long as it is called Today, so that none of you may be hardened by sin's deceitfulness" (Heb. 3:12 – 13). That's a *biblical* description of the relational competency of encouraging communication.

Suffering enters our orbit. Satan tempts us to turn away from God. By pointing one another to our great High Priest, we step in and see to it that not a single brother or sister has an unbelieving heart that is deceived about God's good heart. Biblical encouragement doesn't say, "Buck up, buddy, you can get through this!" Biblical encouragement says, "Watch carefully, my friend, because Satan is trying to crop Christ out of your picture. Let's work together to drive a stake in the heart of Satan's lies so you can cling by faith to the good heart of God!"

> Encouraging biblical communication says, "Watch carefully, my friend, because Satan is trying to crop Christ out of your picture. Let's work together to drive a stake in the heart of Satan's lies so you can cling by faith to the good heart of God!"

Hebrews 10:19 – 25 communicates the same message. Here we read a call to encourage one another toward perseverance that is based on redemptive, relational mind and soul renewal. It is because "we have confidence to enter the Most Holy Place by the blood of Jesus" (Heb. 10:19) and since "we have a great priest over the house of God" (10:21) that we can "draw near to God" (10:22) and "hold unswervingly to the hope we profess" (10:23). And what is our duty to one another in the midst of suffering and in light of our redemption? "Let us consider how we may spur one another on toward love and good deeds. Let us not give up meeting together, as some are in the habit of doing, but let us encourage one another — and all the more as you see the Day approaching" (Heb. 10:24 – 25).

People come to us not so much with "stinking thinking," but with "shrunken narratives." That's why God's Word calls us to stretch people to the larger story — to the story of the God "who raises the dead" (2 Cor. 1:9). We do so through:

+ Stretching People to Christ-Focused Images of God, Self, and Others
+ Stretching People to the Eternal Story
+ Stretching People to See Life with Spiritual Eyes

Stretching People to Christ-Focused Images of God, Self, and Others

Emilio and Maria, like every person who has ever lived, seek to answer three vital identity questions:

+ What is my image of God?
+ What is my identity in Christ?
+ What do Christlike relationships with others look like?

These three questions are always vital. In the midst of suffering, they take on an air of urgency because Satan uses our suffering to challenge our confidence in who God is, who we are in Christ, and how we love others like Christ.

That's why biblical encouragement begins with stretching people to Christ-focused images of God, self, and others. The life and ministry of Vibia Perpetua illustrates encouraging communication. Perpetua is known as the first female martyr of the church. Barely over twenty, a mother of an infant child, the daughter of an unbelieving father, the wife of an absent husband, and a very recent convert to Christ, Perpetua is jailed and told that unless she recants her confession of faith made at her baptism, she will be killed.[73]

Refusing to recant, she is imprisoned. While in prison, Perpetua pens the story of her life.

On the first page she shares her purpose by explaining that her book was "Written expressly for God's honor and people's encouragement."[74] Even on her way to martyrdom, Perpetua answers the question, "What do Christlike relationships with others look like?" Her answer — Christlike relationships are focused on healing encouragement that glorifies God and ministers to others.

In a moment we'll learn how Perpetua's Christ-focused view of God and of herself empowered her to have this Christlike motivation in her relationships with others. But first, let's consider, as we are commanded to do in Hebrews 10:24 – 25, some interactions with Emilio and Maria that could spur them on toward love and good deeds. You've been climbing in the casket with them, you've been helping them to renew their minds redemptively and relationally, and now you trialogue with them:

- Sometimes couples going through a diagnosis of cancer can grow apart instead of closer together. Emilio and Maria, how can the two of you be each other's spiritual friend and encouragement partner as you go through this together?
- It's easy and even understandable to become self-focused and only family-focused as you face this. Yet, as we discussed, in Christ you are God's heroes. How can the two of you encourage one another to minister to others during this time? That would be heroic, wouldn't it!

Perpetua was able to maintain a focus of encouraging others because of her Christ-centered image of God. As she and her fellow converts were being marched to their death, they were witnessing to the crowd. We're told, "They were exhorting the people, warning them to remember the judgment of God."[75]

If anyone ever had an excuse to focus on *life is bad*, it was Perpetua. If anyone could be tempted to crop Christ out of the picture, at this moment it would have been Perpetua. Instead, she remembers the future and focuses on the *eternal character of God* — our *God of holy love* who guarantees that while in this life things can go horribly wrong and be terribly unjust, from God's perspective, all will be well. Like Perpetua and her band of brothers and sisters, we need to cling to our image of God's holy love — that he is simultaneously and continuously in control and caring, all-powerful and infinitely loving, above us and near us.

In suffering, Emilio and Maria, like all of us, are forced to face two great questions about God:

- "God, *do you care?*" — Questions about God's love.
- "God, *are you in control?*" — Questions about God's holiness.

Every problem of the soul includes a distorted, unbalanced answer to these two questions about God's infinitely perfect character. To know the God of peace and the peace of God, we must know God in the fullness of his *holy love*, in the perfection of his *affectionate sovereignty,* and in the beauty of who he is as *the Lion and the Lamb.*

Perpetua understood what Emilio and Maria needed to grasp deep in their hearts — that God cares (loving) and he is in control (holy). Perpetua grasped God's good heart because of the cross of Christ, "the event in which

God makes known his holiness and his love simultaneously, in one event, in an absolute manner." The cross "is the only place where the loving, forgiving merciful God is revealed in such a way that we perceive that his holiness and his love are equally infinite."[76] The Christ of the cross answers the question, "How can the holy love of God come to terms with the unholy lovelessness of man?"[77] The cross is where the kindness and severity of God meet. "Divine love triumphs over divine wrath by divine self-sacrifice."[78]

Perpetua understood and clung to her image of who she was *in Christ*. Toward the end of her life, others took over the writing of her life story. They describe her final moments. "Perpetua followed with a quick step as a true spouse of Christ, the darling of God, her brightly flashing eyes quelling the gaze of the crowd."[79]

On her way to death, with her eyes she shut the mouths of the boisterous pagan crowd. How? By clinging to the image of *who she was in Christ*. To them she was entertainment. To Christ she was the darling of God.

When Emilio and Maria are hurting, when Satan crops Christ out of the picture, we must remind them Whose they are: they belong to the God of holy love. And we must remind them who they are: in Christ they are the beloved of God. Paul prays in Ephesians 3 that the Ephesians, together with all the saints — and Emilio and Maria — grasp that they are *infinitely loved by their infinitely loving and holy God.*

Stretching People to the Eternal Story

Encouraging communications also stretch people to the eternal story. Ponder how Perpetua and her friends accomplished this. Perpetua's friend and fellow martyr, Felicitas, was pregnant. According to Roman law, she could not be executed until after her baby was born. Her fellow Christian martyrs hated that she would have to be martyred alone. Of them it was written, "Her friends were equally sad at the thought of abandoning such a good friend to travel alone on the same road to hope."[80] Felicitas joined them in praying that she would give birth early so that she could be executed with them. And that's exactly what occurred.

Amazing! Most of us would plead for every extra hour possible. Most of us would not perceive the road to death by the sword to be the *road to hope*. They did. And they perceived that in the body of Christ, we are to travel this road *together*, not alone.

Shirley and I experienced this truth recently. Two close friends who were struggling with deep grief left the sanctuary in the middle of our morning worship service. Noticing this, Shirley and I exited also. Meeting them in the foyer, we spent the next hour crying, praying, and sharing. Several times they told us, "We're so sorry you had to miss church." We kept responding, "We're not missing church; we are *doing* church. We are *being* the church together with you."

Perpetua, Felicitas, and their friends shared Paul's Romans 8 perspective that suffering today is not worthy of being compared to the glory that shall be revealed in heaven. *Eternal hope provides an eternal perspective.* Witnesses watching their final hours shared this testimony. "The day of their victory dawned, and with joyful countenances they marched from the prison arena *as though* on their way to heaven. If there was any trembling, it was from joy, not fear."[81]

The day of their *victory*? Only if one has an eternal perspective! They were able to weave in the eternal truth that we are more than conquerors through him who loves us so. Nothing shall ever separate us from the love of God in Christ — not even death.

Emilio and Maria need to know that they are not traveling alone on the road to hope. They need to know that they are more than conquerors. We need to help them to weave eternal truth into their temporal story by trialoguing about an eternal perspective.

Stretching People to See Life with Spiritual Eyes

In encouraging communication, spiritual friends stretch people to see life with spiritual eyes. Once again, Perpetua is our model. "But that noble woman stubbornly resisted even to the end. Perpetua was singing victory psalms *as if* already crushing the head of the Egyptian."[82]

We need more *as if* living. "As if" living looks at life with spiritual eyes, with faith eyes, and not with eyeballs only. It relates our final victory to our current battles. It does what Perpetua was able to do. It does what Elisha did. Remember the story? He and his servant are surrounded, vastly outnumbered by the enemies of God. Elisha, with spiritual eyes, sees that those who are with him are more than those who are with the enemy. His servant surely thought that Elisha had finally lost it. And then Elisha prays, "O Lord, open his eyes so he may see" (2 Kings 6:17).

We need to pray for Emilio and Maria, "Open the eyes of their heart, Lord." And we need to trialogue with them in ways that encourage them toward *as though* and *as if* living. Maybe it would sound something like this ...

"Emilio and Maria, we've just read 2 Kings 6:15 – 17. Elisha's servant was terrified because of the overwhelming odds against them. You've been honest about your situation and candid about your fears — and I'm so glad you have been. Elisha is saying to you, 'Don't be afraid. See with spiritual eyes the victory you have in God.' Christ is saying to you, 'Don't let your hearts be overwhelmed by trouble. You are more than conquerors in me.' What do you see when you look at your situation with spiritual eyes? How is your perspective different when you look at this diagnosis through the lens of faith? What does victory in this situation look like when you view it and perceive it through eternal glasses?"

Notice how encouraging communication uses God's Word to light our spiritual friends' paths. We tend to use the Scriptures like a floodlight that we shine directly *in* someone's eyes immediately after they have been wandering in the dark. What happens? They're shocked and become even more blinded. That's not how we use God's Word. Instead, it is a flashlight that we hold together to shine *on* their path so they can see with spiritual eyes God's comfort, encouragement, and direction along their healing journey — so they can know God as their *Parakaletic Encourager*.

Scriptural Treatment Planning: Pursuing Christlikeness

What are we trying to produce through our biblical counseling ministry? How could we describe the *aim, goal, purpose,* or *intended result* of our counseling? When we're sitting down with suffering people like Emilio and Maria, what do we hope the Spirit will accomplish through our personal ministry of the Word?

These are important questions not just for counselors, but for all those engaged in gospel ministry. Of course, there are various biblical ways to answer these questions, but I want to point our attention to Paul's words in Galatians 4:19 and Colossians 1:28 – 29: "My dear children, for who I am again in the pains of childbirth *until Christ is formed in you*" (emphasis added); "We proclaim him, admonishing and teaching everyone with all wisdom, *so that we may present everyone perfect in Christ. To this end* I labor, struggling with all his energy, which so powerfully works in me" (emphasis added).

Christlikeness is our ultimate goal in our intense labor as biblical counselors. But what does that look like? In chapter 2, I described it as *our inner life increasingly reflecting the inner life of Christ*. I noted that for us to move toward that goal, we must have a comprehensive scriptural understanding of the inner life, of the heart. Knowing who God designed us to be provides us with our target or goal in counseling. Figure 8.1 sketches the chambers of the heart. This summary portrait of the heart served in chapter 2 as our guide in trialoguing with people so that we could understand their situation and their soul. In this chapter, it serves as our guide as we develop scriptural treatment plans.

Maturing as a Biblical Counselor

Counseling Others

- Picture yourself counseling Emilio and Maria. You've been engaged in the sustaining/climbing in the casket process. You've been journeying with them in the healing process of redemptive, relational mind and soul renewal. In the "spaghetti relationship" of gospel-centered counseling, you are now engaged in encouraging communications.

1. Biblical encouragement says, "Watch carefully, my friend, because Satan is trying to crop Christ out of your picture. Let's work together to drive a stake in the heart of Satan's lies so you can cling by faith to the good heart of God!"

   a. How would this description of biblical encouragement impact how you interact with Emilio and Maria?

   I would be very watchful for indications

   b. How could this description of biblical encouragement impact our relationships at church, how our small groups function, our husband and wife relationships, etc.?

   Improved greatly

2. In stretching Emilio and Maria to Christ-focused images of God, self, and others:

   a. How could you help them to explore their image of God as a God of holy love—so they could grasp that they are infinitely loved by their infinitely loving and holy God?

   Reviewing Scripture

b. How could you help them to see themselves as beloved sons and daughters of God and as saints who are more than conquerors?

c. How could you help them to explore what it would look like for them, in the midst of their suffering, to encourage others toward love and good deeds?

3. In stretching Emilio and Maria to the eternal story, how could you weave (not in a preaching-at but in a trialogue-with way) eternal truth into their temporal story so that eternal hope provides them with an eternal perspective?

4. In encouraging communication, spiritual friends stretch people to see life with spiritual eyes. How could you help Emilio and Maria to relate their final victory to their current battle?

5. Encouraging communication uses God's Word to light our friends' paths. With Emilio and Maria, rather than using the Scripture like a floodlight that you shine directly in their eyes (preaching at them), how could you use Scripture as a flashlight that you all hold together (trialogue) to shine on their path so they can know God as their Encourager?

While it is essential that we understand who we are counseling and what they are going through, that's the beginning task of counseling, not the ultimate goal. In biblical counseling, our ultimate goal involves the whole Bible story impacting the whole person's whole story. We move from understanding who they are and what they're going through to helping them to relate Christ's gospel of grace to their life so that they become more like Christ in their inner being and their outer relationships. Thus scriptural treatment planning is so much more than altering the symptoms of a disease, promoting a more balanced personality, or exposing unconscious causes underlying surface

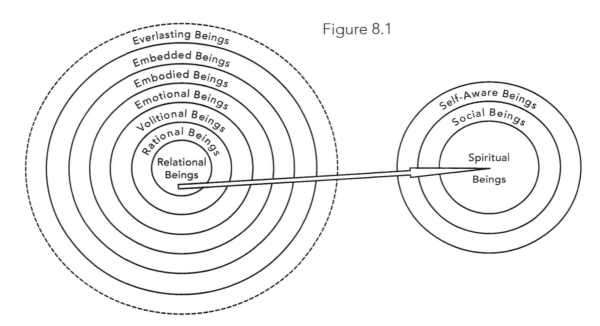

Figure 8.1

symptoms. Scriptural treatment planning cooperates with God in the process of sanctification. Biblical treatment empathizes with (sustaining), encourages (healing), exposes (reconciling), and empowers (guiding) Emilio and Maria so they move toward conformity to Christ. They come to love him more and reflect him better. Those are treatment plans and goals worth pursuing.

We could use figure 8.1 as an academic chart that we soullessly drape over people we are trying to analyze as we move them toward surface solutions. Or we can and should use the biblical portrait behind figure 8.1 as a relational map that we soulfully use to understand people, diagnose heart problems, and journey with people toward soul-u-tions — biblically and lovingly.

Scriptural treatment planning cooperates with God in the process of sanctification by empathizing with (sustaining), encouraging (healing), exposing (reconciling), and empowering (guiding) counselees so they move toward conformity with Christ.

When we're sitting in front of Emilio and Maria and the complexity and intensity overwhelm us, where do we focus? Often in a biblical counseling meeting we're wondering, "Where are we in the counseling process? Where should we go next?" We answer these questions by understanding the biblical view of the heart.

The Scriptures teach that people are everlasting, embedded, embodied, emotional, volitional, rational, relational, self-aware, social, and spiritual beings. This biblical reality provides the comprehensive map that we compassionately follow to help the whole person to put off living according to the old heart and to put on living according to the new Christlike heart.

Yes, biblical counseling is an art. However, we could make it so much art that we lose sight of the truth behind the art — the biblical truth about image bearers in a fallen world. Even the best artists follow a few aesthetic principles and obey a few basic rules of "design." So let's simplify and apply figure 8.1 by relating it to the biblical counseling process of sustaining, healing, reconciling, and guiding. It then becomes our map for eight scriptural treatment planning goals.

Our first focus is discipling people so their inner lives increasingly reflect the inner life of Christ. Our four heart-focused goals are:

- *Relational Heart Goal:* Increasingly loving God with their whole heart (spiritual), increasingly loving others deeply and sacrificially (social), and increasingly resting confidently in who they are in Christ (self-aware).

- *Rational Heart Goal:* Increasingly renewing their mind to view life from God's eternal perspective so Christ's gospel narrative impacts their life story.

- *Volitional Heart Goal:* Increasingly dying to self and living for God and others by pursuing God's purposes with the Holy Spirit's power for God's glory.

- *Emotional Heart Goal:* Increasingly experiencing life deeply and candidly as they soothe their soul in their Savior and manage their moods with a ministry focus.

Our second focus is to journey with people in the biblical counseling process of sustaining, healing, reconciling, and guiding people toward communion with Christ and conformity to Christ. Our four soul care and spiritual direction goals are:

- *Sustaining Heart Goal:* Empathizing with them by climbing in the casket so they know that "it's normal to hurt."
- *Healing Heart Goal:* Encouraging them by celebrating the empty tomb so they know that "it's possible to hope."
- *Reconciling Heart Goal:* Enlightening them by dispensing Christ's grace so they know that "it's horrible to sin but wonderful to be forgiven."
- *Guiding Heart Goal:* Empowering them by fanning into flame the gift of God within them so they know that "it's supernatural to mature."

These are the eight goals of heart-focused scriptural treatment planning. When counseling seems too complex and the "spaghetti relationships" get too messy, return mentally to these eight basic relational targets that God calls every biblical counselor to pursue.

There are some basic ways to keep focused and to drill these goals into our hearts as biblical counselors. They include:

- Biblical Counseling Treatment Plan Record Sheet (appendix 8.1)
- Biblical Counseling Ministry Disclosure Statement and Welcome Form (appendix 8.2)
- Biblical Counseling Self-Evaluation Form (appendix 8.3)
- Biblical Counseling Counselee Evaluation Form (appendix 8.4)
- Biblical Counseling Redeemed Personality Inventory (appendix 8.5)

Biblical Counseling Treatment Plan Record Sheet

See appendix 8.1 for the Biblical Counseling Treatment Plan Record Sheet. This front-back sheet keeps us on track toward biblical goals. Before meeting with a counselee, we can complete the top part of the front side of the sheet. It contains basic "client identification information" as well as our summary regarding where we might focus during this meeting based on our reflections from past meetings. It also has room to record our biblical counseling goals — thus enhancing mutuality in treatment planning.

We can use the middle part of the front page either during a meeting or immediately after (or both). We record here a synopsis of central points that arose and essential insights we gleaned during our meeting.

We can use the bottom of the front page to remind ourselves of directions we and our counselee determined to take between now and the next meeting. We can also begin to work on treatment plans for the upcoming week.

The back of the form uses the eight heart goals as a format for diagnosing how our counselee is doing and to plan treatment as we work with a counselee. Every meeting will not cover every area. We can highlight what was most pertinent, insightful, and moving. Over time, we can collate our records and plans, noting themes and movement on our counselee's path to Christlike maturity.

Biblical Counseling Disclosure Statement (Welcome Form)

See appendix 8.2 for the Disclosure Statement. People often ask, "Do you tell your counselees that these are your goals?" Absolutely. We work together, mutually. Also, ethical integrity demands a disclosure of treatment goals. One of the best ways to accomplish this is through the Biblical Counseling Disclosure Statement distributed and discussed during the first meeting.

This front-back form provides a sample Disclosure Statement explaining our approach and obtaining our counselee's commitment to work from a biblical counseling perspective. It is crucial to spend time explaining and discussing it at the start of a first meeting.

Biblical Counseling Self-Evaluation Form

Wise and humble biblical counselors often record themselves (with their counselee's permission). After recording, we can use the sample Biblical Counseling Self-Evaluation Form (see appendix 8.3) to evaluate ourselves using the eight biblical counseling goals.

The first page is more "quantitative." On it, we list the number of times we focused on a certain aspect of biblical counseling. This is especially helpful for beginning counselors to determine what their natural tendencies lean toward. Of course, some sessions will lend themselves more to sustaining, for instance. So it is important to track our focus over time — over several meetings with a counselee.

The second page of this two-sided form is more "qualitative." Here we evaluate not how many times, but how well we sense we are providing major aspects of biblical counseling. We can also use this form to have other people, like supervisors, professors, lab encouragement partners, and lab mentors, evaluate our counseling.

Biblical Counseling Counselee Evaluation Form

In appendix 8.4 you'll find a Biblical Counseling Counselee Evaluation Form. We can give this to a counselee to evaluate our counseling, especially at the end of our meeting together. This form uses the eight basic treatment goals to assess counseling relational competencies.

Biblical Counseling Redeemed Personality Inventory

The Biblical Counseling Redeemed Personality Inventory (see appendix 8.5) uses the categories of relational (spiritual, social, self-aware), rational, volitional, and emotional heart change as an assessment tool for our counselees to evaluate themselves. This is particularly helpful if used as a pre-evaluation and postevaluation. Counselees assess themselves in each category at the onset of counseling and then again at the end of formal counseling. This helps them to see areas where they are growing. It also helps us as the counselor to see areas where we have been helpful or other areas where we may want to continue to develop our biblical counseling competencies.

All of these forms are aids meant to help us to follow a scriptural treatment planning methodology in biblical counseling. They all are crafted around the eight goals of biblical counseling.

Theo-Dramatic Spiritual Conversations: Healing Theological Trialogues

In *Soul Physicians*, I describe the Bible as a theo-drama: Christ is the Protagonist or Hero, Satan is the antagonist or enemy, and our role as main characters in the drama of redemption is to trust God's good heart and to invite with our words and attract with our lives others to cling to Christ.[83] Theo-drama is another way of describing God's Word as a grand redemptive narrative, with an emphasis on the reality that the whole world is viewing our lives.

The apostle Paul says it like this:

> *Although I am less than the least of all God's people, this grace was given me: to preach to the Gentiles the unsearchable riches of Christ, and to make plain to everyone the administration of this mystery, which for ages past was kept hidden in God, who created all things. His intent was that now, through the church, the manifold wisdom of God should be made known to the rulers and authorities in the heavenly realms, according to his eternal purpose which he accomplished in Christ Jesus our Lord. (Ephesians 3:8–11)*

Self-Counsel and Group or Partner Interaction

1. Use the Biblical Counseling Self-Evaluation Form (appendix 8.3), both sides, to evaluate your biblical counseling.

   a. You can use it based on your most recent biblical counseling meeting (whether you have a recording or not, though a recording is most helpful). Or you can use it based on how you see your overall biblical counseling competencies at this point.

   b. Based on your self-assessment, what is your growth plan?

2. With your lab group, or with a your lab partner, use the Biblical Counseling Counselee Evaluation Form (appendix 8.4) to gain feedback on your biblical counseling.

   a. Seek feedback about your overall biblical counseling to this point.

   b. Based on the feedback, what is your growth plan?

Angelic forces stand on tiptoe to gain a glimpse at the church — at us, at our lives. As God accomplishes his eternal plan of redemption, the entire universe watches. We are the main actors and actresses in his drama of redemption. We have the privilege and responsibility to reveal God's good and gracious heart to all creation. When the final curtain draws back on all of history, we will be on stage declaring and celebrating the truth of Christ's victory narrative.

In sustaining, our spiritual conversations focus on joining our counselees in candor about their suffering as they move toward comfort in Christ. Our trialogues help our counselees to face their suffering *with* Christ.

Now, in healing, our counselees have turned to face Christ. Our theo-dramatic spiritual conversations focus on journeying with our counselees toward communion with Christ, leading to conformity to Christ that celebrates Christ. Our trialogues help our counselees to cling to Christ as their Encourager (communion), to respond to their suffering like Christ by loving God and others (conformity), and to worship and glorify Christ in the midst of their suffering (celebration).

> Theo-dramatic spiritual conversations focus on journeying with our counselees toward communion with Christ, leading to conformity to Christ that celebrates Christ.

With one foot pivoting in our counselee's earthly story, our other foot is pivoting in God's heavenly story. We merge the two realities through stretching our counselee to the scriptural story as we engage in healing trialogues — the bridge between two worlds.

Infusing Hope

Recall that people typically come to us with shrunken views of God, self, and others. Our theo-dramatic trialogues begin in hope-based interactions as we journey with our counselees from these shrunken views to Christ-focused views of God, self, and others.

+ *Concerning God:* From "Where are your great and precious promises when I really need them?" to "I am infinitely loved by the infinitely holy and loving Christ!"
+ *Concerning Self:* From "I don't have the resources to deal with these problems" to "I can do all things through Christ's resurrection power."

+ *Concerning Others:* From "They're all to blame" to "How can I love even my enemies with Christ's grace?"

From the outset of counseling, we can convey hope by communicating that people's problems are not bigger than Christ and his purposes, resources, and resurrection power. During a first meeting together, we can *combine empathy with encouragement*, engaging in trialogues such as:

+ You've experienced some deep hurts. I'm truly sorry for that. I'm also wondering how you have found the strength in Christ to face these struggles each day . . .

+ You've discussed several things that you have tried, and I sense some exasperation in your voice. In coming here, you've not only added a "second pair of eyes," you've added a brother (sister) in Christ who will help you to add God's perspective. So, already, you've taken a wise step that has changed the way you will handle these issues . . .

+ Though these issues may seem almost insurmountable to you, I believe that through Christ, you can do all things. You can change no matter how entrenched the patterns seem. What goes through your mind as you hear me say those words?

+ These are hard issues. They've grown over time. However, with your commitment and God's resources, we can see lasting changes. Would it be okay if I prayed for you right now, asking God to fill you with his hope, love, faith, and power?

Encouraging Progress and Responsibility

Hope in Christ is more than a feeling. It is a conviction that should motivate action. Hope should lead to progressive sanctification — growth in Christ. Throughout our meetings and especially at the end of sessions, we help our counselees to pursue Christ-empowered change through trialogues like:

+ *Relational/Spiritual:* As you leave here today and as you're making progress, how will you be relating to Christ differently? Seeing Christ differently? Depending on his power more?

+ *Relational/Social:* As you leave here today and as you're making progress, how will you be relating to others differently — in a more Christlike way?

+ *Relational/Self-Aware:* As you leave here today and as you're making progress, how will you be seeing yourself differently in Christ?

+ *Rational:* As you leave here today and as you're making progress, how will you be thinking differently — with the mind of Christ?

+ *Volitional:* As you leave here today and as you're making progress, what will you be doing differently? How will your goals and purposes be more like Christ in Philippians 2:1 – 5?

+ *Emotional:* As you leave here today and as you're making progress, how will you manage your moods differently? Soothe your soul in your Savior?

We always want to link growth to Christ's power so that counselees are Christ-sufficient and not self-sufficient. When counselees report good news, celebrate and respond with trialogues like:

+ That's awesome! How have you been cooperating with Christ to change your mind-set about who God is to you in the midst of your suffering?

+ That is so great! How have you been tapping into Christ's resurrection power so that you've been able to live out Philippians 2:1 – 5 like that?

Encouraging Communion with Christ

In sustaining, our spiritual conversations revolve around helping counselees like Emilio and Maria to honestly face life by admitting, "Life is bad. It's normal to hurt." In healing, our spiritual conversations revolve around helping Emilio and Maria to face life face-to-face with Christ by acknowledging, "God is good. It's possible to hope." Some sample trialogues could include:

+ What are you longing for from God right now? If Christ were to walk into the room right now, what would you want from him?

+ What would it be like to worship God in the middle of this? What would it be like for you to turn to Christ in the middle of this? How is all of this helping you to cling to Christ, to depend on him, to hunger and thirst for him?

+ What would it look like for you to rest in God right now? For you to surrender to God? To trust instead of work, to wait instead of demand?

We understand the battle for who will capture the heart — Christ or Satan. To help Emilio and Maria to face that battle, we trialogue in ways that expose the truth that God is good even when life is bad.

+ If you had one word or image to describe God right now, what would it be?

+ If Christ were in this chair, what do you think you would be talking about? What would you want to ask, say, or do? What do you imagine him saying or doing?

+ God is all-powerful, holy, and in control of everything. He's loving, fatherly, accepting, gracious, and good. What impact do these characteristics of God have on you as you face this?

+ Tell me how it impacts you to know that Christ is suffering with you right now. That he is praying for you now.

+ In the middle of this, how do you relate to the image of God as your loving Father?

+ God promises to work all things together for good for his children. What are your thoughts about his promise? What do you think about that passage now?

+ What good purposes has God already provided to you or in you through these events?

Encouraging Conformity to Christ

Communion with Christ in suffering results in conformity to Christ as we handle suffering. Here are some sample trialogues to help Emilio and Maria to respond to suffering in a Christlike way.

+ Picture Christ going through what you're going through. How do you imagine him handling this?

+ How have you been able to cooperate with God's grace to show such patience during all of this? Such love? Grace? Endurance? Hope? Strength?

+ Wow! That's amazing. I'm so impressed with your attitude. Tell me how you've learned to handle this. How are you able to display that fruit of the Spirit? Keep your mind on Christ?

- Who do you suppose is watching you and wondering, "How's she/he doing this?" What would you tell them?
- We've talked about how the "whole world is watching" when God's child suffers. They're watching to see if God's heart is trustworthy. What message do you want to send?

We could introduce the theo-drama imagery to Emilio and Maria and then coauthor a heroic narrative that honors Christ.

- Why do you think the two of you were you chosen for this journey?
- What unique gifts do you each bring?
- Who is the enemy here?
- Who are your comrades in arms? Fellow pilgrims? How could you work together?
- Tell me how you fight to maintain the faith perspective that God is faithful.
- Tell me about the future you hope for. Write the end of the book for me and tell me how the story ends.

Stretching Scriptural Explorations: Healing Biblical Trialogues

We use Scriptures in sustaining to encourage people to face their troubling story with courageous integrity. In healing, we use Scriptures to encourage people to face their faith story with hope in Christ. Stretching scriptural explorations relate God's truth to our counselee's life to encourage them to apply Christ's story of hope to their story of hurt.

> Stretching scriptural explorations relate God's truth to our counselee's life to encourage them to apply Christ's story of hope to their story of hurt.

The process of stretching scriptural explorations is the same as with sustaining, however the focus differs. Now we explore Scriptures (and they are vast) that produce a trialogue that confirms that it's possible to hope because God is good even when life is bad. We stretch our counselees from their shrunken smaller story perspective to Christ's larger, eternal perspective.

Counseling One Another

- If you are working through this material individually, then respond to the following theo-dramatic trialogues in writing.

- If you are working through this material in a lab small group, then with the entire group, or with a lab partner, or with the lab facilitator counseling one group member, or with a lab member counseling another lab member, use the following theo-dramatic trialogues as a starting place for giving and receiving biblical counsel.

1. Thinking about a situation you are facing where you want to find Christ's healing hope, how have you found the strength in Christ to face this situation each day?

   By remembering and reminding myself about the promises that God has made to help me. ie. I Jn 1:9

2. Picture Christ going through what you're going through. How do you imagine him handling this?

   With confidence and faith in a good wise & loving Father

3. God is all-powerful, holy, and in control of everything. He's loving, fatherly, accepting, gracious, and good. What impact do these characteristics of God have on you as you face this?

   Gives me a powerful hope to face the trial

4. What would it be like to worship God in the middle of this? What would it be like for you to turn to Christ in the middle of this?

   Strengthening   Encouraging and But maybe hard at first to take your eyes off of yourself

5. As you face this situation, leave here today, and as you're making progress:

   a. How will you relate to Christ differently? See Christ differently? Depend on his power more?

b. How will you relate to others differently—in a more Christlike way?

Yes, with more grace + patience

c. How will you see yourself differently in Christ?

d. How will you think differently—with the mind of Christ?

e. What will you be doing differently? How will your goals and purposes be more like Christ in Philippians 2:1–5?

f. How will you manage your moods differently? How will you soothe your soul in your Savior?

A Sample Pattern for Scriptural Explorations

Remember the model from sustaining: explore together a relevant biblical narrative or character. Then explore the implications and applications.

- How do you react to this biblical story/psalm/passage?
  - How is it different from your situation? How is it similar?
  - How have you been responding differently? Similarly?
  - What in this story/psalm/passage would you like to add to your story? How do you think you could do that?

- Imagine writing your own story, somewhat like this biblical story/ psalm/passage.
  - What role would God play in your story?
  - What would your relationship to God be like?
  - What role would you play in your story?
  - Who else might be in your story?
  - Are there any characters in this story who remind you of any people in your life?
  - What would the theme of your story be?
  - How would God work your story out for good?
  - How would God give you strength in your story?

Since we want to empower our counselees rather than always directing them to a particular passage that we think is relevant, we can ask:

- What passages have deepened your relationship with God?
- What passages have you found helpful in gaining a new perspective on your situation?
- What Scripture have you found helpful in gaining encouragement and hope as you go through this?

A Biblical Sampler for Stretching Scriptural Explorations

Picture Ashley again (see chapter 6). You've empathized with her deep, dark casket of sexual abuse. And you've helped her to face her own casket by exploring with her 2 Samuel 13. Over the course of many weeks of counseling, you've been moving through the biblical healing process. You've asked her about passages that the Lord has been using in her life to bring her healing hope, and she mentions Isaiah 61. So you begin to trialogue ...

"What are some of the most powerful aspects of that passage for you, Ashley?"

"Right from the beginning I was struck by the phrase, 'The Spirit of the Sovereign LORD ...' (Isa. 61:1). You've mentioned several times 'God's affectionate sovereignty,' and I see in this passage both God's love/affection and his power/sovereignty."

"Where are some of the places you see that?" you ask.

Opening her Bible to the well-worn pages of Isaiah 61, Ashley responds,

"When it says, 'He has sent me to bind up the brokenhearted, to proclaim freedom for the captives and release from darkness for the prisoners, to proclaim the year of the Lord's favor and the day of vengeance of our God, to comfort all who mourn' (Isa. 61:1 – 2). It reminds me of the passage we looked at two weeks ago, Isaiah 40:10 – 11, where God is both the Sovereign Shepherd who is all-powerful and the Good Shepherd who is all-loving. In both passages, God takes care of the abusers — with justice — and takes care of the abused — with gentleness."

"That's a great connection," you remark. "Tell me more about how those two passages impact you, Ashley."

"It was like Christ wrote Isaiah 61:3 just for me. 'And provide for those who grieve in Zion — to bestow on them a crown of beauty instead of ashes, the oil of gladness instead of mourning, and a garment of praise instead of a spirit of despair.'"

Ashley stops, quietly reflects.

You share, "So, you can read it, "I, the Sovereign Lord provide *for Ashley*, who grieves in Chicago, a crown of beauty instead of ashes ...'"

"Absolutely!" Ashley replies.

"I'm struck, Ashley," you continue, "with the phrase 'a garment of praise instead of ... despair.' It was just a few weeks ago we were talking about Tamar's desolation and despair and how you could so powerfully identify with Tamar. And now you are identifying with those in Israel who are comforted and who are praising God. That's amazing. How did Christ carry you to that place?"

Ashley pauses, reflects. "I know a lot of it has to do with another verse in Isaiah that we've discussed. I think Isaiah is becoming my new 'go-to' book! Where it says that in all our distress God too was distressed (Isa. 63:9). I used to keep asking, 'Where was God when I was being abused?' Now I know he suffered with me. And, as we've discussed several times, the ultimate picture that proves that is Christ on the cross. Christ suffers *for* my sin and he suffers *with* me when I'm sinned against. Wow."

Ashley stops. Cries. You cry with her.

After a moment, the two of you celebrate together God's goodness — his good heart. You also spend more time talking about what "beauty instead of ashes" means for Ashley — a conversation that you will return to in future meetings.

Then the two of you pick up where Ashley left off in Isaiah 61. You ask, "Tell me about how the last part of verse 3 'hits you.' 'They will be called oaks of righteousness, a planting of the Lord for the display of his splendor' (Isa. 61:3)."

"Well," Ashley responds, "to think that not too many months ago, I wasn't even 'on speaking terms' with God, and I thought he had no use for me, and now he wants to use me and I want to be used to display his splendor! That's amazing!"

"That is amazing, Ashley," you respond. Several thoughts are going through your mind. One is, how has Ashley been tapping into Christ's resurrection power to move from not speaking *to* God to now speaking *on behalf of God*? The other is, what are some specific ways God is using Ashley to display his splendor? "Could we talk about that?" you ask.

Notice throughout the trialogue how the focus remained on drawing out and stretching Ashley in a process the Holy Spirit had already begun in her heart — healing hope. Ashley's ability to understand and apply God's Word was respected and affirmed. The counselor's role was to join the healing journey that God's Spirit was taking Ashley on through God's Word.

Where We've Been and Where We're Headed

Here's our tweet-size summary of chapter 8.

- We care like Christ by journeying with people to the Christ of the cross.

A shift is coming: from sustaining and healing for suffering to reconciling and guiding for sinning, from biblical soul care to biblical spiritual direction. But remember — all our relational competencies are beneficial for every aspect of the counseling relationship. As we move forward, we'll build on GRACE and RESTS competencies as we help our counselees with two new sets of relational competencies: PEACEE and FAITH.

Maturing as a Biblical Counselor

Counseling Others

1. Using Romans 8, write out a sample trialogue conversation where you engage with a counselee in using the passage to bring healing hope through stretching scriptural explorations.

2. Using 2 Corinthians 4, write out a sample trialogue conversation where you engage with a counselee in using the passage to bring healing hope through stretching scriptural explorations.

6 RECONCILING BIBLICAL COUNSELING COMPETENCIES: PEACEE

PEACEE

Some approaches to counseling focus on suffering and stop there. Others highlight sin and ignore suffering. Gospel-centered counseling addresses both with grace: the evils we have suffered and the sin we have committed. Thus far we've focused on *parakaletic* biblical soul care through sustaining and healing, which focuses on the pain in the soul when we are sinned against. Moving forward, we'll focus on *nouthetic* biblical spiritual direction through reconciling and guiding, which deals with the sin in the heart when we are sinning against God and others.

In chapters 9 and 10, we learn and practice the six skills of reconciling biblical counseling. Here are the student-oriented learning objectives (SOLOs) that will be our target in the healing process.

Active participants in the reading and application of chapters 9–10 will be able to:

+ Expose sin and grace so people see the truth of their adulterous hearts and then see the greater truth of Christ's amazing grace (chapter 9).
+ Be ambassadors of reconciliation who dispense grace by communicating that it's horrible to sin but wonderful to be forgiven (chapter 9).
+ Develop the reconciling relational competency of probing theologically — examining the heart biblically (chapter 9).
+ Develop the reconciling relational competency of exposing heart sins — confronting lovingly and wisely (chapter 9).
+ Develop the reconciling relational competency of applying truth relationally — connecting intimately (chapter 10).
+ Develop the reconciling relational competency of calming the conscience with grace — dispensing grace (chapter 10).
+ Develop the reconciling relational competency of enlightening spiritual conversations — reconciling theological trialogues (chapter 10).
+ Develop the reconciling relational competency of empowering scriptural explorations — reconciling biblical trialogues (chapter 10).

If you are working through *Gospel Conversations* with a group of people, then to meet these learning objectives, you will want to do the following prior to meeting with your small group training lab:

- Chapter 9: Reconciling through Dispensing Grace
  - Read pages 237 to 265.
  - Respond to all questions on pages 239, 243, 255 – 57, and 264 – 65.
  - Read, meditate on, and study Jeremiah 2:11; Romans 5:20 – 6:2; 2 Corinthians 5:17 – 21; 7:8 – 13; Ephesians 4:17 – 19; 2 Timothy 2:22 – 26; Titus 2:11 – 12; and James 4:1 – 4.
  - Optional: Read chapters 8 – 9 of *Gospel-Centered Counseling*.
- Chapter 10: Reconciling through Grace-Maximizing
  - Read pages 267 to 292.
  - Respond to all questions on pages 268, 276 – 77, 281, 287, and 291 – 92.
  - Read, meditate on, and study Hosea 14; Romans 5:1 – 11; 2 Corinthians 2:7 – 11; 6:11 – 13; Hebrews 3:12 – 14; 4:12 – 13; 10:24 – 25.
  - Optional: Read chapters 11 – 12 of *Gospel-Centered Counseling*.

CHAPTER 9

Reconciling through Dispensing Grace

Recall Ashley and the redemptive work that God is doing in her life as she faces her past sexual abuse. Thus far our focus with Ashley has been on her being sinned against. We've climbed in the casket with her as the heat of suffering seeks to drain the life out of Ashley. When scorched by the sun, we've journeyed with Ashley to the Son, who resurrects her hope.

It might seem like a major shift in our counseling with Ashley to move from counseling for suffering to counseling for sinning. However, both are grace focused, sanctification oriented, and compassion filled. Counseling for suffering and sin are also both reality based. Which of us, when facing suffering, has not experienced the temptation to turn away from God in self-sufficiency and to turn inward in our relationships with others in self-centeredness and self-protection?

Additionally, counseling for suffering and sin are both respect-based. We respect Ashley as a suffering daughter of God as we join with her in her troubling story by honoring her pain (sustaining) and as we journey with her in her faith story by honoring her trust in Christ (healing). We also respect Ashley as a new creation in Christ as we join with her in Christ's redemptive story by honoring her capacity to apply the gospel to her temptations (reconciling) and as we journey with her in her grace-in-growth story by honoring her God-implanted desire and power to become more like Christ (guiding).

Maturing as a Biblical Counselor

Self-Counsel and Group or Partner Interaction

- We're moving into a difficult but vital aspect of biblical counseling—talking about personal sin.

1. Why is it easier for many of us to talk about our suffering (about how others have sinned against us) than it is to talk about our own sin?

2. Think back to a time when someone confronted you about sin in an unhelpful way that turned you off and pushed you away from God. What was it about how the person related and talked to you that was unhelpful?

3. Recall a time when someone talked to you about sin in your life in a helpful way that encouraged you to confess your sin and find God's forgiveness. What was it about how the person related and talked with you that was helpful?

4. What is your tendency when you become aware of sin in your life? Do you ignore it, do you become overwhelmed by guilt and despair, or do you confess it and find newness of life in Christ's gracious forgiveness?

Gospel-Centered Biblical Counseling through Reconciling and Guiding

We empathized deeply, connected compassionately, and encouraged Ashley with Christ's healing hope, and she is now sensitive to the work of God in her heart. While we make it plain to Ashley that she was *not* guilty of or responsible for having been abused, we also lovingly and humbly explore with Ashley any possible sinful ways she may be responding to her abuse. We refuse to victimize the victim, but we also refuse to see Ashley simply as a victim. We see her as an active agent and a victor in Christ who can respond to the unholiness of having been abused with the holiness of becoming more like Christ.

In reconciling and guiding, we journey with Ashley toward God's eternal purpose for her. God's mission in the world is to save unholy people and sanctify them. As J. I. Packer explains, "In reality, holiness is the goal of our redemption. As Christ died in order that we may be justified, so we are justified in order that we may be sanctified and made holy."[84]

The Greek word *noutheteo* captures our ministry to Ashley as she victoriously overcomes temptation (reconciling) and becomes more like Christ (guiding). I translate *noutheteo* as *confronting by exposing sin* and *grace out of concern for heart change*. Because we care, and because we know that Ashley was created to be like Christ, we seek to join with the Holy Spirit in enlightening Ashley when she's veered off track and equipping Ashley to get back on track toward Christlikeness.

In helping Ashley through her suffering, she comes to understand that *God is good even when life is bad*. She's able to defeat Satan's lie that *in suffering God is getting back at us*. Now, by grace, she hopes in Christ.

In helping Ashley through her battles with temptation and sin, she comes to understand that *God is gracious even when we are sinful*. She's able to defeat Satan's lie that *God turns his back on us when we turn our back on him*. Now, by grace, she becomes more like Christ.

The grace that saves Ashley is also the grace that changes Ashley.

For the grace of God that brings salvation has appeared to all men [salvation grace]. It teaches us to say "No" to ungodliness and worldly passions, and to live self-controlled, upright and godly lives in this present age [sanctification grace]. (Titus 2:11 – 12)

Robust biblical reconciling and guiding involves *exposing the horrors of sin* and *enlightening to the wonders of Christ's grace while empowering people to apply the supernatural power of Christ's grace to mature them into Christ's likeness*.

Reconciling: Dispensers of Grace

In reconciling, we communicate, *"It's horrible to sin, but wonderful to be forgiven!"* Notice the vital twofold nature of reconciling — it enlightens people to sin *and* to grace. God calls us to be ambassadors of reconciliation (2 Cor. 5:20) who live by and minister according to the reality that where sin abounds, grace super-abounds (Rom. 5:20).

Biblical counselors are *dispensers of grace.* Just as you think about "climbing in the casket" and "celebrating the empty tomb" as summary portraits of sustaining and healing respectively, so when you think about reconciling, picture the summary image of "dispensers of grace." Grace is God's medicine of choice for our disgrace. Biblical counselors give their counselees grace. We dazzle them with grace — with the message of God's holy love that convicts, forgives, welcomes home, renews, and empowers.

Our Need for Grace

Saying that we are dispensers of grace does not mean that we are ignorers of sin. Immediately after the apostle Paul explained that "where sin increased, grace increased all the more" (Rom. 5:20), he addressed a rhetorical question. "What shall we say, then? Shall we go on sinning so that grace may increase?" (Rom. 6:1). Paul's answer: "By no means!" (Rom. 6:2). That's why ambassadors of reconciliation must include the mind-set and the phrase "It's horrible to sin!"

But what makes sin so horrible? Sin is a relational breach where we experience alienation from God because of our spiritual adultery and where we experience separation from one another because of our spiritual self-centeredness. Historically, reconciling has always comprised this dual element: the vertical, our relationship with God; and the horizontal, our relationship with one another. This parallels the greatest commandments — loving God with all our heart and loving one another as we love ourselves.

Sin against God is not just a thief caught in a crime; sin is an adulterer caught in the act. Sin is choosing to love anyone or anything more than God.

And once we turn our hearts away from God — our only satisfying, thirst-quenching, peace-giving spring of living water — we inevitably must turn *to* one another. We worship the creature instead of the Creator (Rom. 1:25). We turn to one another as our substitute gods, and since we are not god, we must fail one another. We are all broken cisterns that can hold no water

(Jer. 2:13). We then turn *on* one another — we kill and we covet; we retaliate and manipulate (James 4:1 – 4).

In relationship to God, sinners are rebellious prodigal children and adulterous wayward spouses. In relationship to one another, sinners are relational murderers and manipulators. That's what's so horrible about sin.

Our Need for Ambassadors of Reconciliation

What makes sin so difficult to defeat is its deceitfulness (Heb. 3:13). Our sin leads us to suppress the truth of our adultery against God and our killing and coveting of one another (Rom. 1:18). After repeated self-deception and truth-suppression, our hearts begin to become hardened and habituated in unbelief (Heb. 3:12 – 13) and our thinking becomes futile and darkened in spiritual blindness (Rom. 1:21).

Unless we respond to conviction from the Word of God, the Spirit of God, and the people of God, we can begin to live according to the pattern of our former unregenerate selves (Eph. 4:17). Darkened in our understanding and separated from the life of God, our hard hearts lose all sensitivity to spiritual reality as we give ourselves over to sensuality to indulge in every kind of impurity with a continual lust for more (Eph. 4:18 – 19).

That is why we need the Holy Spirit — our Divine Counselor who convicts us of guilt in regard to sin, righteousness, and judgment (John 16:8 – 11). That is why we need the Word that exposes and reveals the thoughts and motives of the heart (Heb. 4:12 – 13). And that is why we need the body of Christ — brothers and sisters who see to it that "none of [us] has a sinful, unbelieving heart that turns away from the living God" (Heb. 3:12). And who encourage us daily so that none of us become "hardened by sin's deceitfulness" (Heb. 3:13).

Sustaining is drawing a line in the sand of retreat as we join with sufferers in their suffering. Healing is driving a stake in the heart of Satan's lies and clinging by faith to the good heart of God as we journey with sufferers to Christ. Reconciling is *seeing the truth of my adulterous heart and then seeing the greater truth of Christ's amazing grace.*

Ambassadors of reconciliation engage in redemptive friendships where we dispense Christ's grace to one another, enlightening each other to the truth that it's horrible to sin but wonderful to be forgiven. We center our reconciling message in God coming to retrieve spiritual adulterers. We are in fearful flight from God; God is in passionate pursuit of us. Satan hisses that "God would never forgive and receive an adulterer like *you!*" If we listen to him, if we believe his lie, then we turn away from God, turn on each other, and turn inward toward self-sufficiency, self-trust, self-centeredness, and self-protection. Gospel conversations invite us back to our original shape — turned upward to God and turned outward toward one another.

Ambassadors of reconciliation whisper, "Peace." We remind one another that we have confidence to enter the very presence of God by the blood of Jesus. We have boldness to draw near to God with a sincere heart in full assurance that our Father welcomes the prodigal home and our Spouse welcomes the adulterer home. We're at peace because our guilty conscience has been forgiven and cleansed so that we can hold on to hope because we are held securely by our faithful Father and Husband (Heb. 10:19 – 23).

At peace with God once again, we ponder how we can spur one another on toward love and good deeds — toward loving God and loving one another. We meet together regularly to habitually encourage one another to persevere in pursuing Christ and becoming like Christ (Heb. 10:24 – 25).

Reconciling Relational Competencies: PEACEE

Six reconciling relational competencies are instrumental in helping people find Christ's peace. I define these reconciling relational competencies in several overlapping ways:

- Engaging in redemptive friendships as ambassadors of reconciliation where we dispense grace to one another in the redemptive story.

- Enlightening one another to the twin truths that it's horrible to sin but wonderful to be forgiven.

- Joining with people in Christ's redemptive story by honoring their redeemed capacity to apply the gospel to their temptation and sin.

- Loading the conscience with guilt and lightening the conscience with grace.

- Exposing sin and grace so people see the truth of their adulterous hearts and then see the greater truth of Christ's amazing grace.

Maturing as a Biblical Counselor

Self-Counsel and Group or Partner Interaction

• You want to help your counselees to experience how horrible it is to sin and how wonderful it is to be forgiven. But how about *you*? Is your heart soft to the convicting, exposing ministry of the Spirit of God, Word of God, and the people of God? How well do you receive God's forgiveness—experience his grace? How are you accepting your acceptance? Read Psalms 32 and 51—Psalms of Repentance, Return, and Reconciliation. Then respond to the questions below, applying God's conviction and forgiveness to your life.

1. What are some of the phrases from these two psalms that stand out to you? Why?

2. What sins is the Spirit of God through the Word of God exposing in your life?

3. What is it like for you when you confess your sin and realize that God has wiped your slate clean?

4. Write about a time when God gave you a fresh start.

5. When is the last time you penned a psalm of confession and restoration? What was it like? What would it sound like to pen one now?

6. Spend some time praising God for his generous love and amazing grace.

> Reconciling involves exposing sin and grace so people see the truth of their adulterous hearts and then see the greater truth of Christ's amazing grace.

As with sustaining and healing, it is relatively easy to define reconciling relational competencies, but it takes a lifetime to cultivate them. Over the course of the next two chapters, we'll learn and practice six biblical counseling competencies for reconciling — competencies that I summarize using the acronym *PEACEE*:

- *P* Probing Theologically
- *E* Exposing Heart Sins
- *A* Applying Truth Relationally
- *C* Calming the Conscience with Grace
- *E* Enlightening Spiritual Conversations
- *E* Empowering Scriptural Explorations

Probing Theologically: Examining the Heart Biblically

As we've seen, Hebrews 3:12 – 19 commands us to see to it that no brother or sister in Christ has a sinful, unbelieving heart that turns away from the living God. Hebrews 10:24 – 25 commands us to ponder how to provoke one another to pursue love and good deeds. The reconciling relational competency of probing theologically obeys these commands.

In *A Theology of Christian Counseling*, Jay Adams notes that "all counselors have one goal in common: change." And all counselors "use verbal means to bring about the change."[85] All biblical counseling focuses on helping people to increasingly reflect the image of Christ by speaking, living, and interacting about gospel truth in love.

The modern biblical counseling movement is convinced that God has not placed our sanctification — our growth in Christlike relating, thinking, choosing, and feeling — in the hands of trained and paid professionals. God's plan is that the faithful ministry of every part grows the body into the mature image of Christ.[86]

Let's think about this change process logically and theologically. In order to understand how Christ changes people, we first need to understand who we are and Whose we are. We need to understand people biblically — God's original design for the soul.

Second, before we can understand how Christ changes people, we need to understand why people do what they do. Before we can expose sin, we have to be aware of the nature of sin.

And before we can become aware of sin, we have to ponder and probe what went wrong. We need to diagnose problems biblically — diagnostic categories of sin.

To help us to understand who we are and *Whose* we are, in chapters 6 – 7 of *Gospel-Centered Counseling*, I develop a detailed biblical understanding of image bearers. It follows the four chambers of the heart that I introduced in chapter 2 of *Gospel Conversations*. God designed us as:

- ✦ E: Emotional Beings: Experiencing with Depth — Mood States
- ✦ V: Volitional Beings: Choosing with Courage — Purposes/Pathways
  - ✦ V1: Volitional Being Actions/Behaviors
  - ✦ V2: Volitional Being Heart Motivations
- ✦ RT: Rational Beings: Thinking with Wisdom — Mind-Sets
  - ✦ RT1: Rational Being Beliefs
  - ✦ RT2: Rational Being Images
- ✦ RL: Relational Beings: Loving with Passion — Affections
  - ✦ SA: Self-Aware Being: Conscience/Shalom
  - ✦ SO: Social Being: Community/Fellowship
  - ✦ SP: Spiritual Being: Communion/Worship[87]

To help us to understand what went wrong, in chapters 8 – 9 of *Gospel-Centered Counseling*, I develop a detailed biblical diagnosis of sin in the heart. It probes the four chambers of our sin-sick heart:

- ✦ Fallen Heart Chamber #1: Relational Corruption — Spiritual Adulterers
- ✦ Fallen Heart Chamber #2: Rational Corruption — Heart Idolaters
- ✦ Fallen Heart Chamber #3: Volitional Corruption — Enslaved Destroyers
- ✦ Fallen Heart Chamber #4: Emotional Corruption — Ungoverned Users[88]

An MRI of Our Sin-Sick Heart

To understand how Christ changes people, we first need to understand how sin changes people. Imagine Adam and Eve seconds before the Fall and seconds after. They are the same people, yet totally different.

Before the Fall, they *relate passionately and live in God-dependence* by sacrificing themselves to care for each other and for God's creation — enjoying and exalting God with every breath. After the Fall, everything changes. They *relate selfishly and live self-sufficiently* as they protect themselves by blaming God, one another, and the serpent, as they cover themselves with fig leaves, and as they worship the creature rather than their Creator — they are *spiritual adulterers* (fallen heart chamber #1).

Before the Fall, they *think wisely* by envisioning God as good and seeing with spiritual eyes God's beautiful plan — thinking God's thoughts after him. After the Fall, they *think foolishly and arrogantly* by concluding that their heavenly Father fails to know best and withholds his best and by imagining that their greatest pleasure could be in anything other than God — they are *heart idolaters* (fallen heart chamber #2).

Before the Fall, they *choose courageously* by moving toward one another in total openness and by guarding the garden for God's glory — submitting their wills to God's will. After the Fall, they *choose self-protectively and compulsively* by following a fallen nature enslaved to sin and by pursuing what they mistakenly perceive to be most pleasing — they are *enslaved destroyers* (fallen heart chamber #3).

Before the Fall, they *experience deeply* by feeling their loneliness when apart ("it is not good to be alone") and their joy when together and by enjoying the fullness of life offered by God and one another — experiencing all of life face-to-face with God. After the Fall, they *experience fleshly and shallowly* by running from their fears instead of racing to their forgiving Father, by hiding and suppressing their shame instead of crying out to their Father, and by consuming and using others for their own gain — they are *ungoverned users* (fallen heart chamber #4).

With this theological summary in place, we're now prepared to define the relational competency of probing theologically. Probing theologically involves using a biblical understanding of people and a biblical diagnosis of sin to see to it that no one is hardened by sin's deceitfulness.

> Probing theologically involves using a biblical understanding of people and a biblical diagnosis of sin to see to it that no one is hardened by sin's deceitfulness.

Theologically Guided Ponderings

Picture yourself counseling Ashley. In the spaghetti relationship of biblical counseling, you're now in the terrain of sin and reconciling. Ashley has shared several "styles of relating" that have become somewhat her habitual response to God, people, and life. She sees herself as "perfectionistic" with herself and others — no one ever measures up to her standards, especially not herself. She realizes that she knows little of receiving and giving grace. She also finds herself battling an almost compulsive need for "order" — demanding that everyone does exactly what is expected and everything always be in its place. Anxiety and fear are provoked whenever Ashley's world is not perfectly planned and executed.

As you listen to Ashley, before you even interact with her, you're wanting to interpret her life story from a theological perspective. Rather than theology being irrelevant, it is absolutely relevant to understanding Ashley and diagnosing *the heart issues behind her relational style and emotional symptoms.* You can use the four fallen heart chambers as an X-ray or MRI as you seek to understand Ashley's heart.

Fallen Heart Chamber #1: Relational Corruption — Spiritual Adulterers

Because we know that every social/relational issue ultimately traces back to our spiritual relationship with God, we start by pondering where Ashley may be veering from loving God toward spiritual adultery — trusting in, clinging to, enjoying anything or anyone more than God. As we move from God, the Spring of Living Water, we're all tempted to drink from broken cisterns that hold no water. So as Ashley describes her style of relating, we're asking ourselves and pondering questions related to the spiritual adultery that everyone is tempted toward:

- Why and how is she fleeing from the Father? What is Ashley clinging to and trusting in instead of God?

- What counterfeit lover/love is she pursuing? What false cistern is Ashley trying to drink from?

- What self-sufficient satisfaction is Ashley demanding? Why is she rejecting God-satisfaction? How is her source of nourishment leaving her starved and poisoned? If Ashley trusted God's good heart, how might she be living and relating differently?

+ How could I begin to lovingly, humbly, and boldly expose her false trust? How can I communicate to Ashley the nature of her false lover/loves?

Fallen Heart Chamber #2: Rational Corruption—Heart Idolaters

Because we understand that every person pursues what they *perceive* to be most pleasing and satisfying, we know that Ashley's beliefs and images about God, life, others, and herself are central to her sin and her sanctification. We move from God because we cling to foolish beliefs about God, then the idol factory of our heart manufactures false gods. So as Ashley describes her relationships to God and others, we're asking ourselves and pondering questions related to the heart idolatry that everyone is tempted toward:

+ What faulty, foolish, and contemptuous beliefs and images about God, life, self, and others is Ashley believing? What fabricated sub-versions of God are guiding her mind-set? Where has she lost her awe of God?

+ What specific, unique sinful idol has Ashley carved in her mind? What is she uniquely taking refuge in?

+ How is Ashley suppressing the truth of God, Christ, grace, the gospel, the grand redemptive narrative?

+ How could I lovingly help Ashley to begin to explore the foolish idols of her heart?

Fallen Heart Chamber #3: Volitional Corruption—Enslaved Destroyers

Because we understand that every action is motivated by the goals, purposes, and plans of the heart, we don't focus only on Ashley's external actions, but also on her internal heart motivations. When we give in to false lovers of the soul and foolish idols of the heart, we inevitably become enslaved to self-centered relationships that are dismissive of God, destructive toward others, and damaging to self. So as Ashley describes her relationships to God and others, we're pondering questions related to the habituated, enslaved, destructive patterns of relating that everyone is tempted toward:

+ What cistern is Ashley digging in her attempt to replace God, the Spring of Living Water? What God-sized (infinite) and God-shaped (eternally satisfying) vacuum is she trying to fill with finite, false, and foolish idols?

+ What does Ashley's pattern of behavior indicate about her beliefs about the true source of life?

+ What heart issues might be motivating her manipulation and retaliation (her demands for perfection and order)? How are issues in her heart impacting issues in her home?

+ How could I lovingly help Ashley to begin to understand the root source of her enslaved and destructive behavior?

Fallen Heart Chamber #4: Emotional Corruption—Ungoverned Users

Because we understand that our emotional reactions are in response not simply to our external circumstances but even more so in response to our internal relational affections, relational mind-sets, and volitional purposes, we're committed to tying Ashley's feelings to her heart issues. When we worship false lovers, believe foolish lies, and pursue self-centered goals, we will inevitably mishandle our emotions — they will be ungoverned and self-focused. So as Ashley describes her relationships to God and others, we're pondering questions related to the ungoverned use of emotions that everyone is tempted toward:

+ How is Ashley misusing emotions to quiet the pain in her soul and the sin in her heart?

+ How is Ashley ungoverned in the use of her emotions?

+ How is Ashley living an emotionally demanding life that uses and consumes others?

+ How is Ashley lacking emotional sensitivity to others?

+ How could I lovingly help Ashley to begin to tune in to her feelings? To tune in to how she is misusing her feelings?

Theologically Guided Probing

We start by seeking to diagnose Ashley's heart biblically. As we do, we can now begin to interact, probe, and trialogue with Ashley to help her to begin to understand the issues of her heart.

We must do so in the spirit of Matthew 7:1 – 5. We take the plank out of our eye before we interact with Ashley about the speck in her eye. Since none of us will ever be perfect until our glorification in heaven, this does not mean that we wait until we're perfect before we expose sin in Ashley's heart. Instead, it means that the pattern of our heart is one where we are open to the Spirit of God, the Word of God, and the people of God exposing sin in our heart.

Then we can approach Ashley with a Galatians 6:1 mind-set: "Brothers, if someone is caught in a sin, you who are spiritual should restore him gently. But watch yourself, or you also may be tempted." Biblical counseling and probing theologically is never an "I got you!" moment. It is an "I'm a fellow saint who struggles with suffering and against sin" moment.

In probing with Ashley or any counselee, often it is helpful to "flip" the order of the probes. Instead of starting with the "holy of holies" of the soul — our relational affections and our worship — we start with the "outside of the cup." Before we even address the soul issues, we start with the situational story. And when we address the soul, we move from the emotions to actions, to thoughts, and to desires because most people are more attuned to their feelings and actions than to their thoughts and desires. We journey inward toward the depths of the heart.

Situational: Theologically Guided Probes and Presenting Problems—Circumstances

As we seek to help Ashley with her issues of perfectionism, compulsive order, demandingness, anxiety, and fear, some of the situational areas we might want to probe with her include:

- When did your struggle with _____ begin?
- When is your response worse? Better? With whom is your _____ worse? Better?
- Who is your _____ affecting the most?
- Describe a couple of specific times when your _____ was especially troublesome.
- How are others responding to your _____?

Physical: Theologically Guided Probes and the Body— Embodied Personality

As we begin to get a handle on the situational pattern, then we can begin to address the physical — we are embodied beings. The physical matters. Some of our probes might include:

- How does this struggle with _____ seem to impact you physically?
- When you find yourself getting anxious and fearful because your demands are not being met, how does this tend to impact your body? Your sleep? Appetite? Ability to rest and relax?

Emotional: Theologically Guided Probes and Emotions—Mood States

There is a dual purpose as we begin to address soul issues. First, we want to be sure that we have a comprehensive understanding of the complex emotions, actions, motivations, beliefs, images, and affections swirling about in Ashley's soul. That occurs through more general probes, such as:

+ Describe your anxiety and fear for me.
+ What all are you feeling inside at these times?
+ How are you feeling now as we discuss your _____?
+ How aware are you of your anxiety and fear as it starts to build?
+ How much of a sense of self-control do you feel over anxiety and fear?
+ To what extent is this mood a pattern for you, a common, maybe even a habitual response?
+ Where do you think you learned and developed this pattern of emotional responding?

With a more specific understanding of Ashley's emotional patterns, we can start to probe with Ashley about sin issues related to her relational style and emotional pattern. For instance, we could ask, "Ashley, when you give in to this sinful demandingness, perfectionism, and compulsive maintaining of control, what momentary release from anxiety and fear do you experience?" Or "When you give in to this sinful pattern, where are you surrendering to your feelings, allowing them to control you instead of the Spirit?"

Volitional: Theologically Guided Probes and Actions/Motivations—Purposes/Pathways

We can use general probes to help Ashley and us to have a clear picture of how she responds (actions) and why she responds (motivations) the way she does. Probes related to patterns of behavior include:

+ What do you normally do when you start feeling like this?
+ If you had done exactly what you felt like doing, what would you have done?
+ How do you respond differently with different people?
+ How typical is this pattern of reacting?

Probes related to motivation behind actions include:

+ What were you hoping would happen when you did that?

+ What response do you typically receive when you do that?

+ What would you have liked to have happened when you did that?

+ What does that do for you?

+ Where do you think you learned this way of relating to others?

With a more specific understanding of Ashley's behavioral and motivational patterns, now we can start to probe with Ashley about sin issues related to her relational style and volitional pattern. For instance, we could say, "Ashley, we've looked at Jeremiah 2:13. What cisterns do you think you are digging to quench your thirsts when you give in to this sin?" Or "Ashley, what themes or patterns do you detect in these times when you're clinging to this behavior more than you're clinging to Christ?" Or "Ashley, as you do this, how do you think you might be subtly trying to quench your thirsts in ways that God disapproves of?"

Rational: Theologically Guided Probes and Beliefs/ Images — Mind-Sets

Our actions are motivated by our beliefs and images — our mind-sets. We can use general probes to be sure that we have a clear picture of the beliefs and images that are motivating Ashley's behaviors and leading to her emotions. Probes related to patterns of beliefs include:

+ What do you think was going on inside your mind when you did that?

+ If I had a device recording your mind, what would I have heard?

+ What sentences were flowing through your mind at that moment?

+ What were your thoughts about the other person? God? Life?

Probes related to images include:

+ How would you picture yourself at that moment?

+ If I had a video of your mind at that moment, what images would I have viewed?

+ How do you see yourself in these situations? How do you see God? Others?

+ What book or chapter title would you write to summarize how you saw things at that moment?

With this understanding of Ashley's pattern of beliefs and images, now we can start to probe with Ashley about sin issues related to her rational mind-sets. For instance, "Ashley, what lies do you think you are believing that push the truth about God out of your mind?" Or "Ashley, as you give in to this need to be in control instead of surrendering to God's control, where do you think you are pushing down evidence of God's goodness?" Or "Ashley, how is Satan cropping God out of the picture in these moments of perfectionism?"

Relational: Theologically Guided Probes and Self-Awareness/ Social/Spiritual — Affections

Having worked our way toward understanding Ashley's situation and her soul — her emotions, actions, motivations, beliefs, and images — now we are ready to probe the holy of holies of her soul. We're ready to help Ashley think through her longings, desires, thirsts, and affections — and ways they have become disordered. We're ready to explore Ashley's worship disorder. Probes related to fallen patterns of *self-awareness* include:

+ More than anything else, what did you want at that moment?
+ What are your thoughts about and images of yourself at these times?
+ How do you feel about yourself at these moments?

Probes related to fallen patterns of self-centered *relating to others* (social beings) include:

+ More than anything, what did you want from others at that moment?
+ What were you longing for from the other person?
+ What did you fear from the other person?

Probes related to fallen patterns of *false worship* (spiritual beings) include:

+ How are you viewing God at these moments?
+ Where is God in the picture when you are demanding perfection from others?
+ Where do you suppose you were recruited into this attitude about God?
+ More than anything else, what are you wanting from God at these moments? How are you trying to receive it?

With this understanding of the pattern of Ashley's worship disorder, now we can start to probe with Ashley about sin issues connected to her relational affections. For instance, "Ashley, at that moment, what thirst, hunger, affection, delight, appetite, or desire were you attempting to satisfy?" Or "At the moment of temptation, what do you believe is most satisfying — God or this sin? Why? In what ways?"

Exposing Heart Sins: Confronting Lovingly and Wisely

For someone like Ashley, who has a tender conscience, probing trialogues like the examples on the preceding pages may be all that is needed to enlighten her to her sin and to encourage her to repent and receive Christ's gracious forgiveness. However, that may not be true for all of us (and it may not always be true for Ashley). Some of us stubbornly cling to our false lovers and foolish idols because our hearts have been hardened to and deceived by sin.

In church history, brothers and sisters in Christ responded to hardened deception by lovingly and humbly *loading the conscience with guilt*. I understand that *"guilt"* and *"loading the conscience"* are *not* terms that our modern world appreciates. Even in the church, we are rightfully wary of placing false guilt or worldly shame on people because we are aware of satanic condemnation. That's why, like the apostle Paul in 2 Corinthians 7:8 – 13, we must discern the difference between worldly sorrow that brings death and godly sorrow that leads to repentance and life.

It is this concern for the conscience that should lead us, as it led the Reformers and the Puritans, to expose the horrors of sin. Martin Luther's letter to Count Albert of Mansfield is an example of how Luther approached the task of care-fronting. He had written several times to Count Albert after he became aware that the Count was confiscating mines from those under Luther's pastoral care. When Albert refused to discontinue his practice, Luther wrote him yet another letter of restoration.[89] Notice how Luther's concern for Albert motivated his confrontation. "In short, I am concerned about Your Grace's soul. I cannot permit myself to cease praying for you and being concerned about you, for then I am convinced that I would cease being in the Church."[90] It is the essence of our duty as members of the body of Christ — the church — to speak gospel truth in love to one another.

Luther fulfills the duty of fraternal correction by exposing the discrepancy between who Albert is in Christ and how Albert was living for self.

Maturing as a Biblical Counselor
Self-Counsel

- Here's your *private* opportunity to invite God's Word and God's Spirit to speak into your heart. In responding to the probes below, please feel free to abbreviate or to be "cryptic" in what you write—this is really for *your eyes only and for God, who knows your heart.* If there is a group follow-up time, you would not be asked to share the specifics of the issue you were addressing. Instead, the entire group could be invited to share what the process of heart probing was like, and what work God did in each heart. Also, feel free to move back and forth between questions 1–6. This is not a straitjacket, but a guide, your own spaghetti relationship with God.

1. **Situational Heart Probes**
   Thinking about a current besetting sin, or about a past time of surrender to temptation, prayerfully ponder the following situational probes:

   a. When did my struggle with this temptation begin?

   b. When is my response to the temptation worse? Better? With whom is my response worse? Better?

   c. Who is affected the most by my struggling?

   d. What is going on in my life when this temptation is particularly troublesome?

2. **Emotional Heart Probes**
   Thinking about your emotions/feelings/moods and a current besetting sin, or a past time of surrender to temptation, prayerfully ponder the following heart probes:

   a. Regarding this sin, how am I living to satisfy my immediate pleasure?

b. Regarding this sin, where have I surrendered to my feelings?

c. Relative to this sin, how have I become addicted to pursuing positive feelings or to avoiding negative feelings?

d. When I give in to this sin, what momentary pleasures do I experience? What lasting shame do I experience?

3. **Volitional Heart Probes**

    Thinking about your volition/choices/motivations and a current besetting sin, or a past time of surrender to temptation, prayerfully ponder the following heart probes:

    a. How am I manipulating others to get what I want? Or, when I don't get what I want, how am I retaliating against others for not meeting my demands?

    b. What behavioral themes or motivational patterns do I detect in these times when I am choosing this sin over Jesus?

    c. What do these themes and patterns indicate about my beliefs about the true source of life?

4. **Rational Heart Probes**

    Thinking about your beliefs/images and a current besetting sin, or a past time of surrender to temptation, prayerfully ponder the following heart probes:

    a. What controlling false images of God cloud my thinking when I'm struggling against this sin? What lowly views of God capture my attention?

b. How is Satan cropping God out of the picture? How is Satan cropping in false images of deceptive beauty and seductive temptation?

c. As I give in to this sin, where am I pushing down evidence of God's goodness?

d. How am I belittling God's holy love when I surrender to this sin?

5. **Relational Heart Probes**

Thinking about your affections/thirsts and a current besetting sin, or a past time of surrender to temptation, prayerfully ponder the following heart probes:

a. At the moment of temptation, what affection, delight, appetite, or desire am I attempting to satisfy? What thirst/hunger am I attempting to fill?

b. At the moment of temptation, what false lover am I pursuing? What false cistern am I drinking from? More than anything else, what do I want?

c. What am I clinging to or trusting in instead of God? How am I fleeing from my heavenly Father?

6. As you reflect on your responses to these questions, please don't stop at sin. Turn, no, run to Christ for grace. Apply the words of Milton Vincent: "On my worst days of sin and failure, the gospel encourages me with God's unrelenting grace toward me."[91]

God did many laudable things through Your Grace at the beginning of the gospel: churches, pulpits, and schools were well ordered to the praise and honor of God.... But it appears to me, especially from rumors and complaints that have reached me, that Your Grace has fallen away from such good beginnings and has become a very different person. As Your Grace may well believe, this causes me great heartache on your account.[92]

Luther models a biblical definition of exposing heart sins through confrontation. In biblical care-fronting, we expose heart issues lovingly and wisely by displaying discrepancies between who people are in Christ and how people are living for self.

> Biblical care-fronting exposes heart issues lovingly and wisely by displaying discrepancies between who people are in Christ and how people are living for self.

A Biblical Portrayal of Confrontation: 2 Timothy 2:22 – 26

Timothy is a young pastor charged with shepherding God's flock and confronting wayward sheep (1 Tim. 1:3 – 11). Paul, as Timothy's mentor, doesn't just command Timothy to engage in the difficult process of confrontation. Instead, in 2 Timothy 2:22 – 26, he teaches Timothy the character of the care-fronter, the nature of confrontation, the process of confrontation, the goal of confrontation, and our hope in confrontation.

> *Flee the evil desires of youth, and pursue righteousness, faith, love and peace, along with those who call on the Lord out of a pure heart. Don't have anything to do with foolish and stupid arguments, because you know they produce quarrels. And the Lord's servant must not quarrel; instead, he must be kind to everyone, able to teach, not resentful. Those who oppose him [oppose themselves] he must gently instruct [confront, correct], in the hope that God will grant them repentance leading them to a knowledge of the truth, and that they will come to their senses and escape from the trap of the devil, who has taken them captive to do his will. (2 Timothy 2:22 – 26)*

The Character of the Care-Fronter

Confrontation requires integrity. To confront another, Timothy first has to confront himself. He has to flee (put off) evil desires and pursue (put on) godly affections. He removes the log from his eye by living out of a pure heart, before he confronts the heart of another.

Confrontation also requires humility. Timothy shuns fights, quarrels, and stupid arguments. Instead, he is to be kind and patient toward others, especially with those who are wayward.

Confrontation further requires spirituality. Biblical confrontation is not bold and bullying. It is gentle and patient. In confronting, Timothy practices patience (2 Tim. 2:24 KJV) — he bears up under wrong. When confronting others, they frequently become displeased with him. To bear up without resentment, Timothy needs forbearance.

Timothy is also to confront in meekness (2 Tim. 2:25 KJV). Meekness pictures managed strength released with gentleness, humility, and concern. The meek person neither fights against God nor enters power struggles with others. The meek biblical counselor displays the opposite of self-assertion and self-interest.

The Nature of Confrontation

In 2 Timothy 2:25, Paul commands Timothy to "gently instruct" (confront, correct) those who oppose themselves (author's translation). The phrase "oppose themselves" is from the Greek word for "antithesis" — a contrary position. *Antitasso* means to set oneself against the natural order — God's order. Here in 2 Timothy the word is *antidiatithemenous: anti* — "against," *dia* — "through," and *tithemenous* — "to place." In the middle tense as it is here, it means *to stand opposed to oneself, to place oneself in opposition to oneself.*[93]

As Luther illustrated with Count Albert, confrontation shows Ashley how she is standing opposed to her new self in Christ. It exposes how she is living inconsistently with her new heart. It reveals how she is buying the lie of the works narrative (perfectionism), rather than being rooted in the truth of Christ's grace narrative. Care-fronting points out discrepancies.

The Process of Confrontation

Paul uses the word *paideuonta* ("gently instruct") to describe the process of confrontation. The word relates to schooling, and in this context it emphasizes corrective instruction.[94]

Its root form *paideuo* means to train children. Such child training requires practicality. It also necessitates explanation, as opposed to simply handing down rules by fiat. Much more than mere exhortation to stop a behavior, biblical confrontation involves instruction in the process of heart change leading to behavioral change. That's why Paul tells Timothy that he has to be "able to teach" (2 Tim. 2:24). He needs to skillfully relate doctrine to conduct. He has to wisely relate truth to human relationships.

Of course, all of our teaching and trialogues are Scripture-founded. Luther's interaction with Albert illustrates powerful scriptural confrontation through practical biblical teaching.

> Your Grace too must be aware that you have become cold, have given your heart to Mammon, and have the ambition to become very rich. According to complaints Your Grace is also sharply and severely oppressive to subjects and proposes to confiscate their forges and goods and to make what amounts to vassals out of them. God will not suffer this. Or if he does, he will allow your land to become impoverished and go to ruin, for he can take away what is his own gift without giving an accounting for it; as Haggai says: "Ye have sown much, and bring in little; and he that earneth wages, earneth wages to put it into a bag with holes."[95]

The Goal of Confrontation

The goal of instructive correction (confrontation) is maturity: love out of a pure heart, a good conscience, and a sincere faith (1 Tim. 1:5). Thus the goal is virtue (2 Peter 1:3 – 11): character, not simply content. Biblical instruction/confrontation includes a presentation of a clear worldview (grace narrative) and the implications derived from it (grace relationships). Confrontation promotes spiritual development through personal influence; it is the relational presentation of God's worldview. It skillfully explores any discrepancies between grace narratives and works narratives and grace relationships and works relationships.

Paul further develops the goal of gentle biblical confrontation when he writes "that they may recover themselves" (2 Tim. 2:26, author's translation). Thus the goal is sobriety and sanity. To "recover" means to return to soberness as from a state of delirium where one is under the control of an outside element — the controlling passions of the flesh, intoxicated with false worldviews, and snared by the devil.[96] Confrontation helps Ashley to return to a sound mind — a whole, healthy mind that thinks and lives with peace and integrity.

An additional goal of confrontation is safety — escape from the snare of the devil who has taken them captive to do his will. "Snare" (2 Tim. 2:26 KJV) is a trap that fastens or holds fast, a net, a noose. Various authors used the word for seductive women and for the Trojan horse. A snare is anything that entices with something desirable. It promises pleasure but gives pain. When snared, Ashley is caught in the net of self-deception and captured by the Devil's delusion.

The Hope in Confrontation: Leave the Conviction to God

What happens when, despite our best efforts to expose sin's deceitfulness, people remain blind, hard, and deceived? In such cases, and in all cases, we leave the conviction to God.

That's exactly what Paul teaches his protégé in 2 Timothy 2:24 – 26. He reminds Timothy that the Lord's servant must not quarrel, but instead be kind to everyone — that's care-fronting. Those who oppose him and themselves, he must gently instruct *"in the hope that God will grant them repentance leading them to a knowledge of the truth"* (2:25, emphasis added).

Repentance is between God and our counselee. Our job is to care-front. If we try to force repentance, we will end up in power struggles. Instead, we step aside to allow our counselee to enter into a power struggle with our all-powerful God!

Luther concluded his letter of spiritual counsel to Count Albert with these words, which left the conviction to God:

> Your Grace will know how to take this admonition, for I cannot allow myself to be damned by Your Grace's sin. I desire, rather, that you may be saved together with me, if this be possible. If not, I have at least done my duty and am excused in God's sight. Herewith I commit you to God in all his grace and mercy. Amen.[97]

Notice too who the true enemy is. Ashley is not the ultimate enemy; Satan is. He has taken Ashley captive. In care-fronting, we attack Satan with God's armor rather than attacking Ashley.

Sense Discrepancies by Carefully Hearing the Human Story and God's Story

Let's consider some of the relational competencies necessary for biblical confrontation as we work with Ashley and other counselees. Since Ashley's life of perfectionistic demandingness is not lining up with God's will, we want to sense discrepancies.

Listen for Discrepancies between the Human Story and God's Story

We ask ourselves, as we interact with Ashley:

- How is Ashley failing to see and live out God's grace narrative?
- How is Ashley failing to live out God's grace relationships?
- How is Ashley failing to live like Christ's redeemed image bearer?

Listen for Discrepancies within the Human Story

As we interact, we ponder:

- Where is Ashley seeking false lovers instead of worshiping Christ?
- Where is Ashley following foolish mind-sets rather than wise mind-sets?
- Where is Ashley pursuing self-centered pathways rather than other-centered ones? How is Ashley presenting one goal but pursuing another? Living one lifestyle but claiming another?
- Where is Ashley living according to ungoverned mood states instead of managed moods?

We also seek to perceive:

- Inconsistencies: Mixed messages, goals, thoughts, explanations, and feelings.
- Incongruities: Disparity between two statements, between actions and words, as well as between words and nonverbals.

In all of our listening, we push for specifics: We stay with one event, one issue, or one situation long enough to sense that we were there as an eye-witness.

Provide Feedback Concerning the Discrepancies We Hear

What do we do once we've sensed Ashley's spiritual discrepancies? We present statements that raise the issue of: "On the one hand ... on the other hand ..."

- On the one hand, I hear you saying that you have a deep, abiding trust in God's grace. Yet on the other hand, I sense that your perfectionistic demands on your family and even on yourself are lacking in grace ...

Then we encourage Ashley to confront her own discrepancies:

+ How does this appear to you? What do you make of this? How do you put these two together?

All of these conversations display humility and meekness. God never calls us to cause others to lose face or to sense that we think that we're superior to them. As Paul pointed out, our enemy is Satan, not our counselee.

Luther models this gracious respect. He addressed Albert as a man who was falling away from God, yet he still concentrated on Albert's potential to be restored to God.

> I desire from the bottom of my heart that you may receive in a Christian and gracious way what I write here. God did many laudable things through Your Grace at the beginning of the gospel: churches, pulpits, and schools were well ordered to the praise and honor of God.... For these and other reasons I cannot readily forget Your Grace or cease to pray for you and be concerned for you.[98]

Like Albert, Ashley may respond to our biblical, gentle confrontation in any number of ways. She may meet our confrontation with denial. *"Nope. Not me. Don't see it like that at all."*

She may respond with partial acceptance. This may look like quick agreement and may feel like insincere agreement, or it might take the form of shifting blame or making excuses.

Additionally, she may respond with acceptance and acknowledgment that results in repentance (new attitudes), restitution (new actions), and reconciliation (renewed relationships). If this is her response, we rejoice. If not, we move on to applying truth relationally — the first reconciling relational competency that we develop in chapter 10.

Where We've Been and Where We're Headed

Here's our tweet-size summary of chapter 9.

+ In reconciling, we dazzle our counselees with grace — the message of God's holy love that convicts, forgives, welcomes home, renews, and empowers.

In reconciling, we expose sin *and* we expose grace. We help people to see that it's horrible to sin, but we never leave them there — we always help them to see how wonderful it is to be forgiven. Chapter 10 continues our grace journey.

Maturing as a Biblical Counselor

Self-Counsel and Group or Partner Interaction

1. Ponder some times of confrontation in your own life ...

   a. Have you ever been confronted in a way that felt harsh, controlling, and lacking in love? How did you respond?

   b. Have you ever been confronted in a way that mirrors 2 Timothy 2:22–26—care-fronting? How did you respond?

   c. Have you ever confronted someone in a way that, as you reflect back, was harsh, controlling, and lacking in love? How did the person respond? What could you have done differently?

   d. Have you ever confronted someone in a way that mirrors 2 Timothy 2:22–26—care-fronting? How did the person respond?

2. From the presentation of 2 Timothy 2:22–26 and Paul's teaching on biblical confrontation:

   a. What specifically stands out to you as new and important concepts?

b. What specific applications do you want to make to your life? To your ministry?

Counseling Others

3. Write a series of trialogues with Ashley that explore discrepancies in her life emotionally, volitionally, rationally, and relationally.

CHAPTER 10

Reconciling through Grace-Maximizing

A friend recently said to me, "Biblical counselors have a tendency to be 'sin-maximizers.'" As we interacted, he asserted that the *nouthetic* emphasis on confronting sin at times leads biblical counselors to highlight the exposure of sin — sin-maximizers — to the exclusion of other aspects of pastoral care.

Reflecting on his thinking, another phrase came to my mind as a summary description of what Christ calls biblical counselors to be — "*grace-maximizers.*" In every aspect of biblical counseling by sustaining, healing, reconciling, and guiding, *Christ's gospel of grace* is central.

- Sustaining: It's Normal to Hurt — Christ's Grace to Comfort and Bring Grace to Help in Our Time of Need
- Healing: It's Possible to Hope — Christ's Grace to Bring Encouragement to Us to Hope in Christ's Work in Us
- Reconciling: It's Horrible to Sin — Christ's Grace to Convict Us When We Are Hardened by Sin's Deceitfulness
- Reconciling: It's Wonderful to Be Forgiven — Christ's Grace to Forgive Us as We Return to Him
- Guiding: It's Supernatural to Mature — Christ's Grace to Empower Us as We Put Off the Old Ways and Put On the New Ways in Christ

Maturing as a Biblical Counselor

Self-Counsel and Group or Partner Interaction

1. Read Hebrews 3:12–14. What impact could it make on your life if you had a spiritual friend or two who related to you according to Hebrews 3:12–14?

2. Read Hebrews 4:12–13. What impact could it make on your spiritual life if you and a spiritual friend used God's Word in each other's life the way Hebrews 4:12–13 suggests?

3. Read Hebrews 10:24–25. What impact could it have on your life if you were connected to a group of spiritual friends who consistently related to one another the way Hebrews 10:24–25 suggests?

4. Based on the three preceding passages/questions, what longings are stirring in your soul? What are you motivated to do?

The scriptural purpose of nouthetic biblical counseling through reconciling and guiding is much more than sin-spotting. The beauty of comprehensive biblical counseling is its Christ-focused, gospel-centered emphasis on grace for all of life — in our suffering, our sin, and our sanctification. When we are sinned against, Christ's grace brings healing hope. When we sin against God and others, Christ's grace brings forgiveness and newness of life.

Recall that in reconciling we communicate, *"It's horrible to sin,* but *wonderful to be forgiven!"* If we emphasized only the first half of the reconciling process — it's horrible to sin — then we would be sin-maximizers who become sin-spotters. We would spot a sin, expose a sin, exhort toward change, and move on to the next counselee. But that's not comprehensive, compassionate reconciling that also communicates — it's wonderful to be forgiven!

Rather than being sin-maximizers and sin-spotters, ambassadors of reconciliation are grace-maximizers. We do not minimize suffering or sin, rather we maximize grace as Christ's prescription for our disgrace.

In reconciling, we maximize grace by bringing peace to the conscience that is rightly troubled by sin because it has wrongly breached relationship with God the Father. Recall our memory device for the six reconciling relational competencies:

- *P* Probing Theologically
- *E* Exposing Heart Sins
- *A* Applying Truth Relationally
- *C* Calming the Conscience with Grace
- *E* Enlightening Spiritual Conversations
- *E* Empowering Scriptural Explorations

Applying Truth Relationally: Connecting Intimately

I was counseling a pastor, we'll call him "Ray," who came to me at the encouragement of his elder ministry team. Ray was a younger pastor in his first senior pastoral ministry. The elder team consisted of five spiritually mature men who worked hard at affirming Ray in his ministry. However, whenever they shared any feedback that had the slightest twinge of "something to work on or think about," they felt that Ray became quite defensive. At times his pushback became very intense — he'd label them as disrespectful and disloyal and threaten to "go to a church where I'd be appreciated."

As I listened to Ray's story, I found his perspective to be quite cut-and-dried:

"The elders are spiritually abusing me, and I can do no right in their eyes." Knowing that no elder ministry team perfectly relates to any pastor, there were certainly areas where I could climb in the casket with Ray. However, over time it became clear that the reconciling ministry of exposing sin and enlightening to grace was necessary.

So, former pastor (me) and current pastor (Ray) "probed theologically," looking at Ray's situation and his response from a biblical perspective. Even with a scriptural X-ray of his heart held up for Ray to see, he didn't own his response. So I moved into some gentle care-fronting by exposing heart sins — the discrepancies between Ray's identity in Christ and his way of relating to his brothers in Christ. Ray remained resistant.

We are all tempted toward a stubborn inclination to continue in self-sufficient attitudes (rational heart sin) that lead to self-centered relationships (relational heart sin) maintained by self-protective suppression of the truth (volitional heart sin) (Rom. 1:18 – 32). The beach ball of guilt pops to the surface, but we force it down under the water. Our flesh would rather follow the same old foolish patterns than to put on our new God-dependent wise patterns (Eph. 4:17 – 24).

How do we handle such resistance to repentance? We speak the truth in love by applying the truth relationally as we connect intimately. Because connecting intimately can be so rare, even in biblical counseling, some summary descriptions can help.

- *Relating in the Moment:* Face-to-face relating with our counselee about our counseling relationship.
- *Immediacy:* Dealing with what is taking place in our counseling relationship at the present moment.
- *Relational Patterning:* Discussing the here-and-now between the counselor and the counselee with a view toward implications for other relationships.
- *Staying in the Room:* Rather than discussing only a counselee's relationships to others, you interact about the counselee's way of relating to you.

Applying truth relationally through connecting intimately involves discussing the here-and-now between the counselor and the counselee with a view toward implications for other relationships.

Throughout 1 and 2 Corinthians, Paul models intimate connecting as *he uses his relationship to the Corinthians as a catalyst to expose their relational immaturity.* Witness a beautiful and powerful example from 2 Corinthians 6:11 – 13. "We have spoken freely to you, Corinthians, and opened wide our hearts to you. We are not withholding our affection from you, but you are withholding yours from us. As a fair exchange — I speak as to my children — open wide your hearts also."

Paul follows a foundational principle: How people relate intimately to us mirrors how they relate intimately to others. We can only hide ourselves so long. Eventually, in significant relationships, our words either reveal or betray us, for out of the abundance of the heart, the mouth speaks. We relate in similar ways in all our meaningful relationships. Whatever is central to our style of relating will reflect itself in all our intimate relationships.

The principle holds true *only if* our counseling relationship is truly and purely intimate. If our pastoral ministry, biblical counseling, and spiritual friendships are shallow and merely academic, then we can't expect to detect significant relational patterns. Paul understood that insight alone never delivered anyone (Eph. 4:15; Phil. 1:9 – 11; 1 Thess. 2:8). He believed in and practiced the relational competency of being fully alive and present in his relationships.

Connecting intimately is vital because reality is relational. When we connect intimately with Ray, we become a main character in his life drama instead of remaining simply a reader of his life story. Connecting intimately is powerful because it's rare, even though it's exactly how God designed people to relate (Gen. 2:23 – 25).

The immediacy of our relationship with Ray provides here-and-now tastes of his pain, thirst, sin, and growth. It removes the wall between the two of us and the veil over his eyes, allowing us to catch Ray in the act of spiritual maturity or in the act of fleshly immaturity.

Connecting intimately requires much of us:

+ *Relationally:* We need passionate love to touch soul-to-soul, not as an expert to a client, but as a friend to a friend.
+ *Rationally:* We need the self-awareness and self-confidence to trust our intuition, our gut response, our instincts, our interpretive gifts, and our creative imagination.
+ *Volitionally:* We need the courage to risk the relationship by sharing that impact. We need to be so other-centered that we avoid the all-consuming question, "How am I coming across?" Connecting

intimately requires a sense of "for-ness." "I'm for you. I'm on your side, on your team. I'm here to encourage and empower you."

+ *Emotionally:* We need the openness to experience the impact of our counselee on us right now. We need the vulnerability to deepen our counseling relationship by sharing our counselee's personal impact on us.

Becoming Alive to Our Counselee's Impact on Us

In order to connect intimately with Ray, I had to become alive to his impact on me. This requires me to engage in all the relational competencies explored thus far. These competencies are developmental; they build upon each other. We can't "practice" them in one stage, then toss them out. Intimate connecting requires listening, empathy, etc.

Applying truth relationally requires an additional kind of listening: *listening to our own soul.* I had to trust my gut instinct as I related to Ray. I was asking myself the question: "What do I feel drawn to feel, do, think, and want as we relate?" I was trying to assess the subjective sense of what I was experiencing while we were relating.

With Ray or any counselee, consider some thoughts to probe as we attempt to tune in to a counselee's typical pattern of relating:

+ How do I feel as I relate to Ray? Invited in? Pushed away? Respected? Cared about? Discounted? Mistrusted? Discouraged? Intimidated? Loved?

+ As I relate to Ray, do I sense: Sarcasm? Emotional withdrawal? A critical spirit? The cold shoulder? Defensiveness? Aloofness? Faultfinding? Arrogance? Harshness? Warmth? Trust? Mutuality? Teamwork? Intimacy?

In the modern biblical counseling world, this relational element has not always been emphasized. In fact, at times it has been criticized as subjective and emotional. Let's think about this theologically. Can our emotions be misused and mismanaged? Absolutely. At the same time, can our thoughts be foolish and misguided? Absolutely. Or our thoughts can be wise because our minds are renewed. Likewise, our emotional and relational experience can be an accurate barometer because we are new creations in Christ.

In biblical counseling we use our whole person renewed in the image of Christ — relationally, rationally, volitionally, *and* emotionally — to minister to counselees. In applying truth relationally, we use our experience of how a person relates to us as the current evidence of their pattern of relating to others — either self-centered relating or other-centered relating.

Sharing Our Counselee's Impact on Us

As we do this under the leading of the Spirit, we look for and put into words how Ray is relating to us at this moment. We share how we feel, how we experience Ray right now. "I sense that … It seems like …"

Our sharing is done as a possible reflection of Ray's general pattern of relating. How we relate and how we sense our relationship to Ray becomes a mirror of how Ray relates to others. We want to discuss the possible similar pattern in other relationships, examining how or if our present relationship is an example of Ray's normal style of relating. We help Ray *to see by living an illustration* of how he's relating to God and others. We explore themes, patterns, and styles of relating that either violate or elevate love. Such intimate connecting has the potential to "catch Ray in the act" of sinning against you, making suppression of the truth more difficult.

Experiencing Together Our Impact on One Another

In applying truth relationally, we invite Ray to focus on the here and now, not simply for comparison to his other relationships, but to experience ours deeply. This can lead to a level of intense interaction and open feedback. Invitations to relate intimately can come in many forms.

- Could we discuss what's happening between us right now as we relate?
- How are you experiencing our relationship right now?
- What's going on inside you as we talk?
- How did you feel when _____?
- You seem _____ right now.
- May I share what I'm experiencing right now as we talk? I wonder what we should make of this.

The Process of Applying Truth Relationally

I fear turning something so personal into a "process." More than anything, applying truth relationally by connecting intimately involves our commitment to relate deeply. We refuse to maintain some aloof professional image or a distant pastoral stiffness. Instead, we:

- ◆ Taste the Horrors of Sin
- ◆ Catch the Person Red-Handed
- ◆ Paint the Person a Picture
- ◆ Provide Clarifying Feedback
- ◆ Explore God's Story of Sin, Repentance, and Grace

In *tasting the horrors of sin*, I entered Ray's soul, allowing him to impact me. I found with Ray that every interaction became a deep theological debate — that *he must win*. So I was thinking, "Hmm, at this stage of my life, winning theological debates and making every interaction a competition is not my style. But I sure feel pulled to debate and be competitive. I wonder what's going on between us? Within Ray?" Of course, this took the self-awareness to know how I normally respond and to distinguish my own sinful pattern of relating from Ray's relational sin against me.

Catching the person red-handed required that I keep my relationship with Ray in the room. Instead of focusing on Ray's defensive patterns with his elders, I could share subtle ways that he would become defensive with me. "Ray, I've counseled for three decades now. People give me feedback that I'm a positive encourager whose acceptance and vulnerability make it rather easy for them to receive confrontation from me. Yet right now it seems like you're biting my head off at the slightest implication that there might be something you need to look at ..."

You may be able to imagine what happened at that moment. Ray became defensive when I wondered if he was becoming defensive!

So I continued to stay in the room. "It's happening right now, Ray."

"What's happening right now?" Ray said with more than a twinge of exasperation.

"Even as I try to gently share where you may be defensive with me, you're getting more and more defensive ..."

Ray then became even more defensive and used one of his sinful "defense mechanisms" — theological argumentation. "But Bob, this is just like Paul in 2 Corinthians 12 where he tells the Corinthians that they have driven him to the foolishness of defending his ministry because they should have been commending him instead of attacking him."

Staying in the moment, searching my heart, praying for wisdom, I *painted Ray a picture* by using imagery that fit Ray and our current relationship, "So, Ray, help me to understand if this is your picture of our relationship. Rather than seeing me as a brother or even a father-figure who cares about you and has your best interest at heart, you see me as a 'Corinthian' who is against you and out to get you ..."

By God's grace, Ray melted. He had an "Aha!" moment.

Ray's pattern of sinful defensiveness became so clear to him that I barely needed to move toward *providing clarifying feedback*. But we did wonder aloud together about possible patterns. "Ray, is it possible that this is how you see your elder ministry team and others — as enemies out to get you? If so, I wonder where that comes from and what it might suggest ..."

By *exploring God's story of sin, repentance, and grace*, Ray was able to face God's perspective on his way of relating. Together we explored biblical diagnostic questions such as:

+ What does God's Word say concerning your current way of relating?

+ How would you compare and contrast your way of relating and Christ's way of relating?

+ How would you compare your way of relating with the love chapter in 1 Corinthians 13?

As we applied truth relationally and explored God's Word, the Spirit began to convict Ray about a number of heart sins. Over time Ray came to see his arrogant demandingness that everyone see him and treat him like a super-apostle — like the apostle Paul. He began to recognize a long-standing pattern of self-protective defensiveness. And he began to see how he used theological argumentation to put people in their place — under him!

So we explored God's story of repentance.

+ What would it be like for you, Ray, to take words with you and return to the Lord and confess your sin and ask him to forgive you graciously (see Hos. 14:2)?

+ What would it be like for you to pen a psalm of repentance like a Psalm 32 or 51?

+ What would it be like for you to ask your elders for forgiveness and to rebuild your relationship with them?

Of course, responding to questions like these took Ray and me many hours of gospel-centered counseling and discipleship. They also led us into God's story of grace — which we'll explore in our next relational competency: calming the conscience with grace.

Maturing as a Biblical Counselor

Self-Counsel and Group or Partner Interaction

1. Applying truth relationally through connecting intimately requires a lot of us.

   a. How new or different were these concepts about applying truth relationally?

   b. How easy or hard would it be for you to connect with this level of intimacy? What work might need to occur in your heart in order for you to relate with this other-centered depth and richness?

Counseling Others

2. Use the scenario with Ray and the outline below to complete this exercise in applying truth relationally. Write trialogues that you might use for each of the following skills of connecting intimately.

   a. Taste the Horrors of Sin

   b. Catch the Person Red-Handed

   c. Paint the Person a Picture

   d. Provide Clarifying Feedback

e. Explore God's Story of Sin, Repentance, and Grace

Calming the Conscience with Grace: Dispensing Grace

"But God ..." the two most amazing words in the English language. It's horrible to sin, *but God* offers us his wonderful grace of forgiveness. Gospel-centered biblical counselors must not omit, forget, or minimize the second aspect of the reconciling process: it's wonderful to be forgiven.

In 1 Corinthians 5, Paul confronts the Corinthians for their failure to communicate "it's horrible to sin." But then in 2 Corinthians 2, he confronts them for their failure to live out "it's wonderful to be forgiven." Having finally confronted an erring brother who responded in repentance, Paul commands them: "Now instead, you ought to forgive and comfort him, so that he will not be overwhelmed by excessive sorrow. I urge you, therefore, to reaffirm your love for him" (2 Cor. 2:7 – 8).

Paul then informs us that if we fail to calm the conscience with grace, then we fall victim to and become complicit in Satan's scheme. "... in order that Satan might not outwit us. For we are not unaware of his schemes" (2 Cor. 2:11). Satan is the accuser of Christians, and he accuses us day and night before God (Rev. 12:10).

If Satan can't prevent us from confessing and repenting, then he shifts schemes and tries to deceive us into not receiving God's gracious forgiveness. His lying, condemning, works-oriented narrative is the polar opposite of Christ's truthful, justifying, grace-centered grand narrative.

Because we are aware of Satan's scheme, we practice the spiritual direction art of calming the conscience with grace. This involves applying the living voice of the gospel to people's troubled hearts to encourage them to return home to the forgiving heart and loving arms of their gracious Father.

We calm the conscience by:

+ Enlightening Believers to Understand Their Identity in Christ as Beloved Sons and Daughters
+ Recognizing the Quadralog

- ✦ Providing Tastes of Grace
- ✦ Penning Psalms of Homecoming

Calming the conscience with grace involves applying the living voice of the gospel to people's troubled hearts to encourage them to return home to the forgiving heart and loving arms of their gracious Father.

Enlightening Believers to Understand Their Identity in Christ as Beloved Sons and Daughters

Luther understood the scheme of Satan. This is why Luther not only loaded the unrepentant conscience with guilt, he also lightened the repentant conscience with grace. He did so by applying the living voice of the gospel to people's lives, underscoring the daily, relational significance of Christ's gospel of grace. He models for us the reconciling ministry of enlightening people to their identity as reconciled sons and daughters of God through Christ.

Luther believed that Christians needed to recognize that in their central identity they were loved by God. In one table talk, Luther reflected on his own spiritual struggle and noted that for a long time "I went astray and didn't know what I was about."[99] He continued by saying that what freed him was the realization that he was indeed someone who was loved by God — his core identity was as a beloved child of God. "I began to experience a change when I read about the love of God and what it signifies passively, namely, that by which we are loved by God."[100]

Luther's counseling ministry was thoroughly grace-centered. "Thus the Christian faith differs from other religions in this, that the Christian hopes even in the midst of evils and sins."[101] That's why reconciling communicates, "Even when we are sinful and evil, Christ is gracious and forgiving."

Pastor Ray struggled with accepting his acceptance in Christ. In fact, it was his struggle to receive Christ's grace that made him sinfully defensive in the first place. If his image of God is that of an enemy out to get him, then it should not be surprising that he saw others in the same light. And if Ray sensed that he had to be perfect to receive God's love, then it is not surprising that he fought fiercely against any feedback that suggested even a smidgen of imperfection.

In ministering to Ray, I followed Luther's pastoral care model of magnifying the forgiving heart of our gracious Father.

> For who is able to express what a thing it is, when a man is assured in his heart that God neither is nor will be angry with him, but will be forever a merciful and loving Father to him for Christ's sake? This is indeed a marvelous and incomprehensible liberty, to have the most high and sovereign Majesty so favorable to us. Wherefore, this is an inestimable liberty, that we are made free from the wrath of God forever; and is greater than heaven and earth and all other creatures.[102]

Recognizing the Quadralog

In ministering to Ray, I also sought to help him to recognize the "quadralog." This invented word picks up on the idea of a trialogue and adds to it Satan's role. Every biblical counseling meeting has at least four participants: the counselee, the counselor, the Divine Counselor through the Spirit and Word of God, and the unbiblical counselor — Satan.

Being aware of Satan's role, I asked Ray, "Where were you recruited into this conviction that you have to earn your way to God? It certainly is not what you preach every Sunday, but somehow it has become what you live every Monday through Saturday. It could help if we explored the role of Satan's condemning lies …"

Becoming aware of Satan's condemnation allows us to speak God's truth against those lies. Speaking against Satan's temptation in his own life, Luther wrote:

> You say that the sins which we commit every day offend God, and therefore we are not saints. To this I reply: Mother love is stronger than the filth and scabbiness on a child, and so the love of God toward us is stronger than the dirt that clings to us. Accordingly, although we are sinners, we do not lose our filial relation on account of our filthiness, nor do we fall from grace on account of our sin.[103]

As we recognize Satan's evil presence, and as we become aware of his condemning scheme, we expose his lies and we impart grace. Listen to how Luther did so passionately and perhaps a little crudely.

> It's the supreme art of the devil that he can make the law out of the gospel. If I can hold on to the distinction between law and gospel, I can say to him any and every time that he should kiss my backside. Even if I sinned, I would say, "Should I deny the gospel on this account?"[104]

Providing Tastes of Grace

As we recognize and put off Satan's condemning lies, we need to put on Christ's reconciling truth by providing tastes of grace. Luther explains the powerful relational transaction that occurs when believers speak grace to one another. "The word of a fellow-Christian has wonderful power...." The voices of "brethren and fellow Christians are to be heard and believed as the word and voice of God himself, as though God was speaking to them."[105] God encounters the conscience through his Word mediated through his people.

Luther understood what we must understand: the tormented conscience will lose the battle between the flesh and the Spirit if it is left alone. To one individual experiencing great upheaval of conscience, Luther wrote, "I beseech you by the Lord Christ, as earnestly as I can, not to depend upon yourself and your own thoughts, but to hear the brother in Christ who now speaks to you."[106]

We provide tastes of grace not only by speaking the truth in love but also by living and relating gospel truth in love. With Pastor Ray, just as I needed to catch him red-handed in his sin, he needed to experience me giving him tastes of grace in how I related to him. Once he finally faced his sinful defensiveness, his arrogant self-protectiveness, and his foolish works-oriented self-sufficiency, he expected me to condemn him. When I didn't, when I invited him to receive Christ's grace and to hear my voice reminding him of Christ's grace, I became *Jesus with skin on* for Ray.

Penning Psalms of Homecoming

As important as it was for me to communicate grace to Ray, at some point he had to own, receive, and personalize Christ's grace. I wanted to help Ray to cement his reception of Christ's grace by encouraging him to pen psalms of homecoming. So I gave him the homework assignment of writing his own Psalm 32 or Psalm 51, with a focus on receiving God's forgiving grace.

Enlightening Spiritual Conversations: Reconciling Theological Trialogues

Reconciling spiritual conversations trialogue about biblical wisdom about sin, guilt, confession, repentance, grace, forgiveness, and reconciliation. They seek to enlighten people to the horrors of sin through the conviction of guilt (recognition) and the confession of sin (repentance), and to enlighten people to the wonders of forgiveness through the comfort of grace (reconciliation).

Maturing as a Biblical Counselor

Self-Counselor and/or Counseling One Another

- If you are working through this material individually, then respond to these questions in writing.

- With your lab small group or with a lab encouragement partner, be prepared to work through the following aspects of calming the conscience with grace. Thinking about a besetting sin in your life that you have repented of and, thinking about Satan's lies about Christ's grace, respond to and interact about the following:

1. When in the past has your conscience been calmed with grace by applying the living voice of the gospel to your troubled heart so you were encouraged to return home to the forgiving heart and loving arms of your gracious Father? What was it like? What did God use to bring you to this point of return home?

2. How could you apply to your life the principle of being enlightened to understand your identity in Christ as a beloved son or daughter?

3. How could you apply to your life the principle of recognizing the quadralog?

4. How could you apply to your life the principle of providing (and receiving) tastes of grace?

5. Make the time right now to pen a psalm of homecoming.

> Reconciling spiritual conversations enlighten people to the horrors of sin through the conviction of guilt (recognition) and the confession of sin (repentance), and to enlighten people to the wonders of forgiveness through the comfort of grace (reconciliation).

Hosea 14:1 – 2 powerfully unites conviction, confession, and comfort as it pictures repentance as *relational return*. "Return, O Israel, to the LORD your God. Your sins have been your downfall [conviction]! Take words with you and return to the LORD [confession]. Say to him: 'Forgive all our sins and receive us graciously [comfort].'"

Spiritual Conversations and the Conviction of Guilt: Recognizing the Horrors of Sin

Through probing theologically, exposing heart sin (confronting), and applying truth relationally, we've exposed Ray's heart sinfulness. We've sought to help Ray to recognize the horrors of his sin relationally (he's living like a spiritual adulterer), rationally (he's living like a heart idolater), volitionally (he's living like an enslaved destroyer), and emotionally (he's living like an ungoverned user).

Because of the deceitfulness, hardness, and blindness of sin, before Ray will repent of sin, he must recognize its insanity, see its vileness, and sense its ugliness. John Owen, in his classic work *The Mortification of Sin*, describes what must happen to loosen the hold of sin. "Get a clear and abiding sense upon thy mind and conscience, first, of the guilt, secondly, of the danger, thirdly, of the evil, of that sin wherewith thou art perplexed."[107]

What will motivate Ray to hate sin with a holy hatred? Owen suggests the following principles of loading the conscience with guilt, which we can "translate" into spiritual conversations.

- Have you considered the danger of this particular sin? Do you see the danger of being hardened by its deceitfulness (Heb. 3:12 – 13)? Do you see the danger of the loss of peace with God?
- Have you considered the evil of this sin? How it is spiritual adultery against God the Father? How the Lord Jesus is wounded afresh by it? How it grieves the Holy Spirit?
- Have you considered the absoluteness of God's holiness that this sin betrays?

+ Have you brought this sin to the gospel for further conviction? Have you looked on him whom you have pierced and in bitterness said to your soul, "What have I done? What love, mercy, blood, and grace have I despised and trampled on? Is this the return I make to the Father for his love, to the Son for his blood, and to the Holy Spirit for his grace?"

+ Have you considered the infinite patience and forbearance of God toward you? Have you reminded yourself of his gracious withholding of judgment?

+ Have you prayed for and pursued a constant longing for deliverance from this idol of the heart?

+ Have you pondered what occasions led to your surrendering to this sin? Have you guarded against those occasions?

+ Have you placed faith in Christ for the mortification of this sinful adultery and idolatry?[108]

These spiritual conversations seem foreign and severe to us today because we've lost the spiritual awareness that Owen had. He knew that the defiled imagination glazed, adorned, and dressed the objects of the flesh — making them look beautiful, causing them to seem preferable to God and God's way. He understood that the fleshly imagination darkened the soul like a thick cloud intercepting the beams of God's love and favor.[109] That's why to break sin's hold, we must help one another to see how our heart sins break the heart of God.

Spiritual Conversations and the Confession of Sin: Repentance of the Horrors of Sin

As Ray begins to recognize the horrors of his sin, now, in line with 2 Timothy 2:25 – 26, we want to:

> Gently instruct, in the hope that God will grant them repentance leading them to a knowledge of the truth, and that they will come to their senses and escape from the trap of the devil, who has taken them captive to do his will.

Gentle biblical instruction requires trialoguing about the nature of repentance as *relational return*. It exposes the relational nature of sin and repentance. Some sample trialogues include:

+ Desperate, despairing, and depressed, David repented and then pleaded for rest in the presence of his forgiving God (Psalms 32 and 51). What would your prayer of repentance and return sound like?

+ Hosea 14:2 talks about taking words with us as we return to the Lord in repentance. What specific words of repentance is God's Spirit convicting you to share with God the Father?

+ What would it look like for you to return home as the prodigal did? What would you say to the Father?

+ Rather than turning to God, Adam and Eve, in their shame, attempted to run, hide, and cover. Where have you done the same? What would it look like for you to stop your sinful running, hiding, and covering? As you stopped running, hiding, and covering and faced God, what words of repentance would you share with him?

+ What specific confession do you need to make to God about the false lovers of your soul? About the foolish idols of your heart?

Our sin is always first and foremost against God. However, we also sin against one another. Some sample trialogues help us to ponder how to encourage one another to confess our sin and make restoration.

+ Who do you need to ask to forgive you? Specifically, for what?

+ Given your specific pattern of sin, what would reconciliation look like for you and _____?

+ What will restitution look like in this relationship?

Spiritual Conversations and the Comfort of Grace: Receiving the Wonders of Forgiveness—Reconciliation

Picture yourself having exposed Ray's pattern of heart sin and having exhorted him to repent. But then imagine the agony if you were to leave Ray convicted of such sin, but uncomforted by Christ's grace. Having been enlightened to the nature of repentance, Ray needs to be enlightened to the nature of grace. Terms you've read should now leap across the pages of your mind: "lightening the conscience with grace," "dispensers of grace," and "it's wonderful to be forgiven."

Since repentance is relational return, then what's so amazing about grace is that when we return to God, he receives us! As prodigal sons and daughters, when we return home, our Father sees us from a long way off, is filled with compassion for us, runs to us as his sons and daughters, throws his arms around us, kisses us, and celebrates with us! As adulterous spouses, when we repent and return to our faithful Husband, he shows his love to his wife again though we have been adulterers. He heals us, binds our wounds, revives us, restores us, and receives us graciously so we may live in his presence!

Three categories summarize the types of trialogues to master in order to help Ray to grasp the wonders of forgiveness:

+ Calm the Conscience
+ Assure the Conscience
+ Comfort the Conscience

Calm the Conscience

Since little counsel can be received when the conscience is in intense turmoil, biblical counselors refuse to let sin overwhelm the conscience. The worst sin of all is denying grace. Therefore, the worst thing that we can do is to allow Satan to overwhelm Ray so that he despairs of grace in the midst of his sin. Sin can be forgiven, but believing that sin can't be forgiven leaves Ray hopelessly despairing. Satan tempts Ray to deny Christ's claims, claiming instead that his sin is greater than Christ's forgiveness. To calm Ray's conscience, we help him to distinguish between law and gospel.

+ Where were you recruited into the idea that God is angry with you and rejects you when you sin? Who modeled this idea for you? Does it seem to square with your understanding of the Bible? Of grace? Of the cross? Of Christ?

+ Christ always loves you and accepts you. What scriptural meditation can you use to keep this truth in the forefront of your mind?

+ What does the Bible suggest that you do when you feel overwhelmed by sin and crushed by guilt?

Assure the Conscience

The spirit of bondage enslaves the fleshly conscience, causing it to feel that it's still under the weight of the law and the condemnation of God, whom it views as a harsh Judge. The Spirit of sonship liberates the spiritual conscience, causing it to understand that it's now under the freedom of grace and the forgiveness of God, whom it correctly views as a merciful heavenly Father. The Spirit of sonship frees the conscience from fear, releasing it to trust. Knowing these truths, Ray could benefit from the following spiritual conversations:

+ Throughout the Scriptures (Rom. 5:1–11; 8:1–39; Gal. 3:1–29; 5:1–26), God tells us that we have peace with him through Jesus Christ. When do you experience his peace to the greatest extent? What are you doing differently when you experience his peace?

- Tell me about your experience of God's peace. What is it like for you? I'm wondering how peace with God motivates you to love God and others.

- The Bible assures us that we're no longer under condemnation. The spirit of bondage to guilt has been defeated. We've been set free to experience the Spirit of sonship — forgiveness, acceptance, and liberty. How are you allowing the Spirit of sonship to reign in your heart? By faith, how can you accept your acceptance in Christ?

Comfort the Conscience

The Bible teaches that believers are priests (1 Peter 2:1 – 8) and that God commands Christians to confess their sins one to another (James 5:13 – 20). Throughout church history, believers knew mutual confession as *consolatio fratrum* — the mutual consolation of the brethren through private confession.

> When we have laid bare our conscience to our brother and privately make known to him the evil that lurked within, we receive from our brother's lips the word of comfort spoken by God himself. And if we accept this in faith, we find peace in the mercy of God speaking to us through our brother.[110]

We encourage Ray to confess his hidden sins, and, speaking on behalf of Christ and based on the Word of God, we urge him to accept his acceptance in Christ. We can help Ray to experience a comforted conscience through trialogues like:

- Tell me about times when you've experienced God's forgiveness. What was it like? How did it happen?

- What Scriptures have you turned to to find Christ's forgiveness? Grace? Love? Friendship?

- The Bible talks so much about God's grace, forgiveness, and acceptance of us based on our faith in Christ's death for our sins. When are you most aware of and impacted by these truths? What does God seem to do to bring you to these points of awareness? How do you tend to be cooperating with God as he brings you to these points of awareness?

- Who offers you human tastes of grace that somehow mirror God's infinite grace?

Maturing as a Biblical Counselor

Self-Counsel and Group or Partner Interaction

- Think about a besetting sin you are battling or have battled in the past. Perhaps you will want to ponder the same sin battle you reflected about on page 281. With this besetting sin in mind, respond to the following:

1. Conviction of Guilt and Recognition of the Horrors of Sin: work through the trialogues developed from John Owen to bring the power of the Spirit's conviction to bear on your heart (pages 282–83).

2. Confession of Sin and Repentance of the Horrors of Sin: work through the trialogues about repentance as relational return, applying them to your heart sin and your relationship to Christ (pages 283–84).

3. Comfort of Grace and Receiving the Wonders of Forgiveness—Reconciliation: work through the trialogues about calming your conscience, assuring your conscience, and comforting your conscience, applying them to your acceptance of Christ's grace and forgiveness (pages 284–86).

Counseling Others

- Picture yourself counseling Ray, who has come to a point of repentance. However, he's struggling to receive God's forgiveness and to accept Christ's acceptance.

4. Write your own sample spiritual conversations that *calm* his conscience.

5. Write your own sample spiritual conversations that *assure* his conscience.

6. Write your own sample spiritual conversations that *comfort* his conscience.

Empowering Scriptural Explorations: Reconciling Biblical Trialogues

With reconciling spiritual conversations, we use biblical wisdom principles to enlighten people to guilt, sin, repentance, and grace. With reconciling scriptural explorations, we use specific biblical passages to trialogue about the horrors of sin through the conviction of guilt (recognition) and the confession of sin (repentance), and to trialogue about the wonders of forgiveness through the comfort of grace (reconciliation). We'll use one Old Testament passage (Hos. 14) and one New Testament passage (Luke 15) as sample scriptural explorations addressing all of these categories.

> Reconciling scriptural explorations use specific biblical passages to trialogue about the horrors of sin through the conviction of guilt (recognition) and the confession of sin (repentance), and to trialogue about the wonders of forgiveness through the comfort of grace (reconciliation).

Using Hosea 14 to Trialogue about Guilt, Sin, Repentance, and Forgiveness

Here are some sample scriptural explorations we could use from Hosea 14.

- Hosea describes repentance as a relational return to the Lord. How does picturing repentance as a relational return impact your confession?
- In the context of Hosea, relational return portrays an adulterous spouse returning in repentance to her faithful husband. How does this imagery impact your thoughts about your sin? About repentance? About God's forgiving grace?
- Hosea 14:2 tells us to take words with us. Our repentance is to be specific. What specific words of repentance is God calling you to speak?
- Hosea 14:2 also says to pray, "Forgive all our sins." How many sins do you need to ask the Lord for forgiveness of? How confident are you in God's grace — do you believe that he will forgive and receive you when you confess your sins?
- Hosea 14:2 also says that as we confess our sins, we are to pray, "Receive us graciously." What does that say to you about how amazing Christ's grace is to you?

- Hosea 14:3 describes our sin as worshiping false gods. What false gods is the true God calling you to repent of?

- After talking about worshiping false gods, Hosea 14:3 says that in the true God the fatherless find compassion. Do you believe that God is your Father of compassion, the God of all comfort, and the Savior of all grace and forgiveness?

- In Hosea 14:4, God promises to heal your waywardness and to love you freely. What does it mean to you that when you confess your sin, God forgives you, heals you so you can overcome sin, and loves you freely?

Using Luke 15 to Trialogue about Guilt, Sin, Repentance, and Forgiveness

Here are some sample scriptural explorations we could use from Luke 15 and the parable of the prodigal son and the forgiving father.

- In Luke 15 in the parable of the prodigal son, the younger son disrespected his father by demanding his inheritance while his father was still alive. He put himself first and, in essence, wished his father dead. How have you been putting yourself before God in your sin?

- The younger son attempted to quench his spiritual, God-shaped thirst with the things of the world. How have you been digging broken cisterns and rejecting God, your Spring of Living Water?

- The younger son came to his senses, seeing the folly of his sin. What does it look like for you to come to your senses and see the folly of your sin?

- The younger son went to the father and confessed — relational return. What will your relational return to your Father look like and sound like?

- The father races to the son, embraces the son, accepts the son, forgives the son, receives the son back into the family, and celebrates with the son. Are you prepared to receive God's gracious acceptance like that?

- Even as the father was racing to the son, hugging him, kissing him, and receiving him, the son continued to say he was unworthy to be a son. In what ways do you find it difficult to accept the grace of sonship?

+ In the parable, God presents himself as a Father who longs for his son, rushes out to meet him, embraces him, and celebrates with him. How is this image of God similar to your image of God? Dissimilar? What do you suppose accounts for the difference?

+ What difference would it make in your life if you saw God as a Father willing to forgive and longing to celebrate with you?

+ How would you compare and contrast yourself with the prodigal son? With the elder brother?

Where We've Been and Where We're Headed

Here are two tweet-size summaries of chapter 10, and really of all of *Gospel Conversations.*

+ Christ calls biblical counselors to be *grace-maximizers.*

+ In every aspect of biblical counseling by sustaining, healing, reconciling, and guiding, *Christ's gospel of grace* is central.

The grace that convicts (it's horrible to sin) and welcomes home (it's wonderful to be forgiven) is also the grace that empowers us to say "No!" to sin and "Yes!" to Christlikeness (it's supernatural to mature). Chapters 11 – 12 take us on the guiding journey of growth in grace.

Maturing as a Biblical Counselor

Self-Counsel and Group or Partner Interaction

- Think about a besetting sin you are battling or have battled in the past—perhaps you will want to ponder the same sin battle you reflected about on pages 281 and 287. With this besetting sin in mind, respond to the following interactions:

1. Use some of the sample scriptural explorations from Hosea 14 to help you to work through the guilt/sin (conviction), repentance (confession), and forgiveness process (comfort) (pages 288–89).

2. Use some of the sample scriptural explorations from Luke 15 to help you to work through the guilt/sin (conviction), repentance (confession), and forgiveness process (comfort) (pages 289–90).

Counseling Others

3. Select one Old Testament passage and use it to create trialogues where you interact about conviction, guilt, sin, repentance, grace, and forgiveness.

4. Select one New Testament passage and use it to create trialogues where you interact about conviction, guilt, sin, repentance, grace, and forgiveness.

5 GUIDING BIBLICAL COUNSELING COMPETENCIES: FAITH

FAITH

In my counseling ministry, guiding has brought me the most joy. Sustaining and climbing in the casket is a privileged calling from God. Healing and celebrating the empty tomb is a wonderful honor. Reconciling and dispensing grace is an amazing blessing. Yet for me, guiding and fanning into flame the gift of God is the capstone. It offers the opportunity to see the fruit of biblical counseling — Christlikeness. It offers the chance to be a disciple-making coach and equipper.

In chapters 11 and 12 we learn and practice the five skills of guiding biblical counseling. Here are the student-oriented learning objectives (SOLOs) that will be our target in the healing process.

Active participants in the reading and application of chapters 11 – 12 will be able to:

- ✦ Engage in redemptive friendships as disciple-makers, equippers, mentors, and coaches who fan into flame the gift of God (chapter 11).

- ✦ Empower saints to apply the supernatural power of Christ's grace to mature them into Christ's likeness (chapter 11).

- ✦ Develop the guiding relational competency of fanning into flame the gift of God — envisioning our new identity in Christ (chapter 11).

- ✦ Develop the guiding relational competency of authoring empowering narratives — putting on new covenant living (chapters 11 and 12).

- ✦ Develop the guiding relational competency of insight-based action plans — cocreating homework that works (chapter 12).

- ✦ Develop the guiding relational competency of target-focused spiritual conversations — guiding theological trialogues (chapter 12).

- ✦ Develop the guiding relational competency of heroic scriptural explorations — guiding biblical trialogues (chapter 12).

If you are working through *Gospel Conversations* with a group of people, then to meet these learning objectives, you will want to do the following prior to meeting with your small group training lab:

- ✦ Chapter 11: Guiding through Fanning into Flame the Gift of God
  - ✦ Read pages 297 to 322.
  - ✦ Respond to all questions on pages 299, 306 – 7, 312 – 13 and 322.

- Read, meditate on, and study John 21; 2 Corinthians 3:18; 4:16 – 18; Galatians 5:1 – 3; Ephesians 1:1 – 23; 5:26 – 27; Philippians 3:10; Colossians 3:1 – 11; 2 Timothy 1:6 – 7; and 2 Peter 1:3 – 11.
- Optional: Read chapters 11 – 12 of *Gospel-Centered Counseling*.
- Chapter 12: Guiding through Grace for Growth
  - Read pages 323 to 352.
  - Respond to all questions on pages 324, 332 – 33, 341 – 42, 346 – 48, and 352.
  - Read, meditate on, and study Romans 6:1 – 14; 8:28 – 39; Ephesians 3:15 – 21; Colossians 1 and 3:1 – 16.
  - Optional: Read chapters 15 – 16 of *Gospel-Centered Counseling*.

CHAPTER 11

Guiding through Fanning into Flame the Gift of God

W e've been engaging in the personal ministry of the Word with folks like Trudy and Tony, Pastor Carl, Emilio and Maria, Ashley, and Pastor Ray. They've come to us as saints, sons, and daughters who are facing suffering and battling against sin on their journey toward sanctification — likeness to Christ.

In sustaining, we've climbed in the casket, empathizing with these folks so they know that "it's normal to hurt." We've joined with them in their troubling stories as they have invited Christ into their casket experiences.

In healing, we've celebrated the empty tomb — the resurrection — encouraging them toward the conviction that in Christ "it is possible to hope." We've journeyed with them in their faith story toward Christ and increased Christlikeness.

In reconciling, we've dispensed grace — Christ's amazing grace — enlightening them to the twin convictions that "it's horrible to sin but wonderful to be forgiven." We've joined with them in Christ's redemptive story as they have become aware of sin, confessed sin, repented of sin, been amazed by grace, and received Christ's grace for their disgrace.

Trudy and Tony, Pastor Carl, Emilio and Maria, Ashley, and Pastor Ray have been recipients of Christ's healing hope for their hurt and Christ's amazing grace for their hardness. What more is there to do, right? Have our final counseling session and send them on their way?

That's what we might do if we align with Western cultural norms. We typically see counseling exclusively as a *problem-centered reactive response* to

Maturing as a Biblical Counselor

Self-Counsel and Group or Partner Interaction

1. Who has been a disciple-maker and mentor in your life? Who has been able to stir up and fan into flame the gifts of God within you? Describe what this person is like.

2. How has this person discipled you to become more like Christ? How has this person stirred you up to love and to do good deeds?

3. What impact has this person had on your life? How has this person made a difference in your life and ministry?

Counseling Others

4. Who have you been a disciple-maker and mentor for? Who have you stirred up to love and to do good deeds?

5. How have you ministered in this person's life to help the person to become more like Christ? How have you fanned into flame the gift of God in this person by stirring them up to love and to do good deeds?

trouble. We either react in counseling to trouble in the world — suffering. Or we react to trouble in the heart — sinning. In this model, counseling is removed from the daily flow of one-another church discipleship ministry.

Guiding: Fanning into Flame

Comprehensive biblical counseling, on the other hand, sees counseling *as* discipleship. When we are a church *of* biblical counseling, then everyone in the congregation engages regularly in *sanctification-focused proactive discipleship* as we each speak gospel truth in love to comfort one another and to see to it that no one lives according to an unbelieving heart.

When a brother or sister faces struggles that seem to require more intensive individual focus, then, as part of the overall, ongoing discipleship ministry of the church, they can seek *sanctification-focused personal discipleship* — what we call in our culture "counseling." But notice that it is not problem-focused reactive counseling, but sanctification-focused personal discipleship.

In this model, after sustaining, healing, and reconciling, it makes perfect sense to continue to meet with Trudy and Tony, Pastor Carl, Emilio and Maria, Ashley, and Pastor Ray for *sanctification-focused progressive discipleship* — guiding. And it makes perfect sense that whenever we have our final commencement meeting (I do not like "termination" as the term for a final counseling meeting), then Trudy and Tony, Pastor Carl, Emilio and Maria, Ashley, and Pastor Ray seamlessly continue with the whole church in *sanctification-focused progressive discipleship.*

How Christ Changes People

But how does this sanctification growth happen? What is the power for progressive change? Typically in biblical counseling, we have talked about *how people change.* I suggest that we tweak that language in an important way: *how Christ changes people.* We can only change because of Christ's saving grace that has already changed us and because of Christ's sanctifying grace that motivates and empowers us to change.

I developed in detail in *Gospel-Centered Counseling* that our salvation not only forgives our sin (justification) but also reconciles us to God (reconciliation). Our salvation changes us by implanting a new heart within us (regeneration) and embedding new resurrection power in us to be victorious over sin (redemption).[111]

How does the phrase "how Christ changes people" impact how we counsel people? In thinking about the relationship between our salvation and our sanctification, some summarize it like this: "Sanctification is the art of getting used to our justification." In *Gospel-Centered Counseling*, I suggested a more biblically robust description: "Sanctification is the art of applying our justification, reconciliation, regeneration, and redemption."[112]

If sanctification is simply the art of getting used to our justification, then guiding would either be unnecessary or consist only of reminders of our salvation. We would focus on the "indicatives" of our salvation (what Christ has done for us and who we are in Christ), rather than having an equal focus on the "imperatives" of our salvation (how we live for and grow into the image of Christ).

Interestingly, Luther, who many look to for this "indicative-only approach," did *not* practice this approach. While Luther (and I) believed that reminders of our salvation and meditation on the indicatives are essential motivators for growth in grace, Luther (and I) practiced a both/and approach of faith active in love.[113] In response to grace by faith (indicatives) and empowered by grace, we actively grow in grace as we love God and others (imperatives).

Others see sanctification as imperative-only — "try harder." Apart from grace motivation and grace empowerment, this approach to sanctification matches what the apostle Paul preaches *against* in Galatians 3:3. "Are you so foolish? After beginning with the Spirit, are you now trying to attain your goal by human effort?" If this is our view of sanctification, then "guiding" becomes little more than spotting a sin, confronting a sin, exhorting behavioral change.

The biblical approach to sanctification is a both/and approach. Christ's grace is *both* a salvation grace *and* a sanctification grace. We highlight *both* the indicatives of our salvation (Christ has already changed us) *and* the imperatives of our sanctification (Christ is empowering us to increasingly reflect his image). We must *both* understand our salvation *and* have a role to play in applying our salvation.

Progressive Sanctification

Many Christians have simply given up on sanctification. I'm convinced this is partially because we've misdefined sanctification either as being exclusively of God ("let go and let God," the indicative-only approach) or as self-effort obedience ("try harder," the imperative-only approach).

I'm also convinced that many have given up on sanctification partially because we've made the goal so otherworldly and mystical. The Bible makes it so this-worldly, so human. Sanctification is Pastor Ray as a human being increasingly becoming like Christ in his relating, thinking, choosing, and feeling. Our *target* is the heart — a heart that increasingly relates like, thinks like, chooses like, acts like, and responds to feelings like Christ does. Sanctification is both what Ray is and what Ray is becoming. Ray is a regenerated human *being* and he is a sanctified human *becoming* — becoming more like Jesus.

Jay Adams recognized this truth decades ago in his foundational work, *The Christian Counselor's Manual*. "Be what you are. Basic to the New Testament concept of motivation is the task of becoming what you are. In a real sense we are not merely human *beings*, but also human *becomings*."[114]

In *Gospel-Centered Counseling*, I unite a robust understanding of our salvation and our sanctification into the following definition:

> Sanctification is the grace-motivated and grace-empowered art of applying our justification, reconciliation, regeneration, and redemption so that our inner life increasingly reflects the inner life of Christ (relationally, rationally, volitionally, and emotionally) as we put off the old dead person we once were and put on the new person we already are in Christ (relationally, rationally, volitionally, and emotionally).[115]

Rather than stopping after sustaining, healing, and reconciling, we seamlessly and joyfully move into guiding, which historically and biblically has focused on maturity in Christ. In guiding, we journey with counselees in their growth-in-grace story, empowering them to tap into Christ's resurrection power that is already at work in their new heart. People learn and apply the gospel truth that "it's supernatural to mature." Christ's grace changes people and empowers them to mature into his likeness — becoming more like him in how we relate, think, choose, act, and respond to our feelings.

Sustaining is drawing a line in the sand of retreat as we join with sufferers in their suffering. Healing is driving a stake in the heart of Satan's lies and clinging by faith to the good heart of God as we journey with sufferers to Christ. Reconciling is seeing the truth of my adulterous heart and then seeing the greater truth of Christ's grace. Guiding is *empowering saints to apply the supernatural power of Christ's grace to mature them into Christ's likeness.*

We've pictured sustaining as *climbing in the casket*; healing as *celebrating the empty tomb*; and reconciling as *dispensing grace*. We can picture guiding as *fanning into flame the gift of God*. God has planted within us the same resurrection power that raised Christ from the dead (Eph. 1:5 – 23). The apostle Paul made it the goal of his sanctification to "know Christ and the power of his resurrection" (Phil. 3:10). In guiding, we help people to tap into, apply, and avail themselves of the resurrection power that is already in them. We stir up the new creation they already are in Christ.

Paul stirred up and fanned into flame the gift of God in Timothy with these words:

> I have been reminded of your sincere faith, which first lived in your grandmother Lois and in your mother Eunice and, I am persuaded, now lives in you also. For this reason I remind you to fan into flame the gift of God, which is in you through the laying on of my hands. For God did not give us a spirit of timidity, but a spirit of power, of love and of self-discipline. (2 Timothy 1:5 – 7)

Timothy was a believer, a new creation in Christ. As a babe in Christ, Paul encouraged him to grow up into Christlikeness.

Peter takes the same discipleship and guiding approach in 2 Peter 1:3 – 11. He starts by highlighting our new identity in Christ — our new nature as new creations.

> His divine power has given us everything we need for life and godliness through our knowledge of him who called us by his own glory and goodness. Through these he has given us his very great and precious promises, so that through them you may participate in the divine nature and escape the corruption in the world caused by evil desires. (2 Peter 1:3 – 4)

Peter doesn't stop there. He fans into flame our new heart with these words:

> For this very reason, make every effort to add to your faith goodness; and to goodness, knowledge; and to knowledge, self-control; and to self-control, perseverance; and to perseverance, godliness; and to godliness, brotherly kindness; and to brotherly kindness, love. For if you possess these qualities in increasing measure, they will keep you from being ineffective and unproductive in your knowledge of our Lord Jesus Christ. But if anyone does not have them, he is nearsighted and blind, and has forgotten that he has been cleansed from his past sins." (2 Peter 1:5 – 9)

Peter starts and ends with our identity in Christ as new creations. He insists that we avoid gospel amnesia — forgetting who we are in Christ. He also insists that we avoid gospel inertia — apathetically refusing to grow up in Christ.

Someone once asked Gutzon Borglum, the creative genius behind the presidential carvings on Mount Rushmore, "How did you ever create those faces out of that rock!?" Borglum replied, "I didn't. Those faces were already in there. Hidden. I only uncovered them."

Christian, the face of Jesus is already in there. *In you!* This is the essence of regeneration. God originates within us a new disposition toward holiness. Christlikeness is etched within. The divine nature is embedded in our new nature (2 Peter 1:3 – 4; Col. 3:1 – 11).

In sanctification, we yield to and cooperate with the Holy Spirit who uncovers the Christ who dwells within. To grow in Christ, we need to *understand and apply* who we are in Christ. Once we are clear on the new person we are in Christ, we continue by faith active in love as we cooperate with the Divine Architect, who daily transforms us increasingly into the image of Christ (2 Cor. 3:18; 4:16 – 18). In guiding, it is our joyful privilege to join with our brothers and sisters in Christ on their grace-in-growth journey.

Guiding Relational Competencies: FAITH

Five guiding relational competencies are instrumental in helping people to live out their faith active in love. I define these guiding relational competencies in several overlapping ways:

- Engaging in redemptive friendships as disciple-makers, equippers, mentors, and coaches where we fan into flame the gift of God in one another during the growth-in-grace story.
- Equipping one another to understand and apply the truth that it's supernatural to mature.
- Journeying with people in their growth-in-grace story by empowering them to tap into Christ's resurrection power that is already at work in their new heart.
- Combatting gospel amnesia by reminding people of their identity in Christ and combatting gospel inertia by reminding people of their calling to become like Christ.
- Stirring up the new creation that Christians already are in Christ so we live lives of faith active in love.
- Empowering saints to apply the supernatural power of Christ's grace to mature them into Christ's likeness.

As with sustaining, healing, and reconciling, it is relatively easy to define guiding relational competencies, but it takes a lifetime to cultivate them. Over the course of the next two chapters, we'll learn and practice five biblical counseling competencies for guiding — competencies that I summarize using the acronym *FAITH*:

- ◆ *F* Fanning into Flame the Gift of God
- ◆ *A* Authoring Empowering Narratives
- ◆ *I* Insight-Based Action Plans
- ◆ *T* Target-Focused Spiritual Conversations
- ◆ *H* Heroic Scriptural Explorations

FAITH is a reminder that in guiding, we seek to equip Christians to live a life of faith active in love. We fan into flame the new creation in Christ that we already are. So when you think about guiding spiritual competencies, think FAITH.

> Guiding involves empowering saints to apply the supernatural power of Christ's grace to mature them into Christ's likeness.

Fanning into Flame the Gift of God: Envisioning Our New Identity in Christ

Why don't we grow like Christ in increasing measure? What causes us to be ineffective and unproductive in our knowledge of Christ? Recall that Peter answered those questions by diagnosing the core reason why our new heart grows sickly: *gospel amnesia*. We are nearsighted and blind, having forgotten that we have been *cleansed* from our past sins (2 Peter 1:8 – 9).

The Greek word Peter chooses for "cleansed" is the same word Paul uses in Ephesians 5:26 when he casts an amazing vision for who we are to and in Christ. Christ loved the church and gave himself up for her "to make her holy, cleansing her by the washing with water through the word, and to present her to himself as a radiant church, without stain or wrinkle or any other blemish, but holy and blameless" (Eph. 5:26 – 27).

> Fanning into flame involves prayerfully catching and personally casting a new covenant vision of who Christian counselees are in Christ, because to grow in Christ we must understand and apply who we are in Christ.

Think about those truths in your own life — when you've given in again to yet another besetting sin. Think about it in the life of your counselees — when they have been caught in a sin and experience the shame that goes with such exposure. At that moment, do you, do I, do our counselees see ourselves as loved by Christ (our new nurture) and holy in Christ (our new nature)? At that moment of conviction of sin, do we have an even deeper conviction of grace so that we see ourselves as the beloved of Christ, as the bride of Christ, as loved sons and daughters of the Father (our new nurture)? At that moment of repentance, do we so grasp grace that we see ourselves as holy, cleansed, washed, radiant, without stain or wrinkle or any other blemish, and blameless (our new nature)?

We need to and we can if we will engage with one another in fanning into flame our new identity in Christ. Fanning into flame involves prayerfully catching and personally casting a new covenant vision of who Christian counselees are in Christ, because to grow in Christ we must understand and apply who we are in Christ.

Applying a Biblical Theology of Salvation: "I Believe in the New Covenant"

Think about Pastor Ray and his previously defensive heart and arrogant self-sufficiency. We've probed theologically with Ray, helping him to diagnose four sinful chambers of his heart. We've exposed his heart sin through confronting him lovingly and wisely and through connecting intimately as we've applied truth relationally. By God's grace, as we've engaged in spiritual conversations and scriptural explorations, Ray has confessed his sins to God, repented of his heart sins, and started a restitution and restoration process with his elders and others. He's begun to put off his old ways. And when Satan whispers to Ray, "God won't forgive you; he doesn't accept or love you!" we've sought to calm Ray's conscience with grace. We've reminded him of his new nurture — he is loved by God, forgiven (justification), and welcomed home (reconciled).

But Satan's not done with his whispering campaign. He taunts Ray with new innuendos and insinuations. Satan hisses at Ray: "The saying is right; 'You're not perfect, *just* forgiven.' That's *all* you are — forgiven but still filthy! Welcomed home but still worthless! A spiritual wreck. A washout! Ugly. Despicable you!"

Maturing as a Biblical Counselor

Counseling Others and Group or Partner Interaction

1. We discussed tweaking the phrase "how people change" to "how Christ changes people." How could your counseling be affected by emphasizing the phrase "how Christ changes people"?

2. We suggested that the phrase "sanctification is the art of getting used to our justification" is incomplete. We suggested a more robust description: "Sanctification is the art of *applying* our justification, reconciliation, regeneration, and redemption." How could your counseling be impacted by emphasizing this more robust understanding of sanctification?

3. We suggested that we have made the goal of sanctification too otherworldly and too mystical. We further suggested that the Bible makes our target very clear: our heart to become increasingly like Christ in how we relate, think, choose, act, and respond to our feelings. How could your counseling be changed if we emphasized this "heart target"?

4. We developed from 2 Timothy 1 and 2 Peter 1 the biblical reality that we are already changed—we have a new nature—we are babes in Christ. And we developed from these passages that we also have a calling to grow up in Christ. How could your counseling be impacted by this twin focus on new creations in Christ called to grow up in Christ?

---

5. We illustrated from Gutzon Borglum and developed from 2 Corinthians 3:18; 4:16–18; Colossians 3:1–11; 2 Timothy 1:5–7; and 2 Peter 1:3–4 the truth that the image of Christ is already in the Christian. We need to stir up and fan into flame the new person we already are. How could your counseling be impacted by this mind-set?

If Peter were Ray's gospel-centered counselor, it is at this moment that Peter would cast a new covenant vision of Ray. Peter would remind Ray that by virtue of Christ's new covenant, he not only has a new relationship with Christ, he has a new heart. Christ won Ray's heart *and* cleansed Ray's heart. Ray has a new nurture (who he is *to* Christ) *and* a new nature (who he is *in* Christ).

Peter would remind Ray that as a result of the new covenant, he's not "just forgiven." He's forgiven *and* cleansed — given a new heart (regeneration) and a new power (redemption) so that he can live a new life of purity — a grace-empowered life of faith active in love.

We shouldn't be surprised that Peter would counsel us concerning overcoming gospel amnesia and inertia. It's the exact counsel that Peter needed and received from the Divine Counselor — Christ. Peter had been at the empty tomb and then later been in the presence of the resurrected Christ (John 20). Yet he still needed Christ to cast a vision for his *usefulness* for gospel-centered ministry. In fact, Peter needed three reminders: feed my lambs, take care of my sheep, feed my sheep (John 21:15 – 17).

Jesus puts an exclamation point on his vision, fanning it into flame by envisioning for Peter "the kind of death by which Peter would glorify God. Then he said to him, 'Follow me!'" (John 21:19). Imagine that. The one who denied Christ at Christ's death would glorify Christ by his own death. The one who turned his back on Christ would now spend the rest of his life as a faithful, useful follower of Christ.

Praying for a Biblical Vision of Our Christian Counselee: Physicians of a New Heart

What if for three years we had built into Peter our vision, and then he betrayed us? What would *our* vision of Peter be?

Before we can cast a vision of our counselees as a new creation in Christ, we have to envision them with a new covenant vision. That's easier said than done sometimes. By the very nature of counseling in our culture, people tend to come to counselors at their worst. We see them devastated and broken by suffering. We view them beaten down and beaten up by sin — doing some pretty ugly and evil things. And sometimes in their pain and in their sin, they cause us pain as they sin against us. That's why we need to prayerfully ask the Lord to give us a biblical vision of who they are in and to Christ.

We also need to ask the Lord to give us a new vision of our role as counselors. When we're counseling Christians, we're not just physicians of the soul. We're physicians of a *new* heart. New covenant counselors counsel Christians as Christians, not as if they were still old creations. New covenant counselors believe what the Bible teaches — we have already been changed from the inside out. We have all things necessary for godly living. We are not perfected, but we are cleansed, changed, and empowered.[116] New covenant counselors focus on the implications of the reality that *Christ changes people*.

As we pray about being new covenant counselors, we need to think like new covenant counselors. As we counsel, we can be prayerfully pondering:

+ Do I see myself as a physician of a new heart? As a new covenant counselor? As a gospel-applying counselor?

+ What evidence of a new heart — new Christlike relating, thinking, choosing, acting, and responding to emotions — do I see that I can fan into flame? What Christlike character do I already witness that I can affirm and stir up?

+ What do I already see my counselee offering others which, if stirred up, could grow mightily? What victory over sin do I already detect that I can fan into flame?

+ What strengths does my counselee have that, if surrendered to God, could powerfully advance the kingdom?

+ How has God uniquely designed my counselee? What passions do I see flowing from my counselee's life? Where does my counselee seem to find great joy? What ministry seems most natural for my counselee?

If we're counseling Ray, we connect with the uniqueness already stamped into his makeup by the Holy Spirit. Then we envision what the Spirit has designed Ray to become. As we *catch* a glimpse of what he is and could become in Christ, then we're able to *cast* that vision.

Casting a Biblical Vision of Our Christian Counselees

Because people come to us hurting and hardened, it's easy for them to see themselves only through their suffering and sin. We need to cast a biblical vision of their *universal* identity in Christ and of their *unique* identity in Christ.

Casting a Vision of Our Universal Identity in Christ

By "universal" identity in Christ, I mean those aspects of who we are in Christ that apply to every Christian. In *Soul Physicians*, I provide two charts, each with hundreds of verses paraphrasing who all believers are *in* Christ (our new nature — our sainthood) and who all believers are *to* Christ (our new nurture — our sonship).[117] Our counselees grow in grace as they meditate on and apply these verses, as they grasp who they are in and to Christ.

Maria Stewart understood this concept. As a twenty-eight-year-old widowed, ex-enslaved African American woman, converted just one year earlier, she marched into the office of William Lloyd Garrison, the publisher of the abolitionist newspaper *The Liberator*, to insist that he publish her articles addressed to her fellow sisters of the Spirit. Writing in 1831, she envisioned who they were in and to Christ.

> *Many think, because your skins are tinged with a sable hue, that you are an inferior race of beings; but God does not consider you as such. He hath formed and fashioned you in his own glorious image, and hath bestowed upon you reason and strong powers of intellect. He hath made you to have dominion over the beasts of the field, the fowls of the air, and the fish of the sea (Genesis 1:26). He hath crowned you with glory and honor; hath made you but a little lower than the angels (Psalms 8:5).[118]*

No one was telling young black women in 1831 that they were bearers of God's image with reason and strong powers of intellect. No one was telling them they had dominion over anything. No one except Maria Stewart. She cast a vision that helped countless young black women to understand their identity in Christ.

God calls physicians of the new heart to be like Maria Stewart. We trialogue with our Christian brothers and sisters, exploring what God's Word says about their new heart.

Casting a Vision of Our Unique Identity in Christ

We also need to help people to see their *unique* identity in Christ. God formed and fashioned each of us from eternity past with unique personalities, gifts, passions, and desires (Ps. 139:13 – 16). We have each lived a unique life of special experiences that further equip us for ministry that no one else can do.

When I was transitioning from my first pastoral ministry, a good friend named Tim helped me to recognize my unique identity in Christ. He had been a very successful baseball player, making it to AAA — just missing out on a major league career. Yet his father had never seen a single game he played.

Tim knew that I was a baseball fan and that my boyhood hero was Ernie Banks. So during my going-away party, he marched to the microphone holding a paper bag. As he reached in, he reminded everyone who was my boyhood hero, and then looked at me and said, "Bob, unlike my father, you are a giver. You sacrifice to meet people's needs. You love people with Christ's love. I know that ministry can be hard, and I know that there will be future times when people will beat you up and you'll be tempted to doubt your giving heart. When that happens, I want you to remember this gift."

Then Tim pulled out an Ernie Banks autographed baseball. "Let this gift from me remind you of your passion to give to us, of your calling to be a coach who equips others to be givers also. Before your ministry, I wasn't much of a giver. But by God's grace, you've mentored me to be a gift-giver." Tim understands helping people to see their unique identity in Christ.

We can all be like Tim. God designed us to be "en-couragers" — a companion giving our spiritual friends the courage to persevere when they're on the brink of surrender. We facilitate the grace we see by acting as an "awakener" of what is already there. We draw out and stir up by "affirmingly" exposing the supernatural maturity already residing within. Consider several ways we can do just that with folks like Pastor Ray.

Draw Out by Exploring Narratives of Past Exploits

+ Ray, what are some past times when you've put off the old heart — the old ways of relating, thinking, choosing, acting, and feeling — and put on your new Christlike heart?

+ God tells us that he has given us his Spirit of power, love, and wisdom. Ray, tell me about times when you've utilized God's spiritual power, love, and wisdom.

+ When faced with similar situations in the past, what helped to stir up the gift of God within you, Ray?

Draw Out by Exploring Narratives of Current Resources

+ Ray, if you truly saw yourself as a new creation in Christ, which you are, how would you relate, think, choose, act, and feel differently in this situation?

+ Tell me about any unique gifts that you've allowed to lay dormant that you can fan into flame and stir up into action.

+ If there were no time, talent, or financial restraints, what would you do with your life, Ray? How could you start pursuing a little of that now?

Draw Out by Exploring Narratives of Future Exploits

+ Ray, as you leave here today filled with the Spirit, what will you be doing differently? How will you be loving others (relational)? How will you be making wise biblical decisions (rational)? How will you be choosing to live for God and others (volitional)? How will you be soothing your soul in your Savior (emotional)?

+ Imagine that over the next six months, God does a mighty work within your new heart. How will your home life be different? Your work life? Church life? Relationships? Impact on your community?

+ Dream with me. More than anything else, what do you long to do for God? What legacy do you long to leave? What impact do you hope to make? Who is the one you would most want to impact? How will you be *cooperating with God to bring these dreams to fruition?*

Maturing as a Biblical Counselor

Counseling One Another

- If you are working through this material individually, then use the following trialogues to begin to fan into flame the Christlike maturity that is already within your new heart.

- If you are working through this material in a lab small group, then with the entire group, with a lab partner, with the lab facilitator counseling one group member, or with a lab member counseling another lab member, use the following trialogues to begin to fan into flame Christlike maturity in each other.

1. What are some past times you've put off the old heart—the old ways of relating, thinking, choosing, acting, and feeling—and put on the new Christlike heart?

2. If you truly saw yourself as a new creation in Christ, which you are, how would you relate, think, choose, act, and feel differently in this situation?

3. As you leave here today filled with the Spirit, what will you be doing differently? How will you be loving others (relational)? How will you be making wise biblical decisions (rational)? How will you be choosing to live for God and others (volitional)? How will you be soothing your soul in your Savior (emotional)?

4. Imagine that over the next six months, God does a mighty work within your new heart. How will your home life be different? Your work life? Your church life? Relationships? Impact on your community?

5. More than anything else, what do you long to do for God? What legacy do you long to leave? What impact do you hope to make? Who is the one you would most want to have an impact on? How will you be *cooperating with God to bring these dreams to fruition?*

Authoring Empowering Narratives: Putting on New Covenant Living

It's exciting to have a Christ-empowered role in helping Pastor Ray to repent of and begin putting off the old ways he's related, thought, chosen, acted, and handled his emotions. However, putting off must be followed by putting on. It's also a privilege to play a part in helping Ray to envision living out the new person he already is in Christ. But vision needs to be followed by action — faith active in love.

Heart Change and Gospel-Changed Hearts

When we speak of our identity in Christ, we need to embed that reality in the grand gospel narrative. As Michael Horton explains, "The Good News is not just a series of facts to which we yield our assent but a dramatic narrative that replots our identity."[119] Christ's gospel story invades the very core of our life story — our new identity is a gospel identity.

To jog our memories and replot our identities as biblical counselors and as biblical Christians, we need to look beneath the surface at new creations in Christ. We need to take some additional X-rays of the heart — this time not of the sin-sick heart (chapter 9), but of the salvation-cleansed heart.

First, recall the old heart that we had in our fallen state. Remember the heart disease coursing through the sick heart of the degenerate "old man" we were. That old heart was a slave to unrighteousness. The soul was selfish (relational). The mind foolish (rational). The will manipulative (volitional). The emotions ungoverned (emotional).

Now reflect on the new heart of the new creation in Christ. Slave to righteousness. A new soul, free to love sacrificially (relational). A new mind, enlightened to wisdom (rational). A new will, soft and serving (volitional). New emotions, peaceful yet deep (emotional). We can picture our heart change in Christ like this:

- Renewed Heart Chamber #1: Relational — From Spiritual Adulterers to Virgin Brides
- Renewed Heart Chamber #2: Rational — From Heart Idolaters to Grace Narrators
- Renewed Heart Chamber #3: Volitional — From Enslaved Destroyers to Empowering Shepherds
- Renewed Heart Chamber #4: Emotional — From Ungoverned Users to Soulful Psalmists

Renewed Heart Chamber #1: Relational—From Spiritual Adulterers to Virgin Brides

Only in Christ can a spiritual adulterer become a virgin bride of Christ. It's not just that Christ *sees* us like that, as if he's pretending we're something we're not. Christ *made* us like that; he changed our heart.

Our new heart has new affections, longings, and desires — a new *want to*! As a renewed spiritual being, we *want to* worship God in the core of our being. As new social beings, we *want to* sacrificially minister like Christ to others and for Christ. As renewed self-aware beings, we *want to* rest in who we are in Christ.

Renewed Heart Chamber #2: Rational—From Heart Idolaters to Grace Narrators

Satan conned Adam and Eve into believing that God does not know best and that he withholds his best. They, like us in our fallenness, became *heart idolaters*, believing Satan's sub-version of the story, buying the lie that God does not have a good heart.

Our new heart interprets all of life through the lens of grace. Christ's grand gospel narrative provides the spiritual eyes, the 20/20 spiritual vision, the eternal mind-set through which we interpret life. Thus the new, wise heart is a heart we can identify as a "grace narrator" or "grace interpreter."

The old heart was trapped in the snare that kept focusing on this life, on works, and on how we could atone for our sin. But our new heart with new eyes is designed to focus on the life to come, on Christ's grace, and how he's already atoned for everything. So everything we've done and everything that's been done to us ... we can look at with a new grace-oriented mind-set.

Renewed Heart Chamber #3: Volitional—From Enslaved Destroyers to Empowering Shepherds

Our old heart chamber was dead, so our will was dead to God and enslaved to sin. Even the "good" things we chose to do we did self-protectively and compulsively. We pursued what we mistakenly perceived to be most pleasing.

Relationally, God returns our new heart to *purity*. *Rationally*, he returns our new heart to *sanity*. And *volitionally*, he returns our new heart to *vitality*. We're now free and empowered to empower others. Free to serve Christ and others instead of enslaved to serve Satan and ourselves. The volitionally mature saint says, "I find my life by dying to myself, taking up my cross, and following Christ. I am responsible for my actions and the motivations behind them. This is my new other-centered life purpose in Christ."

The old me was truly a slave to sin and self—to the world, the flesh, and the Devil. The new me is able to say "No!" to sin and "Yes!" to God. The old me was enslaved to living for me and trying to manipulate others. The new me is empowered to choose courageously to lovingly and sacrificially serve God and others.

Renewed Heart Chamber #4: Emotional—From Ungoverned Users to Soulful Psalmists

Our fallen heart runs from our fears rather than racing to our forgiving Father. We either suppress our feelings, stuffing them instead of crying out to God, or we express our feelings indiscriminately, throwing them at others like spears.

Our new heart is like a singer in a gospel choir singing the wonderful African American spirituals. In one line she can be singing her heart out about grief and hurt—crying out to Christ. In the very next line she can be singing her heart out about joy and that comin' day when there will be no more tears or cryin'. Our new emotional heart chamber is *not* emotionless. It is emotion-full. And it is emotion-directed—directed toward God. And emotion-purposed—focused on using emotions to advance God's kingdom, not our cause. This renewed chamber of our heart *feels* with *integrity*—wholeness, honesty, candor.

New Covenant Counseling: Targeting the Heart

Much counseling and most counselees aim at the target of changed circumstances and fixed feelings. Gospel-centered counseling has a very different target — the new heart. In the midst of chaotic circumstances and messy emotions, we seek to help Christians to become more like Christ. Specifically, we guide Christians to live out their new heart in each chamber of the heart:

- *Relational Heart Chamber:* To move from spiritual adulterers to virgin brides who worship Christ (relational/spiritual) and put others before self (relational/social) because they are resting in their identity in Christ (relational/self-aware).
- *Rational Heart Chamber:* To move from heart idolaters to grace narrators who interpret life wisely and make decisions filtered through the mind-set of Christ's grand gospel narrative.
- *Volitional Heart Chamber:* To move from enslaved destroyers to empowering shepherds who courageously choose to follow other-centered purposes that are worship- and ministry-focused.
- *Emotional Heart Chamber:* To move from ungoverned users to soulful psalmists who soothe their soul in their Savior and use their emotions to connect with others.

Personal holiness is personal wholeness. The holy and whole person has a heart whose longings and affections (relational) increasingly reflect Christ, whose images and beliefs (rational) increasingly reflect Christ, whose purposes and behaviors (volitional) increasingly reflect Christ, and whose responses to feelings and moods (emotions) increasingly reflect Christ. In authoring empowering narratives, we equip people to put off the old narrative of the old heart and to put on the new narrative of the new heart so they live like new covenant Christians.

In authoring empowering narratives, we equip people to put off the old narrative of the old heart and to put on the new narrative of the new heart so they live like new covenant Christians.

Authoring Empowering Relational/Spiritual Narratives: Putting on New Worship of Christ

Spiritual renewal involves an "affection set" just as rational mind renewal involves a "mind-set." "Set your hearts on things above" (Col. 3:1). "Set" means to seek with desire, to pursue passionately, to desperately desire. "Heart" is a comprehensive biblical term for the inner person, including all the aspects of personhood — affection, cognition, volition, and emotion. Used as it is here with a word of affection, "heart" especially highlights the relational aspect that longs, thirsts, hungers, and desires — the affection set.

How do we fan into flame and stir up Pastor Ray's spiritual appetite so he puts on adoration of God? By helping him to:

+ Taste Spiritual Thirsts
+ Fix His Spiritual Eyes on Jesus
+ Pursue Spiritual Formation

Intervention Interactions to Taste Spiritual Thirsts

+ Ray, as you know, following Jesus never means killing the new you with all your new desires, longings, loves, affections, delights, and passions. The grace of God comes to us, teaching us to say "No!" to worldly passions, but "Yes!" to God and godly passions (Titus 2:11 – 14). What worldly passions is Christ crucifying in you? How is God's grace teaching you to say "Yes!" to him?

+ Only those who acknowledge that they are thirsty will ever drink from the Spring of Living Water (John 4:1 – 42; 6:25 – 71; 7:25 – 44; Rev. 21:6; 22:17). The invitation to come to Jesus is sent to those who are thirsty. What are you thirsty for, Ray? How can Christ quench your deepest thirst?

+ How have the events of the past months invigorated your passion for Christ? Ray, how have the events of the past months reminded you that the only person you can truly count on is Jesus?

Intervention Interactions to Fix Spiritual Eyes on Jesus

+ We pant after God by fixing our eyes on the Author and Finisher of our faith. Our gaze should never be far removed from his scars. "Let us fix our eyes on Jesus, the author and perfecter of our faith, who for the joy set before him endured the cross, scorning its shame, and sat down at the right hand of the throne of God" (Heb. 12:2). Ray, how does gazing at the Christ of the cross draw you nearer to God?

+ God designed us to thirst for him (Ps. 42:1 – 2). Ray, what is it like for you when you pant after God?

+ Our gaze should never be far removed from God's grace. "Therefore, brothers, since we have confidence to enter the Most Holy Place by the blood of Jesus … and since we have a great priest over the house of God, let us draw near to God with a sincere heart in full assurance of faith" (Heb. 10:19, 21 – 22a). Tell me about your gazing on God's grace. What is it like for you, Ray, to draw near to your gracious God? How does God's grace attract you?

Intervention Interactions to Pursue Spiritual Formation

+ To put on our spiritual affections, we need to feed our soul. Feeding our soul involves pursuing spiritual formation through the practice of the classic spiritual disciplines of the faith. Ray, what personal spiritual workout routine are you following to grow in grace?

+ It's through prayer, meditation, fasting, silence, solitude, worship, fellowship, and the like that we connect with Christ, commune with Christ, and become conformed to Christ. Tell me about your practice of any of these. Tell me about any of these that you would like to learn more about or be accountable for practicing.

Authoring Empowering Relational/Self-Aware Narratives: Putting on Our New Identity in Christ

Entrusting ourselves to our good God, we rest knowing who we are *in* Christ and who we are *to* Christ. Our renewed self-awareness is grace-based and Christ-focused. By grace, we gain Christ-esteem. Christ-shalom. "I am who I am because of the great I Am. I am who I am by Christ's grace."

Spiritual health is a soul at peace with itself *in Christ*. The guiding process involves helping counselees like Pastor Ray to view themselves according to Christ-sufficient identities through:

+ Reckoning on Our New Universal Identity
+ Reckoning on Our New Unique Identity

Intervention Interactions to Reckon on Our New Universal Identity

- How do you think it would impact you, Ray, to read, ponder, probe, study, meditate on, and memorize verses that speak about your identity in Christ?

- Ray, what would it do to your sense of self to claim images of yourself as son, saint, more than conqueror, athlete, bride, etc.?

- Ray, what impact might it have on you if you were to meditate on the following concepts? Reckon on your new relationship to God as your forgiving Father: Romans 8:14 – 17; Galatians 3:26 – 4:7. Reckon on your new relationship to Christ as your sacrificial Savior: Ephesians 5:22 – 33. Reckon on your new relationship to the Spirit as your encouraging best Friend: John 14 – 16; 2 Timothy 1:6 – 7.

Intervention Interactions to Reckon on Our New Unique Identity

- Ray, we can build on our new universal identity by gaining insight into our unique identity in Christ. What is the "shape" of your unique soul (Ps. 139:13 – 16)?

  - *Spiritual Gifts:* What spiritual gifts has the Spirit given you? What ministries are you drawn to? Successful in? Excited about? What is the most thrilling thing you've ever done for God? For others?

  - *Hopes:* What are your Christ-implanted dreams? Your desires? What Christ-centered eulogy would you want spoken at your funeral? What epitaph do you want written on your gravestone?

  - *Abilities:* What equipping do you have for God's kingdom? What experiences do you have in ministry? What talents has God given you?

  - *Personality:* What one word summarizes how God uniquely designed you? What one picture captures who you uniquely are in Christ? What images of yourself stand out to you? To others?

  - *Enjoyment:* What are you passionate about? What do you sense God calling you to do for his kingdom? What do you get excited about? If time, talent, and money were no issue, what would you devote your life to?

Authoring Empowering Relational/Social Narratives: Putting on New Christlike Relationships

As relational beings, we are *spiritual* beings designed to relate to God, *self-aware* beings designed to know who we are in Christ, and *social* beings designed to relate to others. Our renewed communion with Christ allows us to experience a new contentment with who we are in and to Christ. Communing with Christ and content in Christ, now we're free to connect selflessly to others.

Our new love for others is a *grace* love. Having received grace from God, having accepted our grace-based acceptance in Christ, we now view and relate to others from a grace perspective. The guiding process involves nourishing our counselees' new sacrificial relationships toward others through:

+ Imitating Christ's Grace Love
+ Engaging in Spiritual Friendship and Engaging in Spiritual Fellowship

Intervention Interactions to Imitate Christ's Grace Love

+ Ray, how is your communion with Christ deepening your desire to connect with others?
+ Filled with God's grace love, Ray, you're now empowered to imitate Christ's grace love. What will it look like in specific relationships to love others with grace? To love others like Christ loves them?

Intervention Interactions to Engage in Spiritual Friendship and Spiritual Fellowship

+ As you know, Hebrews 3:12 – 15 encourages us to develop a spiritual friendship with at least one other person who knows us through and through. Ray, what spiritual friend, or two, are you connecting deeply with who know you well enough to be able to encourage you daily so you're not hardened by sin's deceitfulness?
+ Ray, you also recall that Hebrews 10:24 – 25 exhorts us to engage in spiritual fellowship with a small group of kindred spirits willing to provoke, prod, exhort, and encourage us toward love and good deeds. What small group are you meeting with or could you meet with for these purposes?

Where We've Been and Where We're Headed

Here are two tweet-size summaries of chapter 11.

+ Christ changes people.
+ We can change because of Christ's saving grace that has already changed us and because of Christ's sanctification grace that motivates and empowers us to change.

Ray, who came to counseling at the behest of his elders, had been "curved in upon himself," defensive, self-protective, and arrogantly self-sufficient. By Christ's grace, his old heart of self-sufficiency has melted away and taken on the form of a new heart of Christ-worship. His old heart of defensive self-protecting is giving way to a blossoming new heart of openness and concern for others. His old curved-in heart is now a heart at peace with who he is in Christ and therefore a heart turned upward to God and outward to others. Much good work has occurred, but there's more work ahead. In the next chapter, we'll author further empowering narratives — rationally, volitionally, and emotionally. We'll also develop the guiding competencies of insight-based action plans, target-focused spiritual conversations, and heroic scriptural explorations.

Maturing as a Biblical Counselor
Self-Counsel and Counseling One Another

- Select a sanctification issue that you're pursuing in your spiritual life. With a partner or with your lab small group, interact and apply the following principles of authoring empowering relational narratives to your growth in grace. If you are working through this material individually, then respond to the following questions in writing.

1. Authoring Empowering Relational/Spiritual Narratives: Putting on New Worship of Christ. Interact about and apply intervention interactions concerning:

   a. Tasting Your Spiritual Thirsts (page 317)

   b. Fixing Your Spiritual Eyes on Jesus (pages 317–18)

   c. Pursuing Spiritual Formation (page 318)

2. Authoring Empowering Relational/Self-Aware Narratives: Putting on Our New Identity in Christ. Interact about and apply intervention interactions concerning:

   a. Reckoning on Your New Universal Identity in Christ (pages 318–19)

   b. Reckoning on Your New Unique Identity in Christ (page 319)

3. Authoring Empowering Relational/Social Narratives: Putting on New Christlike Relationships. Interact about and apply intervention interactions concerning:

   a. Imitating Christ's Grace Love (page 320)

   b. Engaging in Spiritual Friendship and Engaging in Spiritual Fellowship (page 320)

CHAPTER 12

Guiding through Grace for Growth

We're moving toward our commencement meeting with folks like Trudy and Tony, Pastor Carl, Emilio and Maria, Ashley, and Pastor Ray. Commencement is a great word, much better than "termination session." Commencement does not picture an end, but a new beginning.

Trudy and Tony, Pastor Carl, Emilio and Maria, Ashley, and Pastor Ray are already new people in Christ. Through gospel-centered counseling, they are increasingly reflecting that newness.

When formal counseling is done, they commence; they continue living out the new creation they are in Christ. There will be more suffering to endure and overcome. More sin to be tempted by and defeat. But they can increasingly understand and apply the truth that they are more than conquerors in Christ. They can increasingly apply the truth that the Spirit of God through the gospel of Christ has made them alive in Christ. Because Christ changed them, they are encouraged and empowered to keep changing by putting off the vestiges of the old heart and putting on the robes of righteousness that clothe their new heart.

A remarkable narrative from black church history captures the essence of applying our newness in Christ — even during the most difficult suffering and enticing temptation. An African American named Charlie had been enslaved by "Master Bill" before the Civil War. Whipped repeatedly, Charlie finally escaped to the North, where he fought for "the Yanks" in the War. Thirty years later, in the 1890s, Charlie, now an old man, visits the town where he had been enslaved.

Maturing as a Biblical Counselor

Self-Counsel and Group or Partner Interaction

- Use the following trialogues to work through a sanctification issue in your life. Consider this page the start of your "Victory Vision Strategy," or your "Warfare Battle Plan," or your "Victory Planning Sheet."

1. What unique spiritual gifts and gospel resources have you allowed to lie dormant that you can now fan into flame and stir into action in order to prevail in your Christian walk?

2. As a Christian, you have a new heart—you are a new creation in Christ relationally, rationally, volitionally, and emotionally. How can this new identity in Christ encourage and empower you toward Christlikeness in this sanctification issue?

3. How can you tap into Christ's resurrection power and God's spiritual resources to be effective against the world, the flesh, and the Devil?

4. How have you worked through similar sanctification issues before in order to come to a point of victory and growth? How did you manage through Christ to resist the influence of sin on those occasions? How were you empowered to say "Yes!" to godliness?

5. As you move forward on track toward victory over the world, the flesh, and the Devil, what will you be doing differently? How will you keep this victory going and growing? How will you be relating, thinking, choosing, and acting differently?

With a large crowd in the downtown area, Charlie and Master Bill spot each other across the street. Master Bill hollers out, "Charlie, do you remember me?"

"Yes, Master Bill, I still remember you."

"Charlie, do you forgive me for how I mistreated you?"

By now a large crowd has stopped to listen to this exchange shouted across the street. Charlie responds that indeed he had forgiven Master Bill years earlier when Charlie became a Christian.

Astonished, with tears in his eyes, Master Bill walks across the street, hand held out, and asks, "How could you forgive me?"

Be amazed by Charlie's response. "I love you as though you never hit me a lick, for the God I serve is a God of love."[120]

Those who interviewed Charlie about this event couldn't understand how Charlie could respond like this. Charlie understood: *Christ changes people.* Here's how he described it in his own words.

> I had felt the power of God and tasted his love, and this had killed all the spirit of hate in my heart years before this happened. Whenever a man has been killed dead and made alive in Christ Jesus, he no longer feels like he did when he was a servant of the devil. Sin kills dead, but the Spirit of God makes alive. I didn't know that such a change could be made, for in my younger days I used to be a hellcat.[121]

From hellcat to heaven saint — that's the power of putting off and putting on! Christ changed Charlie. Grace changed Charlie. And grace kept changing Charlie — even when coming face-to-face with his sinful former slave master. That's the power of sanctification grace.

While Charlie did not have access to professional counseling, he did have access in the black church to powerful one-another ministry — soul care and spiritual direction that helped him to live out his faith.[122] While Charlie's one-another ministers wouldn't have used an acrostic to summarize what they did, I'm quite confident their ministry reflected guiding FAITH:

- *F* Fanning into Flame the Gift of God
- *A* Authoring Empowering Narratives
- *I* Insight-Based Action Plans
- *T* Target-Focused Spiritual Conversations
- *H* Heroic Scriptural Explorations

In chapter 11, we developed the competency of fanning into flame the gift of God and started to develop the competency of authoring empowering narratives — by addressing relational narratives. In chapter 12, we continue by exploring how to author empowering rational, volitional, and emotional narratives.

Authoring Empowering Narratives: Putting on New Covenant Living

Renewed relationally, we worship God, rest in our identity in Christ, and live to love others. With this relational renewal process moving forward, now we're prepared for rational renewal — putting on new mind-sets.

Authoring Empowering Rational Narratives: Putting on New Wise Mind-Sets

In light of the cross, it is insane to doubt God's goodness. Paul's words become our motto. "If God is for us, who can be against us? He who did not spare his own Son, but gave him up for us all — how will he not also, along with him, graciously give us all things?" (Rom. 8:31b – 32).

What is a new mind-set? It is the larger story, the eternal, heavenly perspective on life that says, "Trust God and live!" Our new mind-sets come complete with new vision. Our Divine Physician performed totally successful laser surgery on our eyes so that we no longer look at life with eyeballs only, but with faith eyes.

Listen to Paul's explanation of the mental sanctification process. "Be transformed by the renewing of your mind" (Rom. 12:2). Paul is telling us to experience a metamorphosis. Be like the caterpillar shedding its outer garment and displaying its true inner nature — the beautiful, free, flying butterfly. Transformation draws out our true inner condition and displays it outwardly so that we become what we are. Paul's also informing us of a central source of our transformation — mind renewal.

In biblical mind-set renewal, we assist our counselees, like Pastor Ray, to:

+ Put on the New Mind in Christ
+ Set the Mind on Things Above
+ Reckon on the New Mind-Set

Intervention Interactions to Put on the New Mind in Christ

- Ray, you've taught this before — Paul teaches that renewing our minds is essential in the process of growth in grace (Rom. 12:1 – 2). Let's talk practically about what that process looks like in your life, situation, and relationships.

- As you know, Ray, Paul also teaches that we have to cast off the old, dead non-grace thoughts about life. What are some of your old ways of thinking about this whole situation? What would it look like to throw them out like the ugly skin of a dead cicada?

- Paul also teaches that we have to put on Christ's new, beautiful grace thoughts about life. What metamorphosis in your mind needs to take place regarding how you view God? Your situation? Yourself? Others?

- Paul commands us, saying, "Let the peace of Christ rule in your hearts" (Col. 3:15). We're to make sure that in our thought life, God's truth acts as umpire. We're responsible for making Christ's grace narrative the final arbiter for interpreting every life event. Paul explains how. "Let the word of Christ dwell in you richly as you teach and admonish one another with all wisdom, and as you sing psalms, hymns and spiritual songs with gratitude in your hearts to God" (Col. 3:16). Putting on our new mind-set begins as we allow God's truth about life to govern our thought life. We make a mental decision to allow God's version of reality to take up residence in our mind as we feed on and meditate on his wisdom. Ray, how are you letting Christ's peace umpire in your heart as you reflect on all that has happened over the past weeks and months? In what ways are you allowing God's truth about life to dwell in you richly? To govern your thought life?

Intervention Interactions to Set Their Mind on Things Above

- As you've taught before, Ray, we are to set our mind-set and direct our thinking toward things above, where Christ is seated at the right hand of God, not on earthly things (Col. 3:1 – 2). What would be different if every morning you began the day with a clear mental picture of Christ seated victoriously at the right hand of God, ruling over every event of your life, graciously giving you everything you need for life and godliness?

+ How would your perspective change, Ray, if for every incident you encountered you filtered through the heavenly narrative of Christ your Victor?

+ Let's be specific. A sinful thought enters your mind, Ray. First, you put it off, rooting out every corrupt imagination. Second, you reflect on godly thoughts. You gather up all your experiences of God and call to mind God's truth. Having done that, what would it be like for you to ask: "How can I take on the mind of Christ? How can I have the attitude Christ had? What would Jesus think (WWJT)?"

Intervention Interactions to Reckon on Their New Mind-Set

+ We are to live based on our new mind-set in Christ (Rom. 6:11). When we're trying to make sense of your life, trying to figure life out, we count ourselves dead to sin and take into account Christ's grace perspective. Ray, what would it be like in your recent situation to consider and evaluate your earthly life based on heavenly reality?

+ Ray, what would it be like to reckon on (picture, imagine, see, view) your whole situation from Christ's grace perspective?

Authoring Empowering Volitional Narratives: Putting on New Other-Centered Purposes

We are purposeful beings with a will that chooses to follow certain characteristic pathways and patterns as we engage life. Our renewed wills are freed and empowered to courageously create good for God's glory and to sacrificially empower others.

Thus, volitional wholeness pursues a whole new *purpose*. We put off the futility of trying to make life work on our own for ourselves. We put on the vitality of working for God through Christ. We put off dominating others and put on empowering them. The guiding process involves provoking Ray's new chosen style of shepherding through other-centered interactions by:

+ Yielding to the Spirit
+ Walking in the Spirit

Intervention Interactions to Yield to the Spirit

+ Ray, as you know, we're to put on in our purposes, practices, and behavior what Christ has already resurrected in our wills. We find this power by admitting that we are powerless. The Bible calls it yielding to the Spirit. Yielding to the Spirit begins with our conscious conviction that without God we can do nothing, but that with God we can do all things through Christ who strengthens us. Have you come to the place in your spiritual life, Ray, where you're consciously aware that without God you can do nothing? That through Christ you can do all things?

+ What is it like for you, Ray, when you confess your neediness and absolute dependence on Christ?

Intervention Interactions to Walk in the Spirit

+ Paul speaks of walking in the Spirit, being led by the Spirit, and keeping in step with the Spirit. While each of these terms maintains a distinctive emphasis, the essence is the same. We're to actively appropriate the Spirit's power in our lives. We're to "allow" the Spirit to guide our walk, our way, our pathway — to direct our steps and lead our interactions with others. Ray, what would it be like for you to be involved in a continual conversation where you're always asking, "Spirit, what would other-centered living look like in this situation? What are you calling me to be and to do right now? How would you want me to respond? What way of relating would please you? Help them?"

+ Ray, tell me about times when you've walked in the Spirit, when you've been led by the Spirit, when you've kept in step with the Spirit. What was different about those times?

Authoring Empowering Emotional Narratives: Putting on New Managed Mood States

We can, with integrity, face our feelings and experience life with all its joys and sorrows. God has given us all that we need for emotional life and emotional maturity so that we can put off unmanaged moods and put on new managed mood states.

The guiding process with emotions involves helping folks like Pastor Ray to move toward emotional maturity as image bearers (relational, rational, volitional, and emotional beings). It includes intervention interactions to:

- Soothe Their Soul in Their Savior (Relational Spiritual)
- Acknowledge Their Mood States (Relational Self-Aware)
- Empathize with Others (Relational Social)
- Bring Rationality to Their Emotionality (Rational)
- Courageously Respond to Their Emotions (Volitional)
- Openly Experience Their Emotions (Emotional)

Intervention Interactions to Soothe Their Soul in Their Savior (Relational Spiritual)

- As a spiritual being experiencing intense emotions, we can soothe our soul in our Savior. Ray, what's it been like for you to take your feelings to God in this situation?
- How have you found your Savior's solace during these trying times? Ray, what is different about those times when you do go to God for comfort?

Intervention Interactions to Acknowledge Mood States (Relational Self-Aware)

- As a self-aware being experiencing deep moods, we can admit, understand, label, and accept our mood states. Ray, how would you rate yourself in these areas? Which of these do you find hardest? Easiest? Why?

Intervention Interactions to Empathize with Others (Relational Social)

- As a social being sensing emotions in others, we can empathize with others, sustaining and healing them. Ray, how has your suffering increased your ability to empathize with others who are suffering?
- How are you allowing the comfort you're receiving from God to comfort others?

Intervention Interactions to Bring Rationality to Emotionality (Rational)

- As a rational being, we can bring rationality to our emotionality. We can gain the wisdom to understand some of the causes and the nature of our feelings. We can envision with spiritual eyes imaginative ways to handle our moods. Ray, how well are you bringing rationality to your emotionality?

+ How well are you able to feel your feelings and understand your feelings?
+ Ray, tell me about times during all this that you've been able to manage your moods.

Intervention Interactions to Courageously Respond to Emotions (Volitional)

+ As a volitional being, we can consciously and courageously choose to creatively respond to our emotional states. Ray, tell me about some times when you've done that as you related to others.
+ What are some of the creative and courageous choices you're making as you respond to your moods?

Intervention Interactions to Openly Experience Emotions (Emotional)

+ As an emotional being, we can openly experience whatever we're feeling, being responsive to God and God's world. Thus cooperating with God, the Creator of emotions, we put on emotional integrity, harmony, and honesty. Ray, tell me about your emotional honesty and openness with yourself.
+ Tell me about your emotional honesty and openness with God.

Insight-Based Action Plans: Co-Creating Homework That Works

Paul begins Romans, Ephesians, and Colossians with gospel indicatives — theological truth related to what Christ has done for us and who we are in Christ. Then in Romans 12 – 16, Ephesians 4 – 6, and Colossians 3 – 4, Paul shifts to gospel imperatives — practical insight into how to apply gospel truth to daily life. For example, after explaining to the Ephesians that they are saints with a new nature (Eph. 1 – 3), Paul exhorts them to make specific application to activate their faith (Eph. 4 – 6).

Maturing as a Biblical Counselor

Self-Counsel and Counseling One Another

- Select a sanctification issue that you're pursuing in your spiritual life. With a partner or with your lab small group, interact and apply the following principles of authoring empowering rational, volitional, and emotional narratives to your growth in grace. If you are working through this material individually, then respond to the following questions in writing.

1. Authoring Empowering Rational Narratives: Put on New Mind-Sets. Interact about and apply intervention interactions concerning:

   a. Putting on the New Mind in Christ (page 327)

   b. Setting Your Mind on Things Above (pages 327–28)

   c. Reckoning on Your New Mind-Set (page 328)

2. Authoring Empowering Volitional Narratives: Putting on New Other-Centered Purposes. Interact about and apply intervention interactions concerning:

   a. Yielding to the Spirit (page 329)

   b. Walking in the Spirit (page 329)

3. Authoring Empowering Emotional Narratives: Putting on New Managed Mood States. Interact about and apply intervention interactions concerning:

   a. Soothing Your Soul in Their Savior (Relational Spiritual) (page 330)

   b. Acknowledging Your Mood States (Relational Self-Aware) (page 330)

   c. Empathizing with Others (Relational Social) (page 330)

   d. Bringing Rationality to Emotionality (Rational) (pages 330–31)

   e. Courageously Responding to Your Emotions (Volitional) (page 331)

   f. Openly Experiencing Emotions (Emotional) (page 331)

Insight-based action plans, or homework that works, follows his model. We seek to change lives with Christ's changeless gospel truth by applying Christ-centered theological insight to Christlike daily living.

Like Paul, we want to master the relational competency of helping our counselees apply new covenant truth to the specifics of their daily relationships. We help them to learn the art of faith active in love through:

- Gospel Victory Action Plans
- Grace Narrative Action Plans
- Commencement Summaries

> Insight-based action plans seek to change lives with Christ's changeless gospel truth by applying Christ-centered theological insight to Christlike daily living.

Gospel Victory Action Plans

Out of the abundance of the heart, the mouth speaks. That's not simply true of our counselees, it's true of *us as counselors*. If we truly believe that our Christian counselees are new creations in Christ, saints with a new nature, new covenant believers who have all they need to live godly lives and are supernaturally enabled to mature through Christ's resurrection power, then how will we speak? How will we word our interactions? We should shape our trialogues to communicate our faith in their supernatural ability to live a life of faith active in love. Thus, we can frame our guiding interactions:

- In a Victorious Form
- In a Progressive Sanctification Form
- In a Truth-to-Life Form
- In a Specific Application Form
- In a Faith-Active-in-Love Form

In a Victorious Form

- Ray, what renewed longings will *replace* your old ones in relationship to God? Your relationship to your elders?

+ Ray, what will you be thinking *differently* when an elder gives you constructive feedback? When an elder shares hurtful criticism?

+ Ray, what do you want to be doing *instead* of being defensive?

+ Ray, what new managed moods will you *put on* when you start feeling discouraged?

In a Progressive Sanctification Form

+ *Continuous Past Tense:* Ray, how *were* you victoriously putting off and putting on those new longings for closeness to Christ even when you felt distant from the body of Christ?

+ *Continuous Present Tense:* Ray, how *are* you victoriously renewing your mind as an elder offers you feedback?

+ *Continuous Future Tense:* Ray, how *will* you be victoriously living out your new nature in Christ the next time those old feelings of defensiveness arise?

In a Truth-to-Life Form

+ Ray, as you apply what we've been discussing about trusting in Christ as you relate to your elders, how *will you be progressing* toward victory?

+ Ray, as you leave our time together today and *you're on track* toward applying this truth about you, Christ, and your elders, how will you be relating differently?

In a Specific Application Form

+ Ray, can you tell me *more specifically* how you will be listening non-defensively to your elders?

+ Ray, *exactly* what will you be doing differently the next time those old self-protective feelings tempt you?

In a Faith-Active-in-Love Form

+ Ray, how will *you* cooperate with Christ to make this new response to your elders happen?

+ Ray, how will *you* choose to respond through Christ to your elders? What will *you* be doing victoriously in Christ when that happens?

Grace Narrative Action Plans

When life stinks, our perspective tends to shrink, including our God-perspective. Problems tend to create myopia — shortsighted, noncreative, black-and-white, inside-the-box thinking. Everything looks bleak. Futile. Resources remain unrecognized. People feel stuck and stunted.

Confused, our counselees need focus — grace narrative focus. They need our help to have the power to grasp together with all the saints how wide and long and high and deep is the love of Christ. And to grasp together with all the saints that God is able to do immeasurably more than all that we ask or imagine, according to Christ's resurrection power that is at work within us (Eph. 3:17 – 21).

Grace narrative action plans shine the light of new covenant spiritual theology by:

- Developing Gospel Clarity
- Encouraging Grace-Empowered Responsibility
- Drawing Out Spiritual Resources
- Keeping Accountable in the Body of Christ
- Turning Setbacks into Comebacks; Turning Caskets into Empty Tombs

Developing Gospel Clarity

We seek to help our counselees to clearly see what the issues are, what decisions they need to make, what actions they need to take, what they want, and what God wants in and from them.

- Ray, what do you think God is calling us to focus on today?
- Ray, from a gospel-centered perspective, what do you see as the problem?
- Ray, what do you think the Scriptures suggest you would want to change about your relationship to the elders?
- Ray, what would be a Christlike goal in responding to this issue?

Encouraging Grace-Empowered Responsibility

Once we've helped our counselees to gain gospel clarity and focus, we seek to motivate them toward grace-empowered responsible actions — faith active in love. We can start this by *probing what they will be doing differently when the problem is solved.*

+ Ray, when God answers your prayers for empowerment, what will you be doing differently?

+ Ray, as you leave here today, on track to acting more maturely, what will you be doing differently as you respond to congregational criticism?

With clarity about grace-empowered responsibility, we can *urge them to do a small piece of that faith active in love now.*

+ Ray, since you know how you want to relate to your elders, and since you know you have Christ's power to do that, what will it look like to do that this week?

+ Ray, you've done a great job clarifying the issues biblically and practically. So what would it look like for you to do a small piece of that starting today?

Drawing Out Spiritual Resources

Now we want to evoke spiritual resources, solutions, and strengths. We want to empower our counselees to cooperate with the Spirit to organize the chaos of their life into beautiful shapes and patterns. We can start by *exploring how some growth is already happening.*

+ Ray, tell me about some times when, by the Spirit's power, you're responding differently now. How are you specifically doing that?

+ Ray, I'd love to hear a testimony of a time when, by the Spirit's power, you've already responded more maturely to criticism.

+ Ray, where are you already experiencing some spiritual victory in this area?

Now we can help our counselees to *discover how growth is happening.*

+ Ray, tell me about some times when the problem isn't happening. What is different about these victorious times? What are you doing differently, Ray, when you see God at work?

With a pattern of Christ-dependent victory established, we can encourage our counselees toward progressive sanctification by *doing more of it.*

+ Ray, how will you and God keep this victory going?

+ Ray, how do you predict that you and Christ will keep these successes going?

- Ray, how will you continue to commune with God, connect with Christ, and cooperate with the Holy Spirit to keep this fruit growing?

Then we can *celebrate victory*!

- Ray, that's great! Awesome! Wow! Praise the Lord!
- Ray, what does that say about your surrender to Christ? Your love for Christ? Your dependence on Christ?
- Ray, what does that say about Christ's grace at work in your life? His power? His love? His wisdom?

Keeping Accountable in the Body of Christ

Accountability is vital to growth in grace. We can maintain accountability first by *collaboratively developing application assignments — homework.*

- Ray, of everything we've discussed today, what strikes you as most central to the change process God is working out in your life?
- How could you apply what we've discussed today, Ray?
- What do you think it would look like for you to change in these ways, Ray?
- Ray, specifically, how could you apply these changes in your life and relationships this next week?
- Ray, what homework assignment will you give yourself?
- What are you going to do differently because of our meeting today, Ray?
- Ray, let's talk about how you could apply the insights you've gained today.

Note that these assignments place responsibility on our counselee for thinking about what to do, why to do it, and how to do it. To keep our counselees accountable, we can also *follow-up on homework assignments.*

- So, give me an update, Ray. How did things go with last week's assignment?
- Ray, I'm eager to hear about how you implemented last week's homework.
- What's your report today? Tell me how you were able to apply what you learned last week, Ray.
- I'm interested to hear how you were able to _____.
- So, what was happening this past week that you want to continue doing? Thinking?

- Ray, tell me about your progress in putting off _____ and in putting on _____.

Turning Setbacks into Comebacks; Turning Caskets into Empty Tombs

Sometimes we'll open a meeting eagerly anticipating a positive report on the past week, only to hear negatives. What do we do then? How do we turn setbacks, apparent or real, into comebacks? How do we turn defeat or casket experiences into victory? Sometimes our counselee will live victoriously, but those around our counselee will respond sinfully. *When there are no changes in our counselee's circumstances or relationships, we can reply with:*

- Ray, I'm really sorry to hear that others are responding like this. That has to be hard. Tell me how you felt and responded.
- I'm sorry to hear that, Ray. How have you been able to continue to cope with this?
- How have you continued to make godly choices? How have you renewed your mind even in the middle of old circumstances? How have you kept longing for Christ even when your human longings go unmet?

Sometimes our counselees will indicate that they have seen *no change or growth in themselves.* Before we exhort or confront, *explore further.*

- No? Not even a little, Ray?
- Ray, was there one time when you were able to experience a bit more victory than previously?
- How did you keep matters from getting worse, Ray?

If they still share no positive report, then in the spaghetti relationship of counseling, we can *implement previous reconciling competencies* such as probing theologically, confronting wisely and lovingly, and connecting intimately.

And since reconciling highlights grace, we can also *impart grace while encouraging confession.*

- Ray, have you talked to the Lord about your failure in this area?
- Ray, talk to me about any battles with guilt.
- Tell me about the forgiveness you received when you confessed that to the Lord.

Since we don't want to stop at defeat, we can also *explore what they wish they had done differently.*

- Are there actions, attitudes, or words that you would do differently if you had the week to do over again?
- Ray, what do you think kept you from drawing on God's power to do this?

Since sanctification is a lifelong progressive process, we can also *promote resilience.*

- Ray, what can you learn from last week's setback?
- How can you persevere through these trying times?
- What would you like to do differently this week?

Commencement Summaries

As a counselor, we can take action too. At the end of our biblical counseling meetings, we can develop a biblical counseling commencement summary (see appendix 12.1). This allows us to review the initial goals for our counseling, overview the growth that has occurred, summarize areas for further growth, and record reasons for concluding formal biblical counseling. This information is helpful for us in assessing how well we're using God's gifts. It is also beneficial should our counselee decide to return later for additional meetings.

Target-Focused Spiritual Conversations: Guiding Theological Trialogues

By now it should be second nature — our target in gospel-centered counseling is sanctification. Sanctification aims at the heart. Specifically, sanctification aims at increasingly reflecting the inner life or heart of Christ in all four chambers of the new covenant heart: relational affections, rational mind-sets, volitional purposes, and emotional mood states. Target-focused sanctification involves interacting about how we can increasingly reflect the inner life of Christ by putting on what is already new within us — new affections, new mind-sets, new purposes, and new mood states.

> Target-focused sanctification involves interacting about how we can increasingly reflect the inner life of Christ by putting on what is already new within us — new affections, new mind-sets, new purposes, and new mood states.

Maturing as a Biblical Counselor
Self-Counsel and Counseling One Another

- Select a sanctification issue that you're pursuing in your spiritual life. With a partner or with your lab small group, interact and apply the following principles of insight-based action plans. If you are working through this material individually, then respond to the following questions in writing.

1. Reflecting on this area of growth in your life, interact about gospel victory action plans using concepts and trialogues framed:

   a. In a Victorious Form (pages 334–35)

   b. In a Progressive Sanctification Form (page 335)

   c. In a Truth-to-Life Form (page 335)

   d. In a Specific Application Form (page 335)

   e. In a Faith-Active-in-Love Form (page 335)

2. Reflecting on this area of growth in your life, interact about grace narrative action plans using concepts and trialogues related to:

   a. Developing Gospel Clarity (page 336)

   b. Encouraging Grace-Empowered Responsibility (pages 336–37)

   c. Drawing Out Spiritual Resources (pages 337–38)

d. Keeping Accountable in the Body of Christ (pages 338–39)

e. Turning Setbacks into Comebacks; Turning Caskets into Empty Tombs (pages 339–40)

Spiritual Conversations to Empower Christians to Apply Their Salvation

To grow in Christ, we must understand and apply who we are in Christ. To put on our new attire, we have to understand four "gowns" of salvation: regeneration, redemption, justification, and reconciliation. The following sample trialogues interact about our complete salvation as the basis for our progressive sanctification.

Regeneration Trialogues

+ Through regeneration, you're a new creation in Christ with a new nature. You're a saint. How could this truth impact you in your daily Christian walk? How could you be living differently based on your newness in Christ?

+ Through regeneration, you have new capacities to live purely. You have a new *want-to* and a new *can-do* to live for Christ. What new *want-to* is God stirring in you? What new *can-do* is the Spirit empowering within you?

+ Through regeneration, you have a new heart — a heart to love like Christ, think like Christ, choose and act like Christ, and respond to your emotions like Christ. How could knowing and applying these truths influence how you love God and others? Your thought life? The goals you live for and pursue? Your emotional maturity?

+ Through regeneration, you have new life. You're resurrected with Christ. How is Christ's resurrection power changing you daily? In what specific ways?

Redemption Trialogues

+ Through redemption, Christ has freed you from the power of sin. What sins do you want liberation from?

+ Through redemption, you have freedom from sin and victory over sin. You're more than a conqueror through Christ. What sins do you want to conquer? What victories do you long for? What battles do you want to win?

+ How could knowing that you have the power for victory in Jesus impact your spiritual warfare with the world, the flesh, and the Devil?

Justification Trialogues

+ Through justification, Christ cancels the penalty of sin. He declares you "Not guilty!" because he took your guilt, your punishment. What does this awareness prompt in you? What does this knowledge incite in you?

+ Through justification, peace, shalom, and acceptance reign in your heart. When do you most deeply experience your acceptance in Christ? How does it impact how you relate to others?

+ Through justification, God has given you new peace. He hushes the voices of condemnation in your mind. How could you enjoy and experience your new peace with God through Christ?

+ Through justification, God declares you righteous. Tell me how you will live like the righteous person you already are.

+ Through justification, you enjoy a new boldness — confidence in your victory in Christ. Tell me about the victories you've been winning for Christ. Tell me about the victories you'll continue to win through Christ.

Reconciliation Trialogues

+ Through reconciliation, you're a son/daughter of God the Father. How does this change your thinking about yourself? Your life? Your responsibilities?

+ Through reconciliation, you're Christ's virgin bride. How does that image impact you?

- Through reconciliation, you're the repentant prodigal returned home — forgiven and loved with the Father's lavish grace love. If you kept that image in mind constantly, how would you live?
- Through reconciliation, God adopted you into his forever family. You're his adult child. How do you want to please the Father?

Spiritual Conversations to Empower Christians to Live according to Their New Heart

Before our salvation, we had a fallen personality structure. Relationally we had an adulterous heart, rationally we had a foolish heart, volitionally we had a self-centered heart, and emotionally we had an ungoverned heart. Because of our salvation, believers now have a redeemed personality structure. Relationally we have a pure worshiping heart, rationally we have a wise heart, volitionally we have an other-centered heart, and emotionally we have a soulful heart. We can use a redeemed personality inventory to help our Christian counselees to evaluate their current progress toward Christlikeness in each chamber of their new heart.

Redeemed Personality Inventory: Relational

- How well are you clinging to God/running home to the Father, delighting in and trusting him like a faithful son or daughter?
- To what extent are you enjoying Christ more than any other joy in life?
- To what extent are you depending on the Holy Spirit to empower you to become more like Christ?
- How well are you loving others deeply from the heart?
- To what extent are you resting confidently and comfortably in who you are in Christ?

Redeemed Personality Inventory: Rational

- To what extent are you valuing what God values?
- To what extent do you see God as your chief good and supreme satisfaction?
- How well are you allowing the eternal story to invade your earthly story?
- How well are you stirring up wise and wholesome thinking in your mind?

Redeemed Personality Inventory: Volitional

- To what extent are you finding life by dying to yourself, taking up your cross, and following Christ?

- How well are you living to empower, minister to, and shepherd others?

- To what extent are you asking, "What would courageous trust in Christ look like in my relationships?"

Redeemed Personality Inventory: Emotional

- How well are you practicing emotional self-awareness — admitting, experiencing, and identifying your feelings?

- How well are you practicing emotional self-mastery — soothing your soul in your Savior?

- How well are you practicing emotional maturity — managing your moods with a ministry focus?

- How well are you practicing emotional empathy — recognizing and connecting with emotions in others?

- How well are you practicing emotional savvy — handling your relationships maturely?

Redeemed Personality Inventory: Physical

- To what extent are you admitting your absolute need, body and soul, for God?

- To what extent are you allowing physical frailties to remind you of your need for God?

Heroic Scriptural Explorations:
Guiding Biblical Trialogues

Faith active in love involves trusting God while risking deep relationships with others. In heroic scriptural explorations, we empower our counselees to live out what they already are: more than conquerors!

In heroic scriptural explorations, we'll want to select from among a multitude of passages that could help our counselees to courageously apply God's truth in their lives. Here are just a few sample trialogues from a few sample passages.

Maturing as a Biblical Counselor

Self-Counsel and Counseling One Another

- Assess yourself in each heart category below using the Redeemed Personality Inventory. Then, with a partner or with your lab small group, interact about pursuing continued growth in grace in each area. If you are working through this material individually, then be sure to develop a growth-in-grace plan.

1. Redeemed Personality Inventory: Relational

    a. How well am I clinging to God/running home to the Father, delighting in and trusting him like a faithful son or daughter?

    b. To what extent am I enjoying Christ more than any other joy in life?

    c. To what extent am I depending on the Holy Spirit to empower me to become more like Christ?

    d. How well am I loving others deeply from the heart?

    e. To what extent am I resting confidently and comfortably in who I am in Christ?

2. Redeemed Personality Inventory: Rational

    a. To what extent am I valuing what God values?

b. To what extent do I see God as my chief good and supreme satisfaction?

c. How well am I allowing the eternal story to invade my earthly story?

d. How well am I stirring up wise and wholesome thinking in my mind?

3. Redeemed Personality Inventory: Volitional

a. To what extent am I finding life by dying to myself, taking up my cross, and following Christ?

b. How well am I living to empower, minister to, and shepherd others?

c. To what extent am I asking, "What would courageous trust in Christ look like in my relationships?"

4. Redeemed Personality Inventory: Emotional

a. How well am I practicing emotional self-awareness—admitting, experiencing, and identifying my feelings?

b. How well am I practicing emotional self-mastery—soothing my soul in my Savior?

c. How well am I practicing emotional maturity—managing my moods with a ministry focus?

d. How well am I practicing emotional empathy—recognizing and connecting with emotions in others?

e. How well am I practicing emotional savvy—handling my relationships maturely?

5. Redeemed Personality Inventory: Physical
   a. To what extent am I admitting my absolute need, body and soul, for God?

   b. To what extent am I allowing physical frailties to remind me of my need for God?

In heroic scriptural explorations, we empower our counselees to live out what they already are: more than conquerors!

Scriptural Explorations Based on Romans 6

+ In the moment of temptation, what difference could it make for you to see yourself as co-crucified with Christ to the power of sin?

+ In the moment of temptation, what difference could it make for you to see yourself as co-resurrected with Christ so that the same power that raised him from the dead is in you and available to you to defeat sin?

+ What does it mean in your life to count yourself dead to sin but alive to God in Christ? How do those truths empower you to be victorious in _____?

+ Paul tells us that we do not need to let sin reign in our mortal body. Instead, through Christ's resurrection power at work within us, we can offer ourselves as instruments of righteousness. Tell me about God's reign in specific areas of your life. Tell me about specific relationships where you are offering yourself as an instrument of righteousness.

Scriptural Explorations Based on Romans 8:28–39

+ In Romans 8:28 – 29, God *guarantees* that he uses everything we go through to conform us to the likeness of Christ. How is he using _____ to conform you to the image of his Son?

+ Romans 8:31 tells us that if God is for us, then no one can be victoriously against us. What are you motivated to do for God's kingdom, knowing that he is for you and will give you victory in his kingdom work?

+ In Romans 8:37, Paul tells us that in everything — in our suffering and in our struggle against sin, *we are more than conquerors through him who loved us!* What difference would it make as you face _____ if you arose every day and lived each moment with the image of a spiritual conqueror, a spiritual superhero, embedded on your mind?

Scriptural Explorations Based on Colossians 1

+ In Colossians 1:3 – 5, Paul tells us that in Christ we have faith, hope, and love. Tell me about your faith, hope, and love as you face this situation.

+ How is Christ's gospel of grace bearing fruit and growing in your life?

+ Paul prays that we would be filled with the knowledge of God's will. In what areas do you need the knowledge of God's will?

+ Paul also prays that we would live worthy of the Lord and please him. In this situation, what will it look like to please the Lord? To live worthy of the Lord?

+ Paul also prays that we would be strengthened with God's might according to his glorious power. As you face _____, how is Christ strengthening you with might according to his glorious power?

+ What difference can it make as you face _____ to apply the truth that Christ has rescued you from the dominion of darkness and brought you into the kingdom of the Son he loves?

+ In Colossians 1:15 – 18, Paul tells us that Christ is supreme over *everything*. How can you tap into his absolute supremacy so you can have victory as you face _____?

+ What is it like to realize that you've been reconciled to God, freed from accusation, and seen as holy and without blemish in his sight? How does this impact how you respond to _____?

Scriptural Explorations Based on Colossians 3

+ In Colossians 3:1, Paul tells us that we've already been raised with Christ. As you face temptation, how does it encourage and empower you to know that you are raised with Christ?

+ Paul also says that since we have been raised with Christ, we are to set our hearts on things above. What does it mean to you to set your affections on Christ? What does it look like in this _____?

+ Paul tells us in Colossians 3:3 that we are already dead to our old life. On the basis of the burial of the old person we once were, Paul tells us in verse 5 to put to death whatever belonged to the old way. We are to treat as dead what is already dead! What would that look like as you struggle against _____?

+ In verses 9 and 10, Paul says we have *already* taken off the old self and have *already* put on the new self, which is being renewed in the image of Christ. As you struggle against _____, what will it look like for you to live like the new person you already are?

+ Your new self is being renewed in Christ. How are you cooperating with your renewal?

+ Of the list of virtues in Colossians 3:12 – 14, which do you need to implement? How will you do that in Christ's resurrection power?

+ In Colossians 3:15 – 16, Paul tells us that we tap into Christ's resurrection power by letting the word of Christ dwell in us richly and by teaching and counseling and encouraging one another. How is Christ's gospel truth dwelling in you richly? What brothers and sisters in Christ are you joining for mutual teaching, counseling, and encouragement for victory over _____?

Where We've Been and Where We're Headed

Here's our tweet-size summary for chapter 12.

+ Gospel-centered counselors empower their Christian counselees to apply new covenant truth to the specifics of their daily lives.

Our equipping journey is near the end … No, near the *commencement*. I'll save my concluding, commencing summary of where we're headed for the conclusion … No, let's call it the *commencement*.

Be sure not to miss the commencement or the final section on "Maturing as a Biblical Counselor." The commencement will unite our entire biblical counseling equipping journey. And the final "Maturing as a Biblical Counselor" section will provide you with an opportunity to reflect on all that you've learned. And it will help you to decide what your "next steps" are on your biblical counseling journey. See you at the *commencement*!

Maturing as a Biblical Counselor
Counseling Others

1. Use Ephesians 4:17–32 to craft a series of heroic scriptural exploration trialogues.

2. Use Philippians 4 to craft a series of heroic scriptural exploration trialogues.

How the Body of Christ Cares Like Christ

I've served in four churches, either as a pastor or as an elder. I'm sure you won't be surprised to learn that in each of these roles, one of my areas of shepherding oversight has been the biblical counseling ministry.

One of my first tasks in shepherding the biblical counseling ministry in these churches was moving from a church *with* a biblical counselor to a church *of* biblical counseling. People were delighted to have me offer free counseling. "We have the guy who writes books on this stuff counseling our people!" That's a church *with* a biblical counselor.

In the relational management change process in each church, I began casting a vision with the leadership team for a church *of* biblical counseling. By that, I didn't simply mean that I would equip a team of biblical counselors — though that was certainly part of my vision. However, my vision was larger than that because it was an Ephesians 4 vision.

So, in each church, as a church leadership team, we studied the calling of church leaders to equip God's people to do the work of the ministry so that the whole body would be built up and become more like Christ (Eph. 4:11 – 14). That part was second nature for each of the leadership teams.

In each church, we all truly caught the vision of a church *of* biblical counseling when we tied Ephesians 4:11 – 14 with Ephesians 4:15 – 16. I would ask our leaders the simple question, "What is it, according to Scripture, that we are to equip the saints at our church to do?" Answering that question with Ephesians 4:15 – 16, "the lights went on." One leader paraphrased the passage, saying, "Wow, the specific activity we're to equip our church for is speaking the truth in love so we all grow up in Christ as we build the body up in love!" Another followed up, "The 'work' that each part is to do is the ministry of speaking truth in love so people mature in Christ — that's the definition of biblical counseling!"

In other words, biblical counseling, gospel conversations, soul care, and spiritual direction — whatever label we give it — is not a side ministry done by one or a few. Speaking gospel truth in love, sharing Scripture and soul, biblical counseling *is* the one-another ministry calling of the body of Christ. Christ's vision for the church involves the whole body sharing Scripture and soul in gospel conversations where we help one another to become more like Christ as we endure suffering as overcomers and battle and defeat sin as more than conquerors.

So, here's my commencement challenge for *you* and for the church where *you* minister: Don't let *Gospel Conversations* be the end of your journey. Make it the beginning of your church ministry journey. Catch and cast the vision of every member being a one-another minister who speaks gospel truth in love.

Don't just see yourself as a student of these twenty-one biblical counseling relational competencies. See yourself becoming a teacher, coach, and equipper of a congregation of biblical counselors who minister to one another through gospel conversations. That's Christ's vision for how the body of Christ cares like Christ.

Maturing as a Biblical Counselor
Self-Counsel and Group and Partner Interaction

- Either individually, with a partner, and/or as a group, as you wrap up your formal time of working through *Gospel Conversations*, use this final section of "Maturing as a Biblical Counselor" as your "Commencement Summary" of your equipping time.

1. What are some of the major thoughts, phrases, concepts, pictures, and ideas that you will take with you from your study of *Gospel Conversations*?

2. Of the twenty-one biblical counseling relational competencies, which two, three, or four are you most excited about developing further? Why? How will you go about that?

3. How will your *life* be different because of your application of *Gospel Conversations*? Be as specific as possible.

4. How will your *ministry* be different because of your application of *Gospel Conversations*? Be as specific as possible.

5. If you studied and applied *Gospel Conversations* in a group context:
   a. What has been most meaningful about your time together?

b. A major premise of *Gospel Conversations* is that *we learn to be competent biblical counselors by giving and receiving biblical counseling in community.* How has that proven true in your life? How has the counsel you received and given impacted the person you are becoming and the counselor you are becoming?

6. Dream of how God wants to use you to teach, equip, and coach your congregation to become a church *of* biblical counselors who speak gospel truth in love?

Counseling One Another

7. If you studied and applied *Gospel Conversations* in a group context, then reserve a major portion of your final meeting sharing feedback with one another. Focus your feedback on the Christ-empowered growth you've seen in one another. Specifically share with each other:

a. Over the course of our time together, I've seen Christ change and grow your *life* in the following ways …

b. Over the course of our time together, I've seen Christ change and grow your *ministry* in the following ways …

Biblical Counseling Resources

- Appendix 2.1:   Biblical Counseling Initial Intake Form
- Appendix 2.2:   Biblical Counseling Goals Form
- Appendix 2.3:   Biblical Counseling Personal Information Form
- Appendix 2.4:   Authorization for Release of Information: To
- Appendix 2.5:   Authorization for Release of Information: From
- Appendix 2.6:   Biblical Counseling Consent Form
- Appendix 2.7:   Biblical Counseling Permission to Record and Review Form
- Appendix 8.1:   Biblical Counseling Treatment Plan Record Sheet
- Appendix 8.2:   Biblical Counseling Disclosure Statement (Welcome Form)
- Appendix 8.3:   Biblical Counseling Self-Evaluation Form
- Appendix 8.4:   Biblical Counseling Counselee Evaluation Form
- Appendix 8.5:   Biblical Counseling Redeemed Personality Inventory
- Appendix 12.1: Biblical Counseling Commencement Summary

Appendix 2.1: Biblical Counseling Initial Intake Form

Identification Information

Name: _____ Date: _____

Address: _____

_____

Home Phone: _____ Cell Phone: _____

Email: _____

Age: _____ Gender: _____ Marital Status: _____

Church Membership/Attending: _____

Work Schedule: _____ Work Phone: _____

Referred by: _____

Open to Lay Encouragement and Discipleship with a Biblical Counselor: ☐ Yes ☐ No

Brief Summary of Why the Person Desires Biblical Counseling

Personnel Assignment

☐ 1. Referred to _____

because/for: _____

_____

☐ 2. Scheduled with _____

for one immediate meeting on _____.

☐ 3. Appointment scheduled to complete forms and have initial meeting with

_____ on _____.

Homework Assignment

Use the back of this sheet to provide a brief description of the assignment given to the person to complete before the first meeting.

Appendix 2.2: Biblical Counseling Goals Form

Identification Information

Name: _____

Date: _____

1. Why do you desire to meet with a biblical counselor? What are you hoping for and praying for in coming to see a biblical counselor?

2. Thinking ahead, how will you know that your biblical counseling meetings have been helpful? How will you know that you no longer need to meet?

3. What will be different in your life when your biblical counseling meetings are successful?

4. Suppose that one night, while you were asleep, this issue/problem was solved. How would you know?

5. Have you had other situations similar to this? What have you learned from these situations that might be helpful to you now?

6. What are things like when you are not having this concern/problem? What are you doing differently when you do not have this problem?

7. How will you and God keep these times of victory going?

Appendix 2.3: Biblical Counseling Personal Information Form

Identification Information

Name: _____

Home Phone: _____ Cell: _____ Work Phone: _____

Email: _____

Address: _____

_____

Birth Date: _____ Gender: _____

Education in Years: _____ Occupation: _____

Marital Status: ☐ Single ☐ Married ☐ Separated
☐ Divorced ☐ Widowed ☐ Engaged

Referred Here By: _____

Reason for Seeking Biblical Counseling

Why do you desire to meet with a biblical counselor? _____

_____

_____

How long has this issue existed? _____

Were there any significant events occurring in your life/family's life when this issue began?

_____

_____

What have you done about this issue? _____

_____

How would things be different for you if the issue were remedied? _____

_____

_____

What results are you expecting in coming here for biblical counseling? _____

_____

_____

Marriage and Family Information

Spouse's Name: _____ Phone: _____

Spouse's Email: _____ Birth Date: _____

Spouse's Address: _____

_____

Spouse's Education in Years: _____ Occupation: _____

Date of Marriage: _____ Age When Married: H: _____ W: _____

Is your spouse willing to come for counseling? ☐ Yes ☐ No ☐ Uncertain

Give brief information about any previous marriages: _____

_____

Information about Children

PM*	Name	Age	Gender	Education (Grade)	Marital Status

*Check this column (PM) if child is by previous marriage.

What type of instruction in Christian living is given in your home and by whom?

_____

_____

Who does the disciplining in your home? _____

For what behaviors are your children disciplined? _____

_____

What methods of discipline are currently being used? _____

_____

How do you and your family members communicate that you love each other?

_____

Personality Information

Circle any of the following words that best describe you now:

Active	Shy	Hardworking	Leader	Compulsive
Nervous	Likable	Impulsive	Follower	Excitable
Impatient	Self-Conscious	Often Blue	Sarcastic	Serious
Moody	Jealous	Calm	Self-Confident	Easygoing
Imaginative	Ambitious	Good-Natured	Persistent	Quiet
Introverted	Extroverted	Fearful	Loner	Stubborn

Others: _____

Complete the following sentences:

People who know me think that I am: _____
_____

If they knew the "real me," they would know that I am: _____
_____

What I desire more than anything else in life is: _____
_____

What I fear most in life is: _____
_____

The person I admire most in life is: _____
Because: _____
Is there any other information that you would like us to know?
_____
_____
_____
_____

Health Information

Rate your health: ☐ Very Good   ☐ Good   ☐ Average   ☐ Poor

Weight changes recently: ☐ None   ☐ Lost: _____   ☐ Gained: _____

List all important present or past illnesses, injuries, or disabilities: _____

_____

_____

Date of last medical exam: _____   Report: _____

_____

Physician's name: _____   Contact: _____

Are you presently taking medication?   ☐ Yes   ☐ No

Type: _____

_____

Have you used drugs for other than medical purposes?   ☐ Yes   ☐ No

If yes, explain: _____

Have you ever had any counseling before?   ☐ Yes   ☐ No: When: _____

For: _____

Are you willing to sign a release so your counselor may write for medical or counseling reports?
   ☐ Yes   ☐ No

Religious Background

What church do you attend? _____

How often do you attend church? _____

Are you saved?   ☐ Yes   ☐ No   ☐ Not sure what you mean

What ministries/activities are you involved in at church? _____

_____

How often do you read the Bible/pray? _____

_____

Describe your relationship with Christ: _____

_____

Appendix 2.4: Authorization for Release of Information: To

To:

    (Pastor) _____

    (Church) _____

    (Address) _____

    (City) _____

    (Phone) _____

    (Email) _____

From:

    Name/Address of Facility/Counselor: Counselee's Address at Time of Service:

    _____   _____

    _____   _____

    _____   _____

Re:

Name: _____

DOB: _____ SS #: _____

This signed release authorizes you to furnish Pastor _____ the following:

_____

_____

_____

Please forward the requested information to Pastor _____ at the address listed above. It is understood that this is confidential information and that it will not be released without the written permission of the counselee or guardian.

I understand that I may revoke this authorization, except for the action(s) already taken, at any time. Expiration date, event, or condition after which consent is no longer valid:

_____   _____

(Signature of Counselee or Guardian)   (Date)

_____

(Witness)

Appendix 2.5: Authorization for Release of Information: From

From:

(Pastor)   _____

(Church)   _____

(Address)   _____

(City)   _____

(Phone)   _____

(Email)   _____

To:

Name/Address of Facility/Counselor: Counselee's Address at Time of Service:

_____   _____

_____   _____

_____   _____

Re:

Name: _____

DOB: _____   SS #: _____

This signed release authorizes Pastor _____ to furnish the following:

_____

_____

_____

The requested information will be forwarded to the address listed above. It is understood that this is confidential information and that it will not be released without the written permission of the counselee or guardian.

I understand that I may revoke this authorization, except for the action already taken, at any time. Expiration date, event, or condition after which consent is no longer valid:

_____   _____

(Signature of Counselee or Guardian)   (Date)

_____

(Witness)

Appendix 2.6: Biblical Counseling Consent Form

(Name of Counselee) _____ I have been informed
that the spiritual care I will be receiving from _____
(Name of Biblical Counselor) at _____
(Name of Church) is Christian and biblical in nature. I have also been informed that
_____ (Name of Biblical Counselor) is an encourager and
discipler trained at _____ (Name of Church) as a lay biblical counselor in
the church's Biblical Counseling Ministry.

Under supervision from one of the LEAD trainers, _____
(Name of Biblical Counselor) offers to provide biblical encouragement and discipleship on
personal and relational matters from a spiritual perspective guided by biblical principles. He/she
is *not* trained, authorized, or licensed to provide professional counseling, psychological treatment,
or psychological diagnosis. I understand that if and when I desire and request professional counseling, the church's referral network and contact list will be made available.

I give my consent to _____ (Name of Biblical
Counselor) to discuss any and all of the information that I talk about in our meetings with his/
her supervisor(s) in the Biblical Counseling Ministry.

_____   _____

(Signature)   (Date)

Appendix 2.7: Biblical Counseling Permission to Record and Review Form

I give my permission for _____ (Name of Biblical Counselor) to audio/video record any and all of our biblical counseling meetings and to review these recordings with his/her supervisor and fellow trainees in the church's Biblical Counseling Ministry.

I understand that these recordings will be used only for evaluation and training purposes.

I understand that they will be destroyed when they are no longer needed for these purposes or when I cease meeting with my biblical counselor (whichever comes first).

_____

(Print name)

_____   _____

(Signature)   (Date)

Appendix 8.1: Biblical Counseling Treatment Plan Record Sheet

Counselee's Name: _____

Session Number: _____   Date: _____

Pre-Meeting Information

Counselee's Review/Update/Report:

Biblical Counselor's Review/Summary:

Counselee's Goals:

Biblical Counselor's Goals/Focus:

Biblical Counseling Meeting Notes

Biblical Counseling Post-Session Homework Assignment(s)

Next Meeting Date and Time: _____

Continue on the back with Post-Meeting Assessment and Planning

Biblical Counseling Post-Meeting Assessment and Planning

- Sustaining: "It's Normal to Hurt."
  - Biblical Assessment: I discerned ...
  - Biblical Planning: We need to work on ...

- Healing: "It's Possible to Hope."
  - Biblical Assessment: I discerned ...
  - Biblical Planning: We need to work on ...

- Reconciling: "It's Horrible to Sin but Wonderful to Be Forgiven."
  - Biblical Assessment: I discerned ...
  - Biblical Planning: We need to work on ...

- Guiding: "It's Supernatural to Mature."
  - Biblical Assessment: I discerned ...
  - Biblical Planning: We need to work on ...

- Relationally: Affections — Spiritual, Social, Self-Aware
  - Biblical Assessment: I discerned ...
  - Biblical Planning: We need to work on ...

- Rationally: Mind-Sets — Images, Beliefs
  - Biblical Assessment: I discerned ...
  - Biblical Planning: We need to work on ...

- Volitionally: Purposes/Pathways — Goals, Motivations, Actions
  - Biblical Assessment: I discerned ...
  - Biblical Planning: We need to work on ...

- Emotionally: Mood States — Emotional Awareness, Management, and Ministry Focus
  - Biblical Assessment: I discerned ...
  - Biblical Planning: We need to work on ...

Appendix 8.2: Biblical Counseling Ministry Disclosure Statement (Welcome Form)

Welcome to the Biblical Counseling Ministry of _____ Church. We desire to be used by God to speak his truth in love. We know that the path to maturity is often steep and rough and at times filled with pain and confusion. However, there *are* answers. We believe the Bible is *God's all-sufficient guide for relational living.* There is a route to life. Our Lord is that *way.* Christ is the *truth* who frees us to love. He is the *life* who satisfies the deepest thirsts of our soul.

Ministries Offered

As a *ministry* of _____ Church, our services are *free.* As a discipleship ministry of a *local church*, we offer to you:

- Individual biblical counseling regarding spiritual and personal issues.
- Premarital biblical counseling and marital biblical counseling.
- Family/parental biblical counseling: with children under the age of thirteen we work primarily with the parents and/or with the parents and children.
- Adolescent biblical counseling: with parental consent and involvement.
- Small group discipleship: see our brochure on our various groups.
- A referral network.

Confidentiality

Confidentiality is an important aspect of the biblical counseling relationship, and we will carefully guard the information you entrust to us. All communications between you and our Biblical Counseling Ministry offices will be held in strict confidence unless you (or a parent in the case of a minor) give authorization to release this information. The exceptions to this would be: (1) if a person expresses intent to harm himself/herself or someone else; (2) if there is evidence or reasonable suspicion of abuse against a minor child, elder person, or dependent adult; (3) if a subpoena or other court order is received directing the disclosure of information; (4) when your biblical counselor consults with his/her supervisor; or (5) if a person persistently refuses to renounce a particular sin (habitual unrepentant rebellion against God's Word), and it becomes necessary to seek the assistance of others in the church to encourage repentance, restoration, and reconciliation (see Matthew 18:15 – 20 and our Church Restoration Policy). Our counselors strongly prefer not to disclose personal information to others, and they will make every effort to help you find ways to resolve a problem as privately as possible.

Appointments

Our biblical counselors work by scheduled appointments. Of course, in emergencies, exceptions are made. We need your prompt and consistent participation in your scheduled meetings. Please contact our office twenty-four hours in advance if you must cancel an appointment. This will allow us to schedule another individual during this time. If you will arrive forty-five minutes early for your first appointment, you will then be able to complete all necessary forms. During your initial meeting, you will determine the goals you would like to work toward. After five sessions, you and your biblical counselor will evaluate your progress toward those goals and together determine what further action needs to be taken.

Our Commitments to You in Biblical Counseling

We would like to explain what we mean by *biblical counseling*. Biblical counselors are spiritual friends committed to the historic church roles of *soul care* and *spiritual direction* through:

+ *Sustaining:* Empathizing with your suffering, helping you to understand that *"it's normal to hurt."*
+ *Healing:* Encouraging you to see life from a biblical perspective, helping you to know that *"it's possible to hope."*
+ *Reconciling:* Examining and exposing your current responses to life and suggesting new ways of handling problems, helping you to see that *"it's horrible to sin but wonderful to be forgiven."*
+ *Guiding:* Empowering you to mature through Christ and helping you to grasp that *"it's supernatural to mature."*

Because we care about *you*, our desire is for you to be drawn closer to Christ and to become more like Christ, which we see as *your life increasingly reflecting the life of Christ*:

+ *Relational Maturity:* Loving God wholeheartedly and loving others sacrificially.
+ *Rational Maturity:* Wisely living according to the truth of Christ's gospel of grace.
+ *Volitional Maturity:* Courageously choosing to pursue God's purposes in your life through the Spirit's power.

+ *Emotional Maturity:* Deeply and honestly experiencing life with integrity, fully open to God while managing your moods for God's glory and with a ministry focus.

Your Commitments to Christ, to Yourself, and to Us in Biblical Counseling

We ask that you commit to:

+ Honestly and openly sharing your hurts and struggles.
+ Evaluating your own emotions, actions, motivations, beliefs, and relationships.
+ Actively participating in the growth of renewed emotions, actions, convictions, and desires.
+ Coming to each meeting prepared to review your progress throughout the last week (including the completion of personalized "homework" assignments) and prepared to share your goals for the present meeting.

Growth in Christ requires all the resources of the body of Christ. Therefore, it is essential that those seeking biblical counseling at our church commit to the following:

+ Regular church attendance (at your church or our church).
+ Active participation in Adult Bible Fellowship/Sunday school.
+ Participation in at least one small group (we'll discuss the appropriate group for you).

We ask that you sign below to indicate your understanding of, agreement with, and commitment to our Biblical Counseling Ministry focus as described on these two pages.

_____   _____   _____

(Your Name)   (Parent, If a Minor)   (Date)

Recording Self-Evaluation Part I: Interaction Log

1. Record the number of times your interactions focused upon:

   a. Sustaining: *"It's normal to hurt."* _____

   b. Healing: *"It's possible to hope."* _____

   c. Reconciling:

      (1) Part A: *"It's horrible to sin."* _____

      (2) Part B: *"It's wonderful to be forgiven."* _____

   d. Guiding: *"It's supernatural to mature."* _____

2. Record the number of times your interactions focused upon:

   a. Relational Longings (Affections):

      (1) Spiritual _____

      (2) Social _____

      (3) Self-Aware _____

   b. Rational Concepts (Mind-Sets):

      (1) Images _____

      (2) Beliefs _____

   c. Volitional Choices (Purposes/Pathways):

      (1) Goals _____

      (2) Actions _____

   d. Emotional Responses (Mood States): _____

   e. Physical Issues (Habituated Tendencies): _____

Recording Self-Evaluation Part II: Personal Assessment

Using the scale below, evaluate yourself in the following biblical counseling areas:

1. I disagree strongly
2. I disagree
3. I'm not sure
4. I agree
5. I agree strongly

_____ *Sustaining:* I listened to and sensed my counselee's hurts.

_____ *Sustaining:* I climbed in the casket with my counselee, empathizing with and embracing my counselee's pain.

_____ *Healing:* I encouraged my counselee to embrace God.

_____ *Healing:* I trialogued (spiritual conversations and scriptural explorations) with my counselee, encouraging him/her to see God's perspective on his/her suffering.

_____ *Reconciling:* I exposed the horrors of my counselee's sin.

_____ *Reconciling:* I shared God's grace, showing how wonderful it is to be forgiven.

_____ *Guiding:* I enlightened my counselee to God's supernatural work of maturity.

_____ *Guiding:* I equipped and empowered my counselee to grow in grace.

_____ *Relational:* I effectively used the concept of "affections" to assess and expose the relational motivations in my counselee's soul.

_____ *Rational:* I effectively used the concept of "mind-sets" to assess and expose the rational direction (images and beliefs) in my counselee's heart.

_____ *Volitional:* I effectively used the concept of "purposes/pathways" to assess and expose the volitional interactions (styles of relating, goals, purposeful behaviors) in my counselee's will.

_____ *Emotional:* I effectively used the concept of "mood states" to assess and expose the emotional reactions in my counselee's moods.

_____ *Truth/Discernment/Scripture:* I used theological insight to understand the spiritual dynamics and root causes related to my counselee.

_____ *Love/Compassion/Soul:* I compassionately identified with my counselee — I was engaged, involved, and related from my soul.

_____ *Overall:* I would go to myself for biblical counseling/spiritual friendship.

Appendix 8.4: Biblical Counseling Counselee Evaluation Form

As biblical counselors, we desire to grow in our ability to speak God's truth in love. Your honest feedback is very helpful to us. Please evaluate your biblical counselor based on the following scale:

1. I disagree strongly
2. I disagree
3. I'm not sure
4. I agree
5. I agree strongly

_____ 1. My biblical counselor listened to and sensed my hurts.

_____ 2. My biblical counselor empathized with and embraced my pain.

_____ 3. My biblical counselor encouraged me to embrace God in my pain.

_____ 4. My biblical counselor encouraged me to see God's perspective on my suffering.

_____ 5. My biblical counselor lovingly, courageously, and humbly exposed areas of sin in my heart.

_____ 6. My biblical counselor helped me to see the wonders of God's grace so I could experience God's forgiveness.

_____ 7. My biblical counselor helped me to see that I can mature only through Christ's resurrection power.

_____ 8. My biblical counselor equipped and empowered me to love like Christ.

_____ 9. My biblical counselor helped me to assess the longings of my soul, exposing the false idols of my heart as well as my soul's thirst for Christ.

_____ 10. My biblical counselor helped me to assess beliefs, exposing foolish beliefs and helping me to renew my mind in Christ.

_____ 11. My biblical counselor helped me to assess the motivations behind my behaviors and helped me to put off the old self and to put on a new person in Christ.

_____ 12. My biblical counselor helped me to assess my moods, assisting me to become more emotionally self-aware and better able to manage my moods.

_____ 13. My biblical counselor used biblical principles to understand the spiritual dynamics and root causes at work in my life.

_____ 14. My biblical counselor compassionately identified with me, engaging me with deep personal involvement and relating to me with Christlike love.

_____ 15. The goals that we set for biblical counseling were successfully met.

_____ 16. Because of our biblical counseling relationship, I love Christ more.

_____ 17. Because of our biblical counseling relationship, I love other people more.

_____ 18. Because of our biblical counseling relationship, I more fully understand my identity in Christ.

_____ 19. I would go to my biblical counselor again for biblical counseling if I needed it.

_____ 20. I would recommend my biblical counselor to others for biblical counseling.

Please use the back to share any additional suggestions, thoughts, questions, or comments.

Your Name: _____

Biblical Counselor's Name: _____

Appendix 8.5: Biblical Counseling Redeemed Personality Inventory

1. Redeemed Personality Inventory: Relational
   a. How well am I clinging to God/running home to the Father, delighting in him, and trusting him like a faithful son or daughter?
   b. To what extent am I enjoying Christ more than any other joy in life?
   c. To what extent am I depending upon the Holy Spirit to empower me to become more like Christ?
   d. How well am I loving others deeply from the heart?
   e. To what extent am I resting confidently and comfortably in who I am in Christ?

2. Redeemed Personality Inventory: Rational
   a. To what extent am I valuing what God values?
   b. To what extent do I see God as my chief good and supreme satisfaction?
   c. How well am I allowing God's eternal story to invade my earthly story?
   d. How well am I stirring up wise and wholesome thinking in my mind?

3. Redeemed Personality Inventory: Volitional
   a. To what extent am I finding life by dying to myself, taking up my cross, and following Christ?
   b. How well am I living to empower, minister to, and shepherd others?
   c. To what extent am I asking, "What would courageous trust in Christ look like in my relationships?"

4. Redeemed Personality Inventory: Emotional
   a. How well am I practicing emotional self-awareness — admitting, experiencing, and identifying my feelings?
   b. How well am I practicing emotional self-mastery — soothing my soul in my Savior?
   c. How well am I practicing emotional maturity — managing my moods with a ministry focus?
   d. How well am I practicing emotional empathy — recognizing and connecting with emotions in others?
   e. How well am I practicing emotional savvy — handling my relationships maturely?

5. Redeemed Personality Inventory: Physical
   a. To what extent am I admitting my absolute need, body and soul, for God?
   b. To what extent am I allowing physical frailties to remind me of my need for God?

Appendix 12.1: Biblical Counseling Commencement Summary

Counselee's Name: _____

Date First Seen: _____   Date Last Seen: _____

Today's Date: _____   Your Name: _____

Summary of Initial Issue(s), Major Goal(s), Biblical Assessment, and Biblical Plans

Summary of Growth/Maturity Resulting from Biblical Counseling Meetings

Insight Concerning Any Unresolved Areas and Suggestions for Continued Growth

Reason(s) for Commencement:

Notes

1. Michael Firmin and Mark Tedford, "An Assessment of Pastoral Counseling Courses in Seminaries Serving Evangelical Baptist Students," 420 – 27.

2. Jay Adams, *A Theology of Christian Counseling*, ix.

3. Robert Kellemen, *Soul Physicians*, 3.

4. Leon Morris, *The First and Second Epistles to the Thessalonians*, 68.

5. Ibid.

6. John Calvin, *Commentary on 1 Thessalonians*, 28.

7. Morris, 79 – 80.

8. Milton Vincent, *A Gospel Primer for Christians*, 22.

9. Morris, 84.

10. Quoted in Morris, 93.

11. Kellemen, *Gospel-Centered Counseling*, 23.

12. Kellemen, *Soul Physicians*, 31 – 46.

13. Michael Horton, *The Gospel-Driven Life: Being Good News People in a Bad News World* (Grand Rapids, MI: Baker Books, 2009), 116.

14. Ibid.

15. Kellemen, *Gospel-Centered Counseling*, 19.

16. Ibid., 20.

17. For an extensive theology of biblical counseling built on a comprehensive biblical understanding of people, see Kellemen, *Gospel-Centered Counseling*, chapters 6 – 7.

18. Drawn from the Biblical Counseling Coalition Confessional Statement: http://biblicalcounselingcoalition.org/about/confessional-statement/.

19. For a comprehensive approach to understanding biblical counseling and physical and social influences on the heart, see Jeff Forrey and Jim Newheiser, "The Influences on the Human Heart," in *Christ-Centered Biblical Counseling*, 123 – 37. Also see Kellemen, *Anxiety*, 39 – 42.

20. For a fuller explanation of our inner life (relational affections, rational mind-sets, volitional purposes/pathways, and emotional mood states), see chapters 6 and 7 of Kellemen, *Gospel-Centered Counseling*.

21. Joseph Durlak, "Comparative Effectiveness of Paraprofessional and Professional Helpers," 80 – 92.

22. J. A. Hattie, C. F. Sharpley, and H. J. Rogers, "Comparative Effectiveness of Professional and Paraprofessional Helpers," 534 – 41.

23. Jeffrey S. Berman and Nicholas C. Norton, "Does Professional Training Make a Therapist More Effective?" 401 – 7.

24. Keith Herman, "Reassessing Predictors of Therapist Competence," 29 – 32.

25. Siang-Yang Tan and Yiu-Meng Toh, "The Effectiveness of Church-Based Lay Counselors," 260 – 67.

26. William Hendriksen, *Galatians and Ephesians*, 224 – 25.

27. Walter Gundmann, *Theological Dictionary of the New Testament*, 3 – 4.

28. Kellemen, *Gospel-Centered Counseling*, chapters 6 – 7.

29. See Jey Adams, *Competent to Counsel*, *The Christian Counselor's Manual*, and *A Theology of Christian Counseling*.

30. William A. Clebsch and Charles R. Jaekle, *Pastoral Care in Historical Perspective*, xii.

31. The use of sinner, sufferer, saint as a way of looking at counselees is commonly used by many in the biblical counseling world, including the Christian Counseling Education Foundation (CCEF).

32. "Sons" and "sonship" are the common biblical/theological terms for our heavenly Father's relationship to us. The terms incorporate *both* males and females and highlight our reconciled relationship with our Father along with all the privileges and responsibilities that flow from that relationship.

33. See chapters 11 – 12 of Kellemen, *Gospel-Centered Counseling*, for a fuller development of our identity in Christ as saints and sons.

34. Frank Lake, *Clinical Theology*, 21.

35. Ibid., 37.

36. To study the historical evidence further, see Kellemen, "Spiritual Care in Historical Perspective"; Kellemen, *Spiritual Friends*; Kellemen and Karole A. Edwards, *Beyond the Suffering*; and Kellemen and Susan M. Ellis, *Sacred Friendships*.

37. John McNeil, *A History of the Cure of Souls*.

38. Ibid.

39. Lake, 25.

40. Martin Luther, *Luther's Letters of Spiritual Counsel*, 338.

41. Margaret Gibson, *The Didascalia apostolorum in English*, 28 – 57.

42. Clebsch and Jaekle, 103.

43. See Kellemen, *Spiritual Friends*; Kellemen and Edwards, *Beyond the Suffering*; and Kellemen and Ellis, *Sacred Friendships*.

44. W. Michaelis, *Theological Dictionary of the New Testament*, 801 – 3.

45. A. T. Robertson, *Word Pictures in the New Testament*, 565.

46. Olaudah Equiano, *The Interesting Narrative of the Life of Olaudah Equiano*, 4, emphasis added.

47. Ibid., 41 – 42.

48. Ibid., 30.

49. Luther, *Luther's Letters*, 204.

50. Octavia Albert, *The House of Bondage*, 2.

51. Ibid., 15.

52. Ibid., 28 – 29.

53. Ibid., 27.

54. Quoted in Thomas Oden, *Classical Pastoral Care*, vol. 3, 8, emphasis added.

55. Gilbert Osofsky, *Puttin' On Ole Massa*, 248.

56. Peter Randolph, *From Slave Cabin to Pulpit*, 113.

57. Chris Castaldo, "Cultivate Gospel Conversations by Listening," The Gospel Coalition, April 17, 2013, http://thegospelcoalition.org/blogs/tgc/2013/04/18/gospel-listening/.

58. Martin Luther, *Luther's Works*, vol. 54, 30.

59. Ibid., 30 – 31.

60. I develop Ashley's story and a biblical counseling response in Kellemen, *Sexual Abuse*.

61. Biblical Counseling Coalition Confessional Statement: http://biblicalcounselingcoalition.org/about/confessional-statement/.

62. Kevin Vanhoozer, *The Drama of Doctrine*, 402.

63. Ibid., 224, 212.

64. Richard Sibbes, *The Bruised Reed*, 63.

65. A. Nebe, *Luther as Spiritual Adviser*, 183.

66. Luther, *Luther's Works*, vol. 42, 124.

67. Nebe, 178.

68. Ibid., 184 – 85.

69. Luther, *Luther's Works*, vol. 16, 214.

70. Luther, *Luther's Works*, vol. 42, 143, 154.

71. Ibid.

72. Luther, *Luther's Letters*, 15.

73. Patricia Wilson-Kastner, et al., "The Martyrdom of Perpetua," in *A Lost Tradition*, 3 – 20.

74. Ibid., 19.

75. Ibid., 27.

76. Emil Brunner, *The Mediator*, 450, 470.

77. John Stott, *The Cross of Christ*, 133.

78. Ibid., 159.

79. Wilson-Kastner, 28.

80. Ibid., 26 – 27.

81. Ibid., 28.

82. Ibid.

83. Kellemen, *Soul Physicians*, 59.

84. J. I. Packer, *Rediscovering Holiness*, 33.

85. Adams, *A Theology of Christian Counseling*, ix.

86. Paul Tripp, *Instruments in the Redeemer's Hands*, xi.

87. Kellemen, *Gospel-Centered Counseling*, 100 – 1.

88. Ibid., 161 – 68.

89. Luther, *Luther's Letters*, 337 – 39.

90. Ibid., 338 – 39.

91. Milton Vincent, *A Gospel Primer for Christians*, 20.

92. Luther, *Luther's Letters*, 338.

93. Ralph Earle, *Word Meanings in the New Testament*, 406.

94. A. T. Robertson, *Word Pictures in the New Testament*, 541.

95. Luther, *Luther's Letters*, 338.

96. Earle, 406.

97. Luther, *Luther's Letters*, 338 – 39.

98. Ibid., 338.

99. Luther, *Luther's Works*, vol. 54, 442.

100. Ibid., 443.

101. Ibid., 70.

102. Luther, *Commentary on Galatians*, 314.

103. Luther, *Luther's Works*, vol. 54, 70.

104. Ibid., 106.

105. Nebe, 181 – 82.

106. Ibid., 217.

107. John Owen, *The Mortification of Sin*, 107.

108. Ibid.

109. Ibid., 53.

110. Luther, *The Bondage of the Will*, 201.

111. See chapters 11 – 12 and 15 – 16 of Kellemen, *Gospel-Centered Counseling*.

112. Ibid., 255.

113. See chapter 6 of Kellemen, "Spiritual Care in Historical Perspective," *Gospel-Centered Counseling*.

114. Adams, *The Christian Counselor's Manual*, 161.

115. Kellemen, *Gospel-Centered Counseling*, 256 – 57.

116. For a detailed biblical explanation of the implications of the new covenant, see chapters 11 and 12 of Kellemen, *Gospel-Centered Counseling*.

117. Kellemen, *Soul Physicians*, 363 – 66, 379 – 84.

118. Marilyn Richardson, *Maria W. Stewart*, 29.

119. Horton, 12.

120. Clifton Johnson, *God Struck Me Dead*, 40 – 41.

121. Ibid.

122. See Kellemen and Edwards, *Beyond the Suffering*.

Bibliography of Sources Cited and Consulted

Adams, Jay E. *The Christian Counselor's Manual: The Practice of Nouthetic Counseling.* Grand Rapids, MI: Zondervan, 1973.

———. *Competent to Counsel: Introduction to Nouthetic Counseling.* Grand Rapids, MI: Zondervan, 1970.

———. *A Theology of Christian Counseling: More Than Redemption.* Grand Rapids, MI: Zondervan, 1979.

Albert, Octavia. *The House of Bondage: Or, Charlotte Brooks and Other Slaves.* New York: Oxford University Press, 1988.

Berman, Jeffrey S., and Nicholas C. Norton. "Does Professional Training Make a Therapist More Effective?" *Psychology Bulletin* 98, no. 2 (1985): 401–7.

Bigney, Brad. *Gospel Treason: Betraying the Gospel with Hidden Idols.* Phillipsburg, NJ: P&R, 2012.

Brunner, Emil. *The Mediator: A Study of the Central Doctrine of the Christian Faith.* London: Westminster, 1947.

Calvin, John. *Commentary on 1 Thessalonians.* Wheaton, IL: Crossway, 1999.

Clebsch, William A., and Charles R. Jaekle. *Pastoral Care in Historical Perspective.* Northvale, NJ: Jason Aronson, 1994.

Cugoano, Quobna O. *Thoughts and Sentiments on the End of Slavery.* New York: Penguin Classics, 1999.

Durlak, Joseph. "Comparative Effectiveness of Paraprofessional and Professional Helpers." *Psychological Bulletin* 86, no. 1 (1979): 80–92.

Earle, Ralph. *Word Meanings in the New Testament.* Peabody, MA: Hendrickson, 2000.

Emlet, Michael R. *CrossTalk: Where Life and Scripture Meet.* Greensboro, NC: New Growth Press, 2009.

Equiano, Olaudah. *The Interesting Narrative of the Life of Olaudah Equiano.* New York: Modern Library, 2004.

Eyrich, Howard, and William Hines. *Curing the Heart: A Model for Biblical Counseling*. Dublin: Mentor, 2002.

Firmin, Michael, and Mark Tedford. "An Assessment of Pastoral Counseling Courses in Seminaries Serving Evangelical Baptist Students." *Review of Religious Research* 48, no. 4 (2007): 420–27.

Forrey, Jeff, and Jim Newheiser. "The Influences on the Human Heart." Chap. 8 in *Christ-Centered Biblical Counseling: Changing Lives with God's Changeless Truth*, ed. by James MacDonald, Bob Kellemen, and Steve Viars. Eugene, OR: Harvest House, 2013.

Gibson, Margaret, trans. *The Didascalia apostolorum in English*. London: Cambridge University Press, 1903.

Gundmann, Walter. "agathos." In *Theological Dictionary of the New Testament*. Edited by Geoffrey Bromiley, 3–4. Grand Rapids, MI: Eerdmans, 1985.

Hattie, J. A., C. F. Sharpley, and H. J. Rogers, "Comparative Effectiveness of Professional and Paraprofessional Helpers." *Psychological Bulletin* 95, no. 3 (1984): 534–41.

Henderson, John. *Equipped to Counsel: A Training Program in Biblical Counseling*. Mustang, OK: Dare 2 Dream Books, 2008.

Hendricksen, William. *Philippians, Colossians, and Philemon*. Grand Rapids, MI: Baker Book House, 1979.

Herman, Keith C. "Reassessing Predictors of Therapist Competence." *Journal of Counseling and Development* 72, No. 1 (1993): 29–32.

Horton, Michael. *The Gospel-Driven Life: Being Good News People in a Bad News World*. Grand Rapids, MI: Baker Books, 2009.

Johnson, Clifton, editor. *God Struck Me Dead: Voices of Ex-Slaves*. Cleveland: Pilgrim, 1993.

Kellemen, Robert W. *Anxiety: Anatomy and Cure*. Phillipsburg, NJ: P&R, 2012.

———. *Biblical Counseling and the Church: God's Care through God's People*. Grand Rapids, MI: Zondervan, 2015.

———. *Equipping Counselors for Your Church: The 4E Ministry Training Strategy*. Phillipsburg, NJ: P&R, 2011.

———. *God's Healing for Life's Losses: How to Find Hope When You're Hurting*. Winona Lake, IN: BMH Books, 2010.

———. *Gospel-Centered Counseling: How Christ Changes Lives*. Grand Rapids, MI: Zondervan, 2014.

———. *Sexual Abuse: Beauty for Ashes*. Phillipsburg, NJ: P&R, 2013.

———. *Soul Physicians: A Theology of Soul Care and Spiritual Direction*. Winona Lake, IN: BHM Books, 2007.

———. "Spiritual Care in Historical Perspective: Martin Luther as a Case Study in Christian Sustaining, Healing, Reconciling, and Guiding." PhD diss., Kent State University, 1997.

———. *Spiritual Friends: A Methodology of Soul Care and Spiritual Direction.* Winona Lake, IN: BHM Books, 2007.

Kellemen, Robert W., and Karole A. Edwards. *Beyond the Suffering: Embracing the Legacy of African American Soul Care and Spiritual Direction.* Grand Rapids, MI: Baker Books, 2007.

Kellemen, Robert W., and Susan M. Ellis. *Sacred Friendships: Celebrating the Legacy of Women Heroes of the Faith.* Winona Lake, IN: BMH Books, 2009.

Kellemen, Robert W., and Jeff Forrey, editors. *Scripture and Counseling: God's Word for Life in a Broken World.* Grand Rapids, MI: Zondervan, 2014.

Lake, Frank. *Clinical Theology: A Theological and Psychiatric Basis to Clinical Pastoral Care.* London: Darton, Longman, & Todd, 1966.

Lane, Timothy S., and Paul David Tripp. *How People Change.* 2nd ed. Greensboro, NC: New Growth Press, 2008.

Luther, Martin. *The Bondage of the Will.* Translated by O. R. Johnston and J. I. Packer. Grand Rapids, MI: Baker Academic, 1957.

———. *Commentary on Galatians.* Translated by P. S. Watson. Grand Rapids, MI: Revell, 1988.

———. "Devotional Writings I." In *Luther's Works,* vol. 42. Translated by Helmut T. Lehmann and Martin O. Dietrich. Philadelphia: Fortress, 1969.

———. *Luther: Letters of Spiritual Counsel.* Edited and translated by Theodore G. Tappert. Vol. 18 of the Library of Christian Classics. J. Baillie, J. T. McNeil, and H. P. Van Dusen, gen eds. Philadelphia: Westminster, 1955.

———. "Sermon on John 18:28." In *What Luther Says,* vol. 1. Compiled by Ewald M. Plass. St. Louis: Concordia, 1959.

———. *Large Catechism.* Translated by Robert Fischer. Philadelphia: Fortress, 1981.

———. "Lectures on Isaiah: Chapters 1 – 39." In *Luther's Works,* vol. 16. Edited by Jaroslaw Pelikan. St. Louis, MO: Concordia, 1969.

———. "The Sermon on the Mount." In *Luther's Works,* vol. 21. St. Louis, MO: Concordia, 1968.

———. "Table Talk." In *Luther's Works,* vol. 54. Edited by Helmut T. Lehmann and Theodore G. Tappert. Philadelphia: Fortress, 1967.

MacDonald, James, Bob Kellemen, and Steve Viars, editors. *Christ-Centered Biblical Counseling: Changing Lives with God's Changeless Truth.* Eugene, OR: Harvest House, 2013.

McNeil, John T. *A History of the Cure of Souls.* New York: Harper & Row, 1951.

Michaelis, W. "pathetos." In *Theological Dictionary of the New Testament.* Edited by Geoffrey Bromiley, 801 – 3. Grand Rapids, MI: Eerdmans, 1985.

Morris, Leon. *The First and Second Epistles to the Thessalonians.* Grand Rapids, MI: Eerdmans, 1959.

Nebe, A., ed. *Luther as Spiritual Adviser.* Translated by C. H. Hays. Philadelphia: Lutheran Publication Society, 1894.

Oden, Thomas C. *Pastoral Counsel.* Vol. 3 of *Classical Pastoral Care.* Grand Rapids, MI: Baker Book House, 1987.

Osofsky, Gilbert, ed. *Puttin' On Ole Massa.* Reprint ed. San Francisco: Harper & Row, 1969.

Owen, John. *The Mortification of Sin.* Ross-Shire, Scotland: Christian Focus, 1996.

———. *Temptation and Sin.* Evansville, IN: Sovereign Book Club, 1958.

Packer, J. I. *Knowing God.* Downers Grove, IL: InterVarsity Press, 1973.

———. *A Quest for Godliness: The Puritan Vision of the Christian Life.* Wheaton, IL: Crossway, 1990.

———. *Rediscovering Holiness: Know the Fullness of Life with God.* Grand Rapids, MI: Baker Books, 2009.

Powlison, David. "Affirmations and Denials: A Proposed Definition of Biblical Counseling." *The Journal of Biblical Counseling* 19, no. 1 (Fall 2000): 18–25.

———. *Seeing with New Eyes: Counseling and the Human Condition Through the Lens of Scripture.* Phillipsburg, NJ: P&R, 2003.

———. *Speaking Truth in Love: Counsel in Community.* Greensboro, NC: New Growth Press, 2005.

Randolph, Peter. *From Slave Cabin to Pulpit.* Chester, NY: Anza, 2005.

Richardson, Marilyn, ed. *Maria W. Stewart: America's First Black Woman Political Writer: Essays and Speeches.* Bloomington, IN: Indiana University Press, 1987.

Robertson, A. T. *Word Pictures in the New Testament.* Nashville: Holman, 2000.

Scott, Stuart, and Heath Lambert, ed. *Counseling the Hard Cases: True Stories Illustrating the Sufficiency of God's Resources in Scripture.* Nashville: B&H Academics, 2015.

Sibbes, Richard. *The Bruised Reed.* Revised ed. Carlisle, PA: Banner of Truth Trust, 1998.

Stott, John. *The Cross of Christ.* Downers Grove, IL: InterVarsity, 1986.

Tan, Siang-Yang, and Yiu-Meng Toh. "The Effectiveness of Church-Based Lay Counselors: A Controlled Outcome Study." *Journal of Psychology and Christianity* 16, no. 3 (1997): 260–67.

Thiebauz, Marcelle. *The Writings of Medieval Women.* New York: Garland, 1994.

Tripp, Paul David. *Instruments in the Redeemer's Hand: People in Need of Change Helping People in Need of Change.* Phillipsburg, NJ: P&R, 2002.

Vanhoozer, Kevin J. *The Drama of Doctrine: A Canonical Linguistic Approach to Christian Doctrine.* Philadelphia: Westminster John Knox, 2005.

Viars, Stephen. *Putting Your Past in Its Place: Moving Forward in Freedom and Forgiveness.* Eugene, OR: Harvest House, 2011.

Vincent, Milton. *A Gospel Primer for Christians: Learning to See the Glories of God's Love*. Bemidji, MN: Focus, 2008.

Wilkerson, Mike. *Redemption: Freed by Jesus from the Idols We Worship and the Wounds We Carry*. Wheaton, IL: Crossway, 2011.

Williams, Sam, and Bob Kellemen. "The Spiritual Anatomy of the Soul." Chapter 7, in *Christ-Centered Biblical Counseling: Changing Lives with God's Changeless Truth*. Edited by James MacDonald, Bob Kellemen, and Steve Viars. Eugene, OR: Harvest House, 2013.

Wilson-Kastner, Patricia, Ronald Castner, Ann Millin, Rosemary Rader, and Jeremiah Reedy, editors. "The Martyrdom of Perpetua," In *A Lost Tradition: Women Writers of the Early Church*. Washington, DC: University Press of America, 1981.

Scripture Index

Gospel-Centered Counseling

How Christ Changes Lives

Robert W. Kellemen

Everyone talks about the personal ministry of the Word, but how do we make one-another ministry truly biblical? *Gospel-Centered Counseling* equips readers to change lives with Christ's changeless truth. It does so by examining life's seven ultimate questions and then guiding readers on a journey that explores the biblical, gospel-centered narrative of:

- The Word: "What is truth?" "Where can I find answers?"
- The Trinity: "Who is God?" "Can I know Him personally?"
- Creation: "Who am I?" "What makes people tick?"
- Fall: "What went wrong?" "Why do we do the things we do?"
- Redemption: "Can I change?" "How do people change?"
- Glorification: "Where am I headed?" "How does our future destiny impact our present reality?"
- Sanctification: "How can I help?" "How can I change lives?"

Bob Kellemen builds on the foundation of the written Word and provides a gospel-centered resource for understanding people, diagnosing problems, and prescribing biblically based solutions.

Gospel-Centered Counseling is the first book in the **Equipping Biblical Counselors** series, a comprehensive relational training curriculum for the local church that provides a model for equipping God's people to change lives with Christ's changeless truth. This two-book series weaves together comprehensive biblical insight with compassionate Christian engagement.